The Last Days and The Book of Revelation

A Scriptural Study Aid

**Prepared and Organized
by
Bruce H. Porter**

ISBN: 9781793269669

INTRODUCTION

The Prophet Joseph Smith stated that whenever God gives a vision of an image, or beast, or figure of any kind, He always holds Himself responsible to give a revelation or interpretation of the meaning thereof, otherwise we are not responsible or accountable for our belief in it@ (TPJS p. 291). As the Apostle Paul stated, 'Eye hath not seen, nor ear heard, neither have entered into the heart of man, the things which God hath prepared for them' (1 Corinthians 2: Verse 9). Prophetic visions might be difficult to record when there is no physical or intellectual conception of what they have seen. In vision, a prophet may see and understand many things simultaneously, as all senses participate in the manifestation. A Prophet might view the heavenly reaction or command, and then the result of that command as an earthly event. When trying to write what he has seen, a prophet must try and put everything in order as he understands it, often trying to record in writing, consecutive and simultaneous events in linear time. Understanding this it must be realized that in the written record the prophet may leap back and forth, sometimes overlapping events, and time periods, making prophecy seem apocalyptic. Visionary tenses are often difficult to decipher, and fall into three categories: 1) narrative past, 2) visionary present, and 3) apocalyptic future. The time line, however, is always the problem as these tenses can change within the same verse, leaving the interpretation obscure. Prophecy is history in reverse, and of the two, prophecy is always more sure, if the understanding is clear.

Elder Bruce R. McConkie has made this statement, in reference to chronological timing in the Book of Revelation:

> *As with all scripture dealing with the events to precede and attend the Second Coming, there is not a perfect chronological recitation of events. That which is to occur in one seal must be related to the things in another, and to give an over-all perspective, things widely separated in time are often spoken of in the same sentence.* (DNTC Vol. III p. 488)

Learning from the Doctrine and Covenants Section 77 everything before Revelation 6:12 should be history. Chapter Six, Verse Twelve will be used as a starting point for the 'Last Days' beginning with the opening of the Sixth Seal.

Thus, the scriptures below reflect an opinion, and only an opinion, as to how they might be better organized for an easier and more fluid understanding. Without question many people, if not most, will disagree with this organization, and outline. Thoughtful disagreement is encouraged, and welcomed if it will lead to more study, and a better understanding of The Book of Revelation.

This work, *The Last Days and the Book of Revelation* has been divided, for the sake of study, into a number of sections or events that are specifically discussed in the scriptures. This is done to assist in the organization of cross references, and corresponding scriptures that relate to the Book of Revelation. It is not suggested or implied that the following list of events and the order, is complete or chronologically correct, however an effort has been made to do so. Some events may be happening concurrent with other events, for example, event # 20 the fall of Babylon may be taking place during a number of other events.

To the right of the List of Events are the Chapters and verses that correspond with that event. Italicized events that have a number and letter are not contained in the Book of Revelation, but, are in other scripture. These are added for a better understanding of the last days and the Book of Revelation.

This text is prepared for use as a scriptural help and study aid for the Book of Revelation and the "last days" events as outlined in scripture. Because of this it has not been formatted in a book form and contains little commentary with an overabundance of scripture. It is my belief that scripture is the best commentary on the scripture.

Each numbered section or Chapter will begin with a short introduction followed by the passages from The Book of Revelation pertaining to that heading or topic. Numbered section with an #a, #b, #c, etc. are elements of the last days that are not specifically discussed in The Book of Revelation but are found in other scripture and are placed in the chronological context of Revelation.

Elements of The Book of Revelation,
And the
Elements of the Last Days

Chapter	Title and Topic	Chapters
1.	The Mission of John.	**10:** 1-11
2.	The War in Heaven.	**12:** 3, 4a; 7-12
3.	The Woman and Child, the Church and Kingdom.	**12:** 1, 2, 4b, 5-6, 13
4.	The Apostasy, The Woman and Child hidden.	**12:** 14-17
5.	The Restoration, The Church and the Wilderness.	**14:** 6-7
6.	The Gospel will cause the fall of Babylon.	**14:** 8
	6a. *The Judgements of God upon the Wicked, and The Restoration of Israel.*	
7.	The Gospel's proclamation to 'Come out of Babylon.'	**18:** 4, 5
	7a. *The Restoration begins the Gathering*	
8.	Satan's influence over the Nations of the Earth.	**13:** 1-18 **14:** 9-11
9.	Babylon the Great which Reigneth over the kings of the Earth.	**17:** 1-18
10.	The Sixth Seal is Opened.	**6:** 12-17
11.	The Sealing of the 144,000.	**7:** 1-8
12.	The Seventh Seal is Opened, Nature in Commotion.	**8:** 1-13
13.	Wars, and Plagues.	**9:** 1-21
14.	The Patience of the Saints.	**14:** 12-13

1

The Mission of John

Revelation Chapter 10

This chapter deals with the mission of the Apostle John as he asked to remain on earth until the Savior would return, and outlines his mission during this time in and apocalyptic way. We begin with Chapter Ten as an introduction to the events of the Last Days, as it deals with John and his responsibility, and not so much with the events. At times, one must ask questions, or imagine what question John would ask to receive a particular part of his revelation. Perhaps, his question amid these chapters would have been: *What will I be doing, during this time?* The response, or answer to the question results in the Ainsert@ of Chapter Ten.

The prophet Ezekiel has a similar vision of the Alittle book@ that must be eaten by the prophet. This chapter of Ezekiel is included below, as an example and cross-reference of a corresponding vision.

Chapter Ten of the Book of Revelation could be called an "insert" chapter, as could other chapters, and passages in the Book of Revelation. Insert chapters or verses are placed among surrounding chapters or passages that deal with last day events, and appear to be out of context. However these 'insert' chapters may be in consequence of unwritten questions that the prophet may have had in mind, or asked.

Tarry until I come

1 AND the Lord said unto me: John, my beloved, what desirest thou? For if you shall ask what you will, it shall be granted unto you.
2 And I said unto him: Lord, give unto me power over death, that I may live and bring souls unto thee.
3 And the Lord said unto me: Verily, verily, I say unto thee, because thou desirest this thou shalt tarry until I come in my glory, and shalt **prophesy before nations, kindreds, tongues and people**
6 Yea, he has undertaken a greater work; therefore I will make him as flaming fire and a ministering angel; he shall **minister for those who shall be heirs of salvation who dwell on the earth.** (D.& C. 7:1-3, 6).

Revelation 10:Verse 1
1 AND I saw another mighty angel come down from heaven, clothed with a cloud: and a rainbow [was] upon his head, and his face [was] as it were the sun, and his feet as pillars of fire:

Revelation 10:Verse 2

2 And **he had in his hand a little book open:** and he set his right foot upon the sea, and [his] left [foot] on the earth,

Revelation 10:Verse 3

3 And cried with a loud voice, as [when] a lion roareth: and when he had cried, seven thunders uttered their voices.

Revelation 10:Verse 4

4 And when the seven thunders had uttered their voices, I was about to write: and I heard a voice from heaven saying unto me, **Seal up those things which the seven thunders uttered, and write them not.**

Revelation 10:Verse 5

5 And the angel which I saw stand upon the sea and upon the earth lifted up his hand to heaven,

Revelation 10:Verse 6

6 And sware by him that liveth for ever and ever, who created heaven, and the things that therein are, and the earth, and the things that therein are, and the sea, and the things which are therein, that there should be time no longer:

Revelation 10:Verse 8

8 And the voice which I heard from heaven spake unto me again, and said, Go [and] take the little book which is open in the hand of the angel which standeth upon the sea and upon the earth.

Revelation 10:Verse 9

9 And I went unto the angel, and said unto him, Give me the little book. And he said unto me, **Take [it], and eat it up;** and it shall **make thy belly bitter, but it shall be in thy mouth sweet as honey.**

Revelation 10:Verse 10

10 And I took the little book out of the angel's hand, and ate it up; and it was in my mouth **sweet as honey: and as soon as I had eaten it, my belly was bitter.**

Revelation 10:Verse 11

11 And he said unto me, **Thou must prophesy again before many peoples,** and nations, and tongues, and kings.

D&C 77:Verse 14

14 Q. **What are we to understand by the little book which was eaten by John**, as mentioned in the 10th chapter of Revelation?

A. We are to understand that it was a mission, and **an ordinance, for him to gather the tribes of Israel**; behold, this is Elias, who, as it is written, must come and restore all things.

---

1 Nephi 14:Verse 18

18 And it came to pass that the angel spake unto me, saying: Look!

1 Nephi 14:Verse 19

19 And I looked and beheld a man, and he was dressed in a white robe.

1 Nephi 14:Verse 20

20 And the angel said unto me: Behold one of the twelve apostles of the Lamb.

1 Nephi 14:Verse 21

21 Behold, **he shall see and write the remainder of these things**; yea, and also many things which have been.

1 Nephi 14:Verse 22

22 And he shall also write concerning the end of the world.

1 Nephi 14:Verse 23

23 Wherefore, the things which he shall write are just and true; and behold they are written in the book which thou beheld proceeding out of the mouth of the Jew; and at the time they proceeded out of the mouth of the Jew, or, at the time the book proceeded out of the mouth of the Jew, the things which were written were plain and pure, and most precious and **easy to the understanding of all men.**

1 Nephi 14:Verse 24

24 And behold, the things which this apostle of the Lamb shall write are many things which thou hast seen; and behold, the remainder shalt thou see.

1 Nephi 14:Verse 25

25 But **the things which thou shalt see hereafter thou shalt not write;** for the Lord God hath ordained the apostle of the Lamb of God that he should write them.

1 Nephi 14:Verse 26

26 And also others who have been, to them hath he shown all things, and they have written them; and they are sealed up to come forth in their purity, according to the truth which is in the Lamb, in the own due time of the Lord, unto the house of Israel.

1 Nephi 14:Verse 27

27 And I, Nephi, heard and bear record, that the name of the apostle of the Lamb was John, according to the word of the angel.

Ezekiel 2:Verse 3a
3 And he said unto me, Son of man, I send thee to the children of Israel . . .

Ezekiel 2:Verse 7
7 And thou shalt speak my words unto them, whether they will hear, or whether they will forbear:

Ezekiel 2:Verse 9
9 And when I looked, behold, an hand [was] sent unto me; and, lo, **a roll of a book [was] therein**;

Ezekiel 2:Verse 10
10 And he spread it before me; and it [was] written within and without: and [there was] written therein lamentations, and mourning, and woe.

Ezekiel 3: Verse 1
1 MOREOVER he said unto me, Son of man, **eat that thou findest; eat this roll,** and go **speak unto the house of Israel.**

Ezekiel 3:Verse 2
2 So I opened my mouth, and **he caused me to eat** that roll.

Ezekiel 3:Verse 3
3 And he said unto me, Son of man, cause thy belly to eat, and fill thy bowels with this roll that I give thee. Then did I eat [it]; and it was **in my mouth as honey for sweetness.**

Ezekiel 3:Verse 4
4 And he said unto me, Son of man, go, **get thee unto the house of Israel, and speak with my words unto them.**

Ezekiel 3:Verse 5
5 For thou [art] not sent to a people of a strange speech and of an hard language, [but] **to the house of Israel;**

2

The War in Heaven

Another 'insert' passage is the War in Heaven doctrine in Chapter Twelve. This passage might be inserted here because of the questions that John might have asked: *Why is there so much evil, death, and destruction in the Last Days?* Or: *Why does the dragon persecute the woman and child?* The reason there is evil in the world to day is because Satan was cast out of heaven in the beginning, and he has made it his goal to destroy the spiritual nature and progression of mankind. He will take the gold and silver of the world, to buy leaders, and preachers, armies, and navies, in order to influence the governmental, and economical powers (chapters 13, and 17) and control the lifestyles and cultures of humanity. Satan knows that the '*culture*' itself, always becomes the greatest threat to the gospel and the righteousness of the saints.

Satan, the devil, the dragon, the beast, and the anti-Christ have two goals: **(1st.) Destroy the true nature of God.** If Satan can convince mankind that God does not have a physical body, then there can be no exaltation. Without a body the Father cannot have a Son. Therefore, God must come to earth 'incarnate' to explain scripture and the doctrine of the Son of God. Thus, the popular or 'historical' concept of the trinity. **(2nd.) Destroy the necessity of the Atonement.** Without the atonement there is no need for repentance, ordinance, or the exercise of faith. All one must do is believe to be *saved*, then Satan 'carefully leadeth them down to hell' and mankind will remain filthy still. If successful in these two goals, Satan will find it easy to convince the offspring of God that a god does not exist. Thus, there will be no need for a Father in Heaven, no need of a Savior or Son of God, which will leave mankind without religious-based morals, and without a purpose and potential for life on earth. Then false doctrines and teachings such as evolution, or even the nonexistence of God can easily be propagated. Life, then, ' is the survival of the fittest or richest, and Satan then can easily convince mankind of his first article of faith that, 'you can have anything in this world for money,' the fundamental and governing rule of Babylon, or this world in which we live. The 'War in Heaven,' a concept and doctrine that can found in many ancient texts, is best described in the **"Discourse on the Abbaton"** by Timothy of Alexandria. This text and others dealing with the fall of Satan will be found in the appendix.

Revelation 12:Verse 7

7 And there was war in heaven: Michael and his angels fought against the dragon; and the dragon fought and his angels,

Revelation 12:Verse 8

8 And prevailed not; **neither was their place found any more in heaven.**

Revelation 12:Verse 9

9 And the great dragon was cast out, that old serpent, called the Devil, and **Satan, which deceiveth the whole world:** he was cast out into the earth, and his angels were cast out with him.

Revelation 12:Verse 10

10 And I heard a loud voice saying in heaven, Now is come salvation, and strength, and the kingdom of our God, and the power of his Christ: for the accuser of our brethren is cast down, which accused them before our God day and night.

Revelation 12:Verse 11

11 And they overcame him by the blood of the Lamb, and by the word of their testimony; and they loved not their lives unto the death.

Revelation 12:Verse 3

3 And there appeared another wonder in heaven; and behold **a great red dragon,** having seven heads and ten horns, and seven crowns upon his heads.

Revelation 12:Verse 4a

4 And **his tail drew the third part of the stars of heaven, and did cast them to the earth:**

Revelation 12:Verse 12b

12 . . .Woe to the inhabiters of the earth and of the sea! for the devil is come down unto you, having great wrath, because he knoweth that he hath but a short time.

Isaiah 14: Verse 12

12! **How art thou fallen from heaven, O Lucifer, son of the morning** How art thou cut down to the ground, which didst weaken the nations!

Isaiah 14: Verse 13

13 For thou hast said in thine heart, I will ascend into heaven, I will exalt my throne above the stars of God: I will sit also upon the mount of the congregation, in the sides of the north:

Isaiah 14: Verse 14

14 I will ascend above the heights of the clouds; I will be like the most High.

Isaiah 14: Verse 15

15 Yet thou shalt be brought down to hell, to the sides of the pit.

Luke 10: Verse 17

17 And the Seventy returned again with joy, saying, Lord, even the devils are subject unto us through thy name.

Luke 10: Verse 18

18 And he said unto them, **I beheld Satan as lightning fall from heaven.**

---

2 Nephi 2:Verse 16

16 Wherefore, the Lord God gave unto man that he should act for himself. Wherefore, man could not act for himself save it should be that he was enticed by the one or the other.

2 Nephi 2:Verse 17

17 And I, Lehi, according to the things which I have read, must needs suppose that **an angel of God, according to that which is written, had fallen from heaven; wherefore, he became a devil, having sought that which was evil before God.**

2 Nephi 2:Verse 18

18 And **because he had fallen from heaven, and had become miserable forever, he sought also the misery of all mankind.**

---

2 Nephi 9: Verse 8

8 O the wisdom of God, his mercy and grace! For behold, if the flesh should rise no more our spirits must become subject to **that angel who fell from before the presence of the Eternal God, and became the devil, to rise no more.**

D&C 29:Verse 36

36 And it came to pass that Adam, being tempted of the devil--for, behold, the devil was before Adam, for **he rebelled against me, saying, Give me thine honor, which is my power; and also a third part of the hosts of heaven turned he away** from me because of their agency;

D&C 29:Verse 37

37 And **they were thrust down, and thus came the devil and his angels;**

D&C 29:Verse 38

38 And, behold, there is a place prepared for them from the beginning, which place is hell.

D&C 29:Verse 39

39 And it must **needs be that the devil should tempt the children of men**, or they could not be agents unto themselves; for if they never should have bitter they could not know the sweet--

---

D&C 76:Verse 25

25 And this we saw also, and bear record, that **an angel of God who was in authority in the presence of God, who rebelled against the Only Begotten Son whom the Father loved and**

who was in the bosom of the Father, was thrust down from the presence of God and the Son,

D&C 76:Verse 26
26 And was **called Perdition**, for the heavens wept over him--he was Lucifer, a son of the morning.

D&C 76:Verse 27
27 And we beheld, and lo, he is fallen! is fallen, even a son of the morning!

D&C 76:Verse 28
28 And while we were yet in the Spirit, the Lord commanded us that we should write the vision; for **we beheld Satan, that old serpent, even the devil, who rebelled against God, and sought to take the kingdom of our God and his Christ--**

Moses 4: Verse 3
3 Wherefore, because that Satan rebelled against me, and sought to destroy the agency of man, . . . **I caused that he should be cast down**;

Moses 4:Verse 4
4 And he became Satan, yea, even the **devil, the father of all lies, to deceive and to blind men, and to lead them captive at his will,** even as many as would not hearken unto my voice.

Abraham 3: Verse 26
26 And they who keep their first estate shall be added upon; and **they who keep not their first estate shall not have glory in the same kingdom with those who keep their first estate;** and they who keep their second estate shall have glory added upon their heads for ever and ever.

Abraham 3: Verse 27
27 And the Lord said: Whom shall I send? And one answered like unto the Son of Mam: Here am I, send me. And another answered and said: Here am I, send me. And the Lord said: I will send the first.

Abraham 3: Verse 28
28 **And the second was angry, and kept not his first estate, and, at that day, many followed after him.**

Jude 6
6 And **the angels which kept not their first estate, but left their own habitation, he hath reserved in everlasting chains under darkness unto the judgment of the great day.**

Ezekiel 28:Verse 1
1 THE word of the LORD came again unto me, saying,

Ezekiel 28:Verse 2

2 Son of man, say unto the prince of Tyrus, Thus saith the Lord GOD; Because thine heart [is] lifted up, and thou hast said, I [am] a God, I sit [in] the seat of God, in the midst of the seas; yet thou [art] a man, and not God, though thou set thine heart as the heart of God:

Ezekiel 28:Verse 3

3 Behold, thou [art] wiser than Daniel; there is no secret that they can hide from thee:

Ezekiel 28:Verse 4

4 With thy wisdom and with thine understanding thou hast gotten thee riches, and hast gotten gold and silver into thy treasures:

Ezekiel 28:Verse 5

5 By thy great wisdom [and] by thy traffick hast thou increased thy riches, and thine heart is lifted up because of thy riches:

Ezekiel 28:Verse 6

6 Therefore thus saith the Lord GOD; Because thou hast set thine heart as the heart of God;

Ezekiel 28:Verse 7

7 Behold, therefore I will bring strangers upon thee, the terrible of the nations: and they shall draw their swords against the beauty of thy wisdom, and they shall defile thy brightness.

Ezekiel 28:Verse 8

8 They shall bring thee down to the pit, and thou shalt die the deaths of [them that are] slain in the midst of the seas.

Ezekiel 28:Verse 9

9 Wilt thou yet say before him that slayeth thee, I [am] God? but thou [shalt be] a man, and no God, in the hand of him that slayeth thee.

Ezekiel 28:Verse 10

10 Thou shalt die the deaths of the uncircumcised by the hand of strangers: for I have spoken [it], saith the Lord GOD.

Ezekiel 28:Verse 11

11 Moreover the word of the LORD came unto me, saying,

Ezekiel 28:Verse 12

12 Son of man, take up a lamentation upon the king of Tyrus, and say unto him, Thus saith the Lord GOD; Thou sealest up the sum, full of wisdom, and perfect in beauty.

Ezekiel 28:Verse 13

13 Thou hast been in Eden the garden of God; every precious stone [was] thy covering, the sardius, topaz, and the diamond, the beryl, the onyx, and the jasper, the sapphire, the emerald, and the carbuncle, and gold: the workmanship of thy tabrets and of thy pipes was prepared in thee in the day that thou wast created.

Ezekiel 28:Verse 14

14 Thou [art] the anointed cherub that covereth; and I have set thee [so]: thou wast upon the holy mountain of God; thou hast walked up and down in the midst of the stones of fire.

Ezekiel 28:Verse 15

15 Thou [wast] perfect in thy ways from the day that thou wast created, till iniquity was found in thee.

Ezekiel 28:Verse 16

16 By the multitude of thy merchandise they have filled the midst of thee with violence, and thou hast sinned: therefore I will cast thee as profane out of the mountain of God: and I will destroy thee, O covering cherub, from the midst of the stones of fire.

Ezekiel 28:Verse 17

17 Thine heart was lifted up because of thy beauty, thou hast corrupted thy wisdom by reason of thy brightness: I will cast thee to the ground, I will lay thee before kings, that they may behold thee.

Ezekiel 28:Verse 18

18 Thou hast defiled thy sanctuaries by the multitude of thine iniquities, by the iniquity of thy traffick; therefore will I bring forth a fire from the midst of thee, it shall devour thee, and I will bring thee to ashes upon the earth in the sight of all them that behold thee.

Ezekiel 28:Verse 19

19 All they that know thee among the people shall be astonished at thee: thou shalt be a terror, and never [shalt] thou [be] any more.

3

The Woman and Child, the Church and Kingdom

Revelation 12:1, 2, 4b, 5-6, 13

The Church, and the Kingdom of God have been the targets of Satan from the days of Adam down to the present time. Revelation 12:13 states that when the dragon, or Satan saw that he was cast unto the earth, following the War in heaven, he has tried to destroy the gospel, the Church, and the Kingdom of God and His Christ, or in the words of John, 'the Woman and her Child.' The woman and the child are hidden in the wilderness for 1,260 years, until the time of the restoration when the church is called out of the wilderness, to come forth in glory.

———————————

Revelation 12:Verse 1
1 AND there appeared a great wonder in heaven; a **woman clothed with the sun, and the moon under her feet, and upon her head a crown of twelve stars:**

Revelation 12:Verse 2
2 And she being with child cried, travailing in birth, and pained to be delivered.

Revelation 12:Verse 4b
and the dragon stood before the woman which was ready to be delivered, for **to devour her child as soon as it was born.**

Revelation 12:Verse 5
5 And she brought forth a **man child, who was to rule all nations with a rod of iron:** and her child was caught up unto God, and [to] his throne.

Revelation 12:Verse 13
13 And when **the dragon** saw that he was cast unto the earth, he persecuted the woman which brought forth the man [child].

Revelation 12:Verse 6
6 And **the woman fled into the wilderness,** where she hath a place prepared of God, that they should **feed her there a thousand two hundred [and] threescore days.**

———————————

JST Revelation 12: verse 7

7 And the dragon prevailed not against Michael, neither the child, nor **the woman which was the church of God, who had been delivered of her pains, and brought forth the kingdom of our God and his Christ**.

D&C 86:Verse 3

3 And after they have fallen asleep (the apostles) **the great persecutor of the church, the apostate, the whore, even Babylon**, that maketh all nations to drink of her cup, in whose hearts the enemy, even Satan, sitteth to reign--behold he soweth the tares; wherefore, the tares choke the wheat and **drive the church into the wilderness.**

4

The Apostasy, The Woman and Child Hidden

Revelation 12:14-17

The Apostasy, and the hiding of the gospel as the 'child was caught up unto God, and [to] His throne' (Rev. 12:5) protects the Kingdom of God, and the plain and precious things contained in the scriptures, until the time of the restoration. The world, the governments, and mankind are not ready to accept the woman and her child. Only in the Meridian of Time could Christ come to his creation and a nation murder their own God. The atonement, crucifixion, and resurrection could only take place at this time in world history. Likewise, only at the time of Joseph Smith could there be a restitution of all things to usher in the Dispensation of the Fullness of Times.

By divine command and power of God, the Prophet Moroni buries the Nephite Records in the earth. The plain and precious truths contained in the Book of Mormon, along with the Gospel of Jesus Christ, are hidden in the wilderness to come forth in the latter days as a Marvelous Work and Wonder. The Lord in his wisdom waits until the time is right, and nations are formed with the laws that will allow the freedom of worship, to restore the Gospel of Jesus Christ to the earth. The end of the famine of the word of God ends as the boy prophet solemnly enters a grove of trees, and receives the First Vision as the 'Woman and Child' come out of the wilderness. There is always the question of the 1,260 years, the 'forty and two months' or even the 'time, times and half times.' A prophetic day is one year, or about 354 days. The 1,260 years should be subtracted from the time of the restoration of the Church, in the year 1830. As one contemplates these dates, it must be remembered that there were Nephite dispensations as well as the major dispensations. Who knows at what date the gospel was officially taken off the earth, if at all, or when the 1,260 years began, or really ended.

Revelation 12:Verse 14
14 And to the woman were given two wings of a great eagle, that she might fly into the wilderness, into her place, where she is **nourished for a time, and times, and half a time, from the face of the serpent.**

Revelation 12:Verse 15
15 And the serpent cast out of his mouth water as a flood after the woman, that **he might cause her to be carried away of the flood.**

Revelation 12:Verse 16
16 And **the earth helped the woman**, and the earth opened her mouth, and swallowed up the flood which the dragon cast out of his mouth.

Revelation 12:Verse 17
17 And the dragon was wroth with the woman, and went to **make war with the remnant of her seed**, which keep the commandments of God, and have the testimony of Jesus Christ.

Isaiah 29:Verse 9
9 Stay yourselves, and wonder; cry ye out, and cry: they are drunken, but not with wine; they stagger, but not with strong drink.

Isaiah 29:Verse 10
10 For the LORD hath poured out upon you the spirit of deep sleep, and hath closed your eyes: the prophets and your rulers, the seers hath he covered.

Daniel 12:Verse 6
6 And [one] said to the man clothed in linen, which [was] upon the waters of the river, How long [shall it be to] the end of these wonders?

Daniel 12:Verse 7
7 And I heard the man clothed in linen, which [was] upon the waters of the river, when he held up his right hand and his left hand unto heaven, and sware by him that liveth for ever that [it shall be] for a **time, times, and an half**; and when **he shall have accomplished to scatter the power of the holy people,** all these [things] shall be finished.

---

2 Thessalonians 2:Verse 1
1 NOW we beseech you, brethren, by the coming of our Lord Jesus Christ, and [by] our gathering together unto him,

2 Thessalonians 2:Verse 2
2 That ye be not soon shaken in mind, or be troubled, neither by spirit, nor by word, nor by letter as from us, as that the day of Christ is at hand.

2 Thessalonians 2:Verse 3
3 Let no man deceive you by any means: for **[that day shall not come], except there come a falling away first, and that man of sin be revealed, the son of perdition;**

2 Thessalonians 2:Verse 4
4 Who opposeth and exalteth himself above all that is called God, or that is worshipped; so that he as God sitteth in the temple of God, shewing himself that he is God.

D&C 86:Verse 1

1 Verily, thus saith the Lord unto you my servants, concerning the parable of the wheat and of the tares:

D&C 86:Verse 2

2 Behold, verily I say, the field was the world, and the apostles were the sowers of the seed;

D&C 86:Verse 3

3 And after they have fallen asleep **the great persecutor of the church, the apostate, the whore, even Babylon**, that maketh all nations to drink of her cup, in whose hearts the enemy, even Satan, sitteth to reign--behold he soweth the tares; wherefore, **the tares choke the wheat and drive the church into the wilderness.**

D&C 86:Verse 4

4 But behold, in the last days, even now while the Lord is beginning to bring forth the word, and the blade is springing up and is yet tender—

5

The Restoration, The Church called out of the Wilderness

Revelation 14: 6-7

The Woman and Child fled into the wilderness to be nourished, and protected by the power of God from the time that Moroni hid up the records, until the heavens were opened again, and the young Joseph speaks to the Father and Son in the Sacred Grove. The heavens rejoice as the angel, having the everlasting gospel, restores and brings forth from the wilderness, the Church and Gospel of Jesus Christ. Prophecy is History in reverse and of the two prophecy is always more sure. One of the great discussions of the gospel and the tribes of Israel is found in Jacob, Chapter Five. The prophet Jacob reads from the Brass Plates the prophecies of Zenos, an unknown prophet in the cannon of scripture until the discovery of the Dead Sea Scrolls. This 'Allegory of the Olive Tree' in Jacob Five is found in the appendix, and should be read in conjunction with these verses below as we are now in 'the last time'.

Revelation 12: Verse 12a
Therefore rejoice, [ye] heavens, and ye that dwell in them. . . .

Revelation 14:Verse 6
6 And I saw another angel **fly in the midst of heaven, having the everlasting gospel** to preach unto them that dwell on
the earth, and to every nation, and kindred, and tongue, and people,

Revelation 14:Verse 7
7 Saying with a loud voice, Fear God, and give glory to him; for the **hour of his judgment is come:** and worship him that made heaven, and earth, and the sea, and the fountains of waters.

D&C 33:Verse 3
3 For behold, the field is white already to harvest; and it is the eleventh hour, and the last time that I shall call laborers into my vineyard.

D&C 33:Verse 4

4 And my vineyard has become corrupted every whit; and there is none which doeth good save it be a few; and they err in many instances because of priestcrafts, all having corrupt minds.

D&C 33:Verse 5

5 And verily, verily, I say unto you, that **this church have I established and called forth out of the wilderness.**

D&C5:Verse 12

12 Yea, they shall know of a surety that these things are true, for from heaven will I declare it unto them.

D&C 5:Verse 13

13 I will give them power that they may behold and view these things as they are;

D&C 5:Verse 14

14 And to none else will I grant this power, to receive this same testimony among this generation, in this the beginning of **the rising up and the coming forth of my church out of the wilderness**--clear as the moon, and fair as the sun, and terrible as an army with banners.

D&C 5:Verse 15

15 And the testimony of three witnesses will I send forth of my word.

D&C 5:Verse 16

16 And behold, whosoever believeth on my words, them will I visit with the manifestation of my Spirit; and they shall be born of me, even of water and of the Spirit--

---

D&C 109:Verse 72

72 Remember all thy church, O Lord, with all their families, and all their immediate connections, with all their sick and afflicted ones, with all the poor and meek of the earth; that the kingdom, which thou hast set up without hands, may become a great mountain and fill the whole earth;

D&C 109:Verse 73

73 That **thy church may come forth out of the wilderness of darkness,** and shine forth fair as the moon, clear as the sun, and terrible as an army with banners;

Isaiah 29:Verse 11

11 And the vision of all is become unto you as the words of a book that is sealed, which [men] deliver to one that is learned, saying, Read this, I pray thee: and he saith, I cannot; for it [is] sealed:

Isaiah 29:Verse 12

12 And the book is delivered to him that is not learned, saying, Read this, I pray thee: and he saith, I am not learned.

Isaiah 29:Verse 13

13 Wherefore the Lord said, Forasmuch as this people draw near [me] with their mouth, and with their lips do honour me, but have removed their heart far from me, and their fear toward me is taught by the precept of men:

Isaiah 29:Verse 14

14 Therefore, behold, I will proceed to do a marvellous work among this people, [even] a marvellous work and a wonder: for the wisdom of their wise [men] shall perish, and the understanding of their prudent [men] shall be hid.

Malachi 4:Verse 5

5 Behold, I will send you Elijah the prophet before the coming of the great and dreadful day of the LORD:

Malachi 4:Verse 6

6 And he shall turn the heart of the fathers to the children, and the heart of the children to their fathers, lest I come and smite the earth with a curse.

---

1 Nephi 13:Verse 32

32 Neither will the Lord God suffer that the Gentiles shall forever remain in that awful state of blindness, which thou beholdest they are in, because of the plain and most precious parts of the gospel of the Lamb which have been kept back by that abominable church, whose formation thou hast seen.

1 Nephi 13:Verse 33

33 Wherefore saith the Lamb of God: I will be merciful unto the Gentiles, unto the visiting of the remnant of the house of Israel in great judgment.

1 Nephi 13:Verse 34

34 And it came to pass that the angel of the Lord spake unto me, saying: Behold, saith the Lamb of God, after I have visited the remnant of the house of Israel--and this remnant of whom I speak is the seed of thy father--wherefore, after I have visited them in judgment, and smitten them by the hand of the Gentiles, and after the Gentiles do stumble exceedingly, because of the most plain and precious parts of the gospel of the Lamb which have been kept back by that abominable church, which is the mother of harlots, saith the Lamb--I will be merciful unto the Gentiles in that day, insomuch that I will bring forth unto them, in mine own power, much of my gospel, which shall be plain and precious, saith the Lamb.

1 Nephi 13:Verse 35

35 For, behold, saith the Lamb: I will manifest myself unto thy seed, that they shall write many things which I shall minister unto them, which shall be plain and precious; and after thy seed shall

be destroyed, and dwindle in unbelief, and also the seed of thy brethren, behold, these things shall be hid up, to come forth unto the Gentiles, by the gift and power of the Lamb.

1 Nephi 13:Verse 36
36 And in them shall be written my gospel, saith the Lamb, and my rock and my salvation.

1 Nephi 13:Verse 37
37 And blessed are they who shall seek to bring forth my Zion at that day, for they shall have the gift and the power of the Holy Ghost; and if they endure unto the end they shall be lifted up at the last day, and shall be saved in the everlasting kingdom of the Lamb; and whoso shall publish peace, yea, tidings of great joy, how beautiful upon the mountains shall they be.

1 Nephi 13:Verse 38
38 And it came to pass that I beheld the remnant of the seed of my brethren, and also the book of the Lamb of God, which had proceeded forth from the mouth of the Jew, that it came forth from the Gentiles unto the remnant of the seed of my brethren.

1 Nephi 13:Verse 39
39 And after it had come forth unto them I beheld other books, which came forth by the power of the Lamb, from the Gentiles unto them, unto the convincing of the Gentiles and the remnant of the seed of my brethren, and also the Jews who were scattered upon all the face of the earth, that the records of the prophets and of the twelve apostles of the Lamb are true.

1 Nephi 13:Verse 40
40 And the angel spake unto me, saying: These last records, which thou hast seen among the Gentiles, shall establish the truth of the first, which are of the twelve apostles of the Lamb, and shall make known the plain and precious things which have been taken away from them; and shall make known to all kindreds, tongues, and people, that the Lamb of God is the Son of the Eternal Father, and the Savior of the world; and that all men must come unto him, or they cannot be saved.

1 Nephi 13:Verse 41
41 And they must come according to the words which shall be established by the mouth of the Lamb; and the words of the Lamb shall be made known in the records of thy seed, as well as in the records of the twelve apostles of the Lamb; wherefore they both shall be established in one; for there is one God and one Shepherd over all the earth.

---

1 Nephi 14:Verse 7
7 For the time cometh, saith the Lamb of God, that I will work a great and a marvelous work among the children of men; a work which shall be everlasting, either on the one hand or on the other--either to the convincing of them unto peace and life eternal, or unto the deliverance of them to the hardness of their hearts and the blindness of their minds unto their being brought down into captivity, and also into destruction, both temporally and spiritually, according to the captivity of the devil, of which I have spoken.

---

2 Nephi 27:Verse 6

6 And it shall come to pass that the Lord God shall bring forth unto you the words of a book, and they shall be the words of them which have slumbered.

2 Nephi 27:Verse 7

7 And behold the book shall be sealed; and in the book shall be a revelation from God, from the beginning of the world to the ending thereof.

2 Nephi 27:Verse 8

8 Wherefore, because of the things which are sealed up, the things which are sealed shall not be delivered in the day of the wickedness and abominations of the people. Wherefore the book shall be kept from them.

2 Nephi 27:Verse 9

9 But the book shall be delivered unto a man, and he shall deliver the words of the book, which are the words of those who have slumbered in the dust, and he shall deliver these words unto another;

2 Nephi 27:Verse 10

10 But the words which are sealed he shall not deliver, neither shall he deliver the book. For the book shall be sealed by the power of God, and the revelation which was sealed shall be kept in the book until the own due time of the Lord, that they may come forth; for behold, they reveal all things from the foundation of the world unto the end thereof.

2 Nephi 27:Verse 11

11 And the day cometh that the words of the book which were sealed shall be read upon the house tops; and they shall be read by the power of Christ; and all things shall be revealed unto the children of men which ever have been among the children of men, and which ever will be even unto the end of the earth.

2 Nephi 27:Verse 12

12 Wherefore, at that day when the book shall be delivered unto the man of whom I have spoken, the book shall be hid from the eyes of the world, that the eyes of none shall behold it save it be that three witnesses shall behold it, by the power of God, besides him to whom the book shall be delivered; and they shall testify to the truth of the book and the things therein.

2 Nephi 27:Verse 13

13 And there is none other which shall view it, save it be a few according to the will of God, to bear testimony of his word unto the children of men; for the Lord God hath said that the words of the faithful should speak as if it were from the dead.

2 Nephi 27:Verse 14

14 Wherefore, the Lord God will proceed to bring forth the words of the book; and in the mouth of as many witnesses as seemeth him good will he establish his word; and wo be unto him that rejecteth the word of God!

2 Nephi 27:Verse 15

15 But behold, it shall come to pass that the Lord God shall say unto him to whom he shall deliver the book: Take these words which are not sealed and deliver them to another, that he may show them unto the learned, saying: Read this, I pray thee. And the learned shall say: Bring hither the book, and I will read them.

2 Nephi 27:Verse 16

16 And now, because of the glory of the world and to get gain will they say this, and not for the glory of God.

2 Nephi 27:Verse 17

17 And the man shall say: I cannot bring the book, for it is sealed.

2 Nephi 27:Verse 18

18 Then shall the learned say: I cannot read it.

2 Nephi 27:Verse 19

19 Wherefore it shall come to pass, that the Lord God will deliver again the book and the words thereof to him that is not learned; and the man that is not learned shall say: I am not learned.

2 Nephi 27:Verse 20

20 Then shall the Lord God say unto him: The learned shall not read them, for they have rejected them, and I am able to do mine own work; wherefore thou shalt read the words which I shall give unto thee.

2 Nephi 27:Verse 21

21 Touch not the things which are sealed, for I will bring them forth in mine own due time; for I will show unto the children of men that I am able to do mine own work.

2 Nephi 27:Verse 22

22 Wherefore, when thou hast read the words which I have commanded thee, and obtained the witnesses which I have promised unto thee, then shalt thou seal up the book again, and hide it up unto me, that I may preserve the words which thou hast not read, until I shall see fit in mine own wisdom to reveal all things unto the children of men.

2 Nephi 27:Verse 23

23 For behold, I am God; and I am a God of miracles; and I will show unto the world that I am the same yesterday, today, and forever; and I work not among the children of men save it be according to their faith.

2 Nephi 27:Verse 24

24 And again it shall come to pass that the Lord shall say unto him that shall read the words that shall be delivered him:

2 Nephi 27:Verse 25

25 Forasmuch as this people draw near unto me with their mouth, and with their lips do honor me, but have removed their hearts far from me, and their fear towards me is taught by the precepts of men--

2 Nephi 27:Verse 26

26 Therefore, **I will proceed to do a marvelous work among this people, yea, a marvelous work and a wonder, for the wisdom of their wise and learned shall perish, and the understanding of their prudent shall be hid.**

---

3 Nephi 16:Verse 7

7 Behold, because of their belief in me, saith the Father, and because of the unbelief of you, O house of Israel, **in the latter day shall the truth come unto the Gentiles, that the fulness of these things shall be made known unto them.**

---

3 Nephi 21:Verse 9

9 For in that day, for my sake shall **the Father work a work, which shall be a great and a marvelous work among them;** and there shall be among them those who will not believe it, although a man shall declare it unto them.

D&C 45:Verse 28

28 And when the times of the Gentiles is come in, **a light shall break forth among them that sit in darkness**, and it shall be the fulness of my gospel;

D&C 45:Verse 36

36 And when **the light shall begin to break forth,** it shall be with them like unto a parable which I will show you--

D&C 45:Verse 37

37 Ye look and behold the figtrees, and ye see them with your eyes, and ye say when they begin to shoot forth, and their leaves are yet tender, that summer is now nigh at hand;

D&C 45:Verse 38

38 Even so it shall be in that day when they shall see all these things, then shall they know that the hour is nigh.

D&C 133:Verse 36

36 And now, verily saith the Lord, that these things might be known among you, O inhabitants of the earth, **I have sent forth mine angel flying through the midst of heaven, having the everlasting gospel,** who hath appeared unto some and hath committed it unto man, who shall appear unto many that dwell on the earth.

D&C 133:Verse 37

37 And **this gospel shall be preached unto every nation, and kindred, and tongue, and people.**

D&C 133:Verse 38

38 And **the servants of God shall go forth,** saying with a loud voice: Fear God and give glory to him, for the hour of his judgment is come;

D&C 133:Verse 39

39 And worship him that made heaven, and earth, and the sea, and the fountains of waters--

---

6

The Gospel will Cause the Fall of Babylon

Revelation 14: 8

The great day of Satan's power begins to come to a close with the restoration of the Gospel. As the Church is restored along with the priesthood and the ordinances of salvation and exaltation, Satan increases his onslaught against the righteous members of The Church, and Gospel of Jesus Christ. The Prophet Joseph Smith stated: 'In relation to the kingdom of God, the devil always sets up his kingdom, at the very same time, in opposition to God.' This time, however, the church and gospel will continue to go forth, and destroy the kingdom of the devil. Thus, with the restoration of the Gospel (Rev. 14:6-7) comes the cry that 'Babylon is fallen' (Rev. 14:8) as Samuel the Lamanite declares in the Book of Mormon of the wicked, that their: 'destruction is made sure.' The Gospel comes forth in it's fullness in the great day of Satan's power, and with this restoration, the very foundations of Babylon, the Church of the Devil is shaken. The satanic onslaught must increase in intensity and wickedness. The culture and society must act, and believe, that God does not exist, and that the atoning sacrifice of His Son, is a myth, as scripture is not to be taken seriously. Satan knows that with the restoration of the Gospel of Jesus Christ, his kingdom, the Church of the Devil, shall be destroyed, and great shall be the fall thereof.

Revelation 14:Verse 8

8 And there followed another angel, saying, **Babylon is fallen, is fallen,** that great city, because she made all nations drink of the wine of the wrath of her fornication

---

Isaiah 29:Verse 15
15 Woe unto them that seek deep to hide their counsel from the LORD, and their works are in the dark, and they say, Who seeth us? and who knoweth us?

Isaiah 29:Verse 16
16 Surely your turning of things upside down shall be esteemed as the potter's clay: for shall the work say of him that made it, He made me not? or shall the thing framed say of him that framed it, He had no understanding?

Isaiah 29:Verse 17

17 [Is] it not yet a very little while, and Lebanon shall be turned into a fruitful field, and the fruitful field shall be esteemed as a forest?

Isaiah 29:Verse 18

18 And in that day shall the deaf hear the words of the book, and the eyes of the blind shall see out of obscurity, and out of darkness.

Isaiah 29:Verse 19

19 The meek also shall increase [their] joy in the LORD, and the poor among men shall rejoice in the Holy One of Israel.

Isaiah 29:Verse 20

20 For the terrible one is brought to nought, and the scorner is consumed, and all that watch for iniquity are cut off:

Isaiah 29:Verse 21

21 That make a man an offender for a word, and lay a snare for him that reproveth in the gate, and turn aside the just for a thing of nought.

Isaiah 29:Verse 22

22 Therefore thus saith the LORD, who redeemed Abraham, concerning the house of Jacob, Jacob shall not now be ashamed, neither shall his face now wax pale.

Isaiah 29:Verse 23

23 But when he seeth his children, the work of mine hands, in the midst of him, they shall sanctify my name, and sanctify the Holy One of Jacob, and shall fear the God of Israel.

Isaiah 29:Verse 24

24 They also that erred in spirit shall come to understanding, and they that murmured shall learn doctrine.

---

1 Nephi 14:Verse 14

14 And it came to pass that I, Nephi, beheld the power of the Lamb of God, that it descended upon the saints of the church of the Lamb, and upon the covenant people of the Lord, who were scattered upon all the face of the earth; and they were armed with righteousness and with the power of God in great glory.

1 Nephi 14:Verse 15

15 And it came to pass that I beheld that the wrath of God was poured out upon that great and abominable church, insomuch that there were wars and rumors of wars among all the nations and kindreds of the earth.

1 Nephi 14:Verse 16

16 And as there began to be wars and rumors of wars among all the nations which belonged to the mother of abominations, the angel spake unto me, saying: Behold, the wrath of God is upon the mother of harlots; and behold, thou seest all these things--

1 Nephi 14:Verse 17

17 And when the day cometh that the wrath of God is poured out upon the mother of harlots, which is the great and abominable church of all the earth, whose founder is the devil, then, at that day, the work of the Father shall commence, in preparing the way for the fulfilling of his covenants, which he hath made to his people who are of the house of Israel.

---

1 Nephi 22:Verse 10

10 And I would, my brethren, that ye should know that all the kindreds of the earth cannot be blessed unless he shall make bare his arm in the eyes of the nations.

1 Nephi 22:Verse 11

11 Wherefore, the Lord God will proceed to make bare his arm in the eyes of all the nations, in bringing about his covenants and his gospel unto those who are of the house of Israel.

---

2 Nephi 27:Verse 27

27 And wo unto them that seek deep to hide their counsel from the Lord! And their works are in the dark; and they say: Who seeth us, and who knoweth us? And they also say: Surely, your turning of things upside down shall be esteemed as the potter's clay. But behold, I will show unto them, saith the Lord of Hosts, that I know all their works. For shall the work say of him that made it, he made me not? Or shall the thing framed say of him that framed it, he had no understanding?

2 Nephi 27:Verse 28

28 But behold, saith the Lord of Hosts: I will show unto the children of men that it is yet a very little while and Lebanon shall be turned into a fruitful field; and the fruitful field shall be esteemed as a forest.

2 Nephi 27:Verse 29

29 And in that day shall the deaf hear the words of the book, and the eyes of the blind shall see out of obscurity and out of darkness.

2 Nephi 27:Verse 30

30 And the meek also shall increase, and their joy shall be in the Lord, and the poor among men shall rejoice in the Holy One of Israel.

2 Nephi 27:Verse 31

31 For assuredly as the Lord liveth they shall see that the terrible one is brought to naught, and the scorner is consumed, and all that watch for iniquity are cut off;
2 Nephi 27:Verse 32

32 And they that make a man an offender for a word, and lay a snare for him that reproveth in the gate, and turn aside the just for a thing of naught.

2 Nephi 27:Verse 33

33 Therefore, thus saith the Lord, who redeemed Abraham, concerning the house of Jacob: Jacob shall not now be ashamed, neither shall his face now wax pale.

2 Nephi 27:Verse 34

34 But when he seeth his children, the work of my hands, in the midst of him, they shall sanctify my name, and sanctify the Holy One of Jacob, and shall fear the God of Israel.

2 Nephi 27:Verse 35

35 They also that erred in spirit shall come to understanding, and they that murmured shall learn doctrine.

———————————————————

7

The Gospel's proclamation 'Come out of Babylon'

Revelation 18: 4, 5

With the restoration of the Gospel, comes the cry to 'come out of Babylon.' The righteous are constantly reminded to be not partakers of wickedness, to separate themselves from the midst of wickedness, which is spiritual Babylon. As early as 1831, the Lord issued the command to the Latter-day Saints to come out of Babylon. The restoration of the Gospel is proclaimed as the missionaries are sent forth into the world with the declaration to 'come out of Babylon' and gather together for spiritual and physical safety, as Babylon now is about to be destroyed.

Revelation 18:Verse 4

4 And I heard another voice from heaven, saying, **Come out of her,** my people, that ye **be not partakers of her sins, and that ye receive not of her plagues.**

Revelation 18:Verse 5

5 For her sins have reached unto heaven, and God hath remembered her iniquities.

Isaiah 11:Verse 10

10 And in that day there shall be a root of Jesse, which shall stand for an ensign of the people; to it shall the Gentiles seek: and his rest shall be glorious.

Isaiah 11:Verse 11

11 And it shall come to pass in that day, [that] the Lord shall set his hand again the second time to recover the remnant of his people, which shall be left, from Assyria, and from Egypt, and from Pathros, and from Cush, and from Elam, and from Shinar, and from Hamath, and from the islands of the sea.

Isaiah 11:Verse 12

12 And he shall set up an ensign for the nations, and shall assemble the outcasts of Israel, **and gather together the dispersed of Judah from the four corners of the earth.**

Isaiah 11:Verse 13

13 The envy also of Ephraim shall depart, and the adversaries of Judah shall be cut off: Ephraim shall not envy Judah, and Judah shall not vex Ephraim.

Isaiah 48:Verse 20
20 Go ye forth of Babylon, flee ye from the Chaldeans, with a voice of singing declare ye, tell this, utter it [even] to the end of the earth; say ye, The LORD hath redeemed his servant Jacob.

Jeremiah 50:Verse 4
4 In those days, and in that time, saith the LORD, the children of Israel shall come, they and the children of Judah together, going and weeping: they shall go, and seek the LORD their God.

Jeremiah 50:Verse 5
5 They shall ask the way to Zion with their faces thitherward, [saying], Come, and let us join ourselves to the LORD in a perpetual covenant [that] shall not be forgotten.

Jeremiah 50:Verse 6
6 My people hath been lost sheep: their shepherds have caused them to go astray, they have turned them away [on] the mountains: they have gone from mountain to hill, they have forgotten their restingplace.

Jeremiah 50:Verse 7
7 All that found them have devoured them: and their adversaries said, We offend not, because they have sinned against the LORD, the habitation of justice, even the LORD, the hope of their fathers.

Jeremiah 50:Verse 8
8 **Remove out of the midst of Babylon, and go forth out of the land of the Chaldeans**, and be as the he goats before the flocks.

Jeremiah 50:Verse 9
9 For, lo, I will raise and cause to come up against Babylon an assembly of great nations from the north country: and they shall set themselves in array against her; from thence she shall be taken: their arrows [shall be] as of a mighty expert man; none shall return in vain.

Jeremiah 50:Verse 28
28 The voice of them that flee and escape out of the land of Babylon, to declare in Zion the vengeance of the LORD our God, the vengeance of his temple.

Jeremiah 50:Verse 29
29 Call together the archers against Babylon: all ye that bend the bow, camp against it round about; let none thereof escape: recompense her according to her work; according to all that she hath done, do unto her: for she hath been proud against the LORD, against the Holy One of Israel.

Jeremiah 51:Verse 5
5 For Israel [hath] not [been] forsaken, nor Judah of his God, of the LORD of hosts; though their land was filled with sin against the Holy One of Israel.

Jeremiah 51:Verse 6

6 **Flee out of the midst of Babylon**, and deliver every man his soul: be not cut off in her iniquity; for this [is] the time of the LORD'S vengeance; he will render unto her a recompence.

Jeremiah 51:Verse 7

7 Babylon [hath been] a golden cup in the LORD'S hand, that made all the earth drunken: the nations have drunken of her wine; therefore the nations are mad.

Jeremiah 51:Verse 8

8 Babylon is suddenly fallen and destroyed: howl for her; take balm for her pain, if so be she may be healed.

Jeremiah 51:Verse 9

9 We would have healed Babylon, but she is not healed: forsake her, and let us go every one into his own country: for her judgment reacheth unto heaven, and is lifted up [even] to the skies.

Jeremiah 51:Verse 10

10 The LORD hath brought forth our righteousness: come, and let us declare in Zion the work of the LORD our God.

Jeremiah 51:Verse 11

11 Make bright the arrows; gather the shields: the LORD hath raised up the spirit of the kings of the Medes: for his device [is] against Babylon, to destroy it; because it [is] the vengeance of the LORD, the vengeance of his temple.

Jeremiah 51:Verse 37

37 And Babylon shall become heaps, a dwellingplace for dragons, an astonishment, and an hissing, without an inhabitant

Jeremiah 51:Verse 38

38 They shall roar together like lions: they shall yell as lions' whelps. her whole land shall be confounded, and all her slain shall fall in the midst of her.

Jeremiah 51:Verse 39

39 In their heat I will make their feasts, and I will make them drunken, that they may rejoice, and sleep a perpetual sleep, and not wake, saith the LORD.

Jeremiah 51:Verse 40

40 I will bring them down like lambs to the slaughter, like rams with he goats.

Jeremiah 51:Verse 41

41 How is Sheshach taken! and how is the praise of the whole earth surprised! how is Babylon become an astonishment among the nations!

Jeremiah 51:Verse 42

42 The sea is come up upon Babylon: she is covered with the multitude of the waves thereof.

Jeremiah 51:Verse 43

43 Her cities are a desolation, a dry land, and a wilderness, a land wherein no man dwelleth, neither doth [any] son of man pass thereby.

Jeremiah 51:Verse 44

44 And I will punish Bel in Babylon, and I will bring forth out of his mouth that which he hath swallowed up: and the nations shall not flow together any more unto him: yea, the wall of Babylon shall fall.

Jeremiah 51:Verse 45

45 My people, go ye out of the midst of her, and deliver ye every man his soul from the fierce anger of the LORD.

Jeremiah 51:Verse 46

46 And lest your heart faint, and ye fear for the rumour that shall be heard in the land; a rumour shall both come [one] year, and after that in [another] year [shall come] a rumour, and violence in the land, ruler against ruler.

Jeremiah 51:Verse 47

47 Therefore, behold, the days come, that I will do judgment upon the graven images of Babylon: and

Jeremiah 51:Verse 48

48 Then the heaven and the earth, and all that [is] therein, shall sing for Babylon: for the spoilers shall come unto her from the north, saith the LORD.

Jeremiah 51:Verse 49

49 As Babylon [hath caused] the slain of Israel to fall, so at Babylon shall fall the slain of all the earth.

Jeremiah 51:Verse 50

50 Ye that have escaped the sword, go away, stand not still: remember the LORD afar off, and let Jerusalem come into your mind.

Jeremiah 51:Verse 51

51 We are confounded, because we have heard reproach: shame hath covered our faces: for strangers are come into the sanctuaries of the LORD'S house.

Jeremiah 51:Verse 52

52 Wherefore, behold, the days come, saith the LORD, that I will do judgment upon her graven images: and through all her land the wounded shall groan.

Jeremiah 51:Verse 53

53 Though Babylon should mount up to heaven, and though she should fortify the height of her strength, [yet] from me shall spoilers come unto her, saith the LORD.

Jeremiah 51:Verse 54

54 A sound of a cry [cometh] from Babylon, and great destruction from the land of the Chaldeans:

Jeremiah 51:Verse 55

55 Because the LORD hath spoiled Babylon, and destroyed out of her the great voice; when her waves do roar like great waters, a noise of their voice is uttered:

Jeremiah 51:Verse 56

56 Because the spoiler is come upon her, [even] upon Babylon, and her mighty men are taken, every one of their bows is broken: for the LORD God of recompences shall surely requite.

Jeremiah 51:Verse 57

57 And I will make drunk her princes, and her wise [men], her captains, and her rulers, and her mighty men: and they shall sleep a perpetual sleep, and not wake, saith the King, whose name [is] the LORD of hosts.

Jeremiah 51:Verse 58

58 Thus saith the LORD of hosts; The broad walls of Babylon shall be utterly broken, and her high gates shall be burned with fire; and the people shall labour in vain, and the folk in the fire, and they shall be weary.

Zechariah 2:Verse 6

6 Ho, ho, [come forth], and flee from the land of the north, saith the LORD: for I have spread you abroad as the four winds of the heaven, saith the LORD.

Zechariah 2:Verse 7

7 **Deliver thyself, O Zion**, that dwellest [with] the daughter of Babylon.

---

3 Nephi 20:Verse 41

41 And then shall **a cry go forth: Depart ye, depart ye, go ye out from thence, touch not that which is unclean; go ye out of the midst of her; be ye clean that bear the vessels of the Lord.**

3 Nephi 20:Verse 42

42 For ye shall not go out with haste nor go by flight; for the Lord will go before you, and the God of Israel shall be your rearward.

D&C 133:Verse 1

1 Hearken, O ye people of my church, saith the Lord your God, and hear the word of the Lord concerning you--

D&C 133:Verse 2

2 The Lord who shall suddenly come to his temple; the Lord who shall come down upon the world with a curse to judgment; yea, upon all the nations that forget God, and upon all the ungodly among you.

D&C 133:Verse 3

3 For he shall make bare his holy arm in the eyes of all the nations, and all the ends of the earth shall see the salvation of their God.

D&C 133:Verse 4

4 Wherefore, prepare ye, prepare ye, O my people; sanctify yourselves; gather ye together, O ye people of my church, upon the land of Zion, all you that have not been commanded to tarry.

D&C 133:Verse 5

5 Go ye out from Babylon. Be ye clean that bear the vessels of the Lord.

D&C 133:Verse 6

6 Call your solemn assemblies, and speak often one to another. And let every man call upon the name of the Lord.

D&C 133:Verse 7

7 Yea, verily I say unto you again, the time has come when the voice of the Lord is unto you: Go ye out of Babylon; gather ye out from among the nations, from the four winds, from one end of heaven to the other.

D&C 133:Verse 8

8 Send forth the elders of my church unto the nations which are afar off; unto the islands of the sea; send forth unto foreign lands; call upon all nations, first upon the Gentiles, and then upon the Jews.

D&C 133:Verse 9

9 And behold, and lo, this shall be their cry, and the voice of the Lord unto all people: Go ye forth unto the land of Zion, that the borders of my people may be enlarged, and that her stakes may be strengthened, and that Zion may go forth unto the regions round about.

D&C 133:Verse 10

10 Yea, let the cry go forth among all people: Awake and arise and go forth to meet the Bridegroom; behold and lo, the Bridegroom cometh; go ye out to meet him. Prepare yourselves for the great day of the Lord.

D&C 133:Verse 11

11 Watch, therefore, for ye know neither the day nor the hour.

D&C 133:Verse 12

12 Let them, therefore, who are among the Gentiles flee unto Zion.

D&C 133:Verse 13

13 And let them who be of Judah flee unto Jerusalem, unto the mountains of the Lord's house.

D&C 133:Verse 14

14 Go ye out from among the nations, even from Babylon, from the midst of wickedness, which is spiritual Babylon.

D&C 133:Verse 15

15 But verily, thus saith the Lord, let not your flight be in haste, but let all things be prepared before you; and he that goeth, let him not look back lest sudden destruction shall come upon him.

D&C 133:Verse 16

16 Hearken and hear, O ye inhabitants of the earth. Listen, ye elders of my church together, and hear the voice of the Lord; for he calleth upon all men, and he commandeth all men everywhere to repent.

D&C 133:Verse 17

17 For behold, the Lord God hath sent forth the angel crying through the midst of heaven, saying: Prepare ye the way of the Lord, and make his paths straight, for the hour of his coming is nigh--

The Restoration Begins The Gathering of Israel

The restoration of the gospel, and the translation of the Book of Mormon is the key that opens the door for the Gathering of Israel to Jerusalem and to Zion. The Gospel, coupled with the coming forth of the Book of Mormon and the other scriptures, will signal the gathering, as the title page of the Book of Mormon states:

> Wherefore, it is an abridgment of the record of the people of Nephi, and also of the Lamanites--**Written to the Lamanites, who are a remnant of the house of Israel; and also to Jew and Gentile**--Written by way of commandment, and also by the spirit of prophecy and of revelation--Written and sealed up, and hid up unto the Lord, that they might not be destroyed--To come forth by the gift and power of God unto the interpretation thereof--Sealed by the hand of Moroni, and hid up unto the Lord, to come forth in due time by way of the Gentile--The interpretation thereof by the gift of God.
>
> An abridgment taken from the Book of Ether also, which is a record of the people of Jared, who were scattered at the time the Lord confounded the language of the people, when they were building a tower to get to heaven--**Which is to show unto the remnant of the House of Israel what great things the Lord hath done for their fathers; and that they may know the covenants of the Lord, that they are not cast off forever-- And also to the convincing of the Jew and Gentile that JESUS is the CHRIST, the ETERNAL GOD, manifesting himself unto all nations**--And now, if there are faults they are the mistakes of men; wherefore, condemn not the things of God, that ye may be found spotless at the judgment-seat of Christ.

The restoration is the Great and Marvelous Work upon which time, and the work of God pivots. There are many 'dispensations' of the gospel. The seven major dispensations are: Adamic, Enoch, Noah, Abraham, Moses, Christ or the Meridian of Time, and Joseph Smith or the Dispensation of the Fullness of Times. These are sometimes called the seven major dispensations, however, one must not forget the Book of Mormon. We see the dispensation of Nephi, Alma, Samuel the Lamanite, and Christ. There could be many, knowing nothing of the ten tribes. The dispensation of the fullness of times opens the door for the preparation of the Second Coming of Christ, the gathering of Israel, and the destruction of Babylon, because of the restored Gospel. The servants of the Lord have gone forth, to reap the earth, and to gather Israel from around the world, this Alast time@ as scripture states. The walls of Babylon have begun to crumble, and there can only be one outcome. The Goal of each dispensation has been to establish Zion.

All dispensations failed in this goal, except the dispensation of Enoch, (and perhaps Melchizedek) because of secret oaths and combinations. This dispensation will not fail, Zion will stand and usher Israel into the Millennium, as the secret combinations fall with the whore of all the earth. (See the appendix on Nephi).

Ezekiel 37:Verse 1
1 THE hand of the LORD was upon me, and carried me out in the spirit of the LORD, and set me down in the midst of the valley which [was] full of bones,

Ezekiel 37:Verse 2
2 And caused me to pass by them round about: and, behold, [there were] very many in the open valley; and, lo, [they were] very dry.

Ezekiel 37:Verse 3
3 And he said unto me, Son of man, can these bones live? And I answered, O Lord GOD, thou knowest.

Ezekiel 37:Verse 4
4 Again he said unto me, Prophesy upon these bones, and say unto them, O ye dry bones, hear the word of the LORD.

Ezekiel 37:Verse 5
5 Thus saith the Lord GOD unto these bones; Behold, I will cause breath to enter into you, and ye shall live:

Ezekiel 37:Verse 6
6 And I will lay sinews upon you, and will bring up flesh upon you, and cover you with skin, and put breath in you, and ye shall live; and ye shall know that I [am] the LORD.

Ezekiel 37:Verse 7
7 So I prophesied as I was commanded: and as I prophesied, there was a noise, and behold a shaking, and the bones came together, bone to his bone.

Ezekiel 37:Verse 8
8 And when I beheld, lo, the sinews and the flesh came up upon them, and the skin covered them above: but [there was] no breath in them.

Ezekiel 37:Verse 9
9 Then said he unto me, Prophesy unto the wind, prophesy, son of man, and say to the wind, Thus saith the Lord GOD; Come from the four winds, O breath, and breathe upon these slain, that they may live.

Ezekiel 37:Verse 10
10 So I prophesied as he commanded me, and the breath came into them, and they lived, and stood up upon their feet, an exceeding great army.

Ezekiel 37:Verse 11

11 Then he said unto me, Son of man, **these bones are the whole house of Israel: behold, they say, Our bones are dried, and our hope is lost: we are cut off for our parts.**

Ezekiel 37:Verse 12

12 Therefore prophesy and say unto them, **Thus saith the Lord GOD; Behold, O my people, I will open your graves, and cause you to come up out of your graves, and bring you into the land of Israel.**

Ezekiel 37:Verse 13

13 **And ye shall know that I [am] the LORD, when I have opened your graves, O my people, and brought you up out of your graves,**

Ezekiel 37:Verse 14

14 **And shall put my spirit in you, and ye shall live, and I shall place you in your own land: then shall ye know that I the LORD have spoken [it], and performed [it], saith the LORD.**

The vision of the 'Valley of dry bones' is a prophetic vision of the restoration of Israel, the verses above about this restoration is to come about because of the following verses in this chapter. The Book of Mormon coupled with the Bible become one in the hand to the convincing of Jew and Gentile that Jesus is the Christ

---

Ezekiel 37:Verse 15

15 The word of the LORD came again unto me, saying,

Ezekiel 37:Verse 16

16 Moreover, thou son of man, **take thee one stick, and write upon it, For Judah, and for the children of Israel his companions: then take another stick, and write upon it, For Joseph, the stick of Ephraim, and [for] all the house of Israel his companions:**

Ezekiel 37:Verse 17

17 **And join them one to another into one stick; and they shall become one in thine hand.**

Ezekiel 37:Verse 18

18 **And when the children of thy people shall speak unto thee, saying, Wilt thou not shew us what thou [meanest] by these?**

Ezekiel 37:Verse 19

19 **Say unto them, Thus saith the Lord GOD; Behold, I will take the stick of Joseph, which [is] in the hand of Ephraim, and the tribes of Israel his fellows, and will put them with him, [even] with the stick of Judah, and make them one stick, and they shall be one in mine hand.**

Ezekiel 37:Verse 20
20 And the sticks whereon thou writest shall be in thine hand before their eyes.

Ezekiel 37:Verse 21
21 And say unto them, Thus saith the Lord GOD; Behold, I will take the children of Israel from among the heathen, whither they be gone, and will gather them on every side, and bring them into their own land:

Ezekiel 37:Verse 22
22 And I will make them one nation in the land upon the mountains of Israel; and one king shall be king to them all: and they shall be no more two nations, neither shall they be divided into two kingdoms any more at all:

Zechariah 2:Verse 8
8 For thus saith the LORD of hosts; After the glory hath he sent me unto the nations which spoiled you: for he that toucheth you toucheth the apple of his eye.

Zechariah 2:Verse 9
9 For, behold, I will shake mine hand upon them, and they shall be a spoil to their servants: and ye shall know that the LORD of hosts hath sent me.

---

1 Nephi 13:Verse 42
42 And the time cometh that he shall manifest himself unto all nations, both unto the Jews and also unto the Gentiles; and after he has manifested himself unto the Jews and also unto the Gentiles, then he shall manifest himself unto the Gentiles and also unto the Jews, and the last shall be first, and the first shall be last.

---

1 Nephi 14:Verse 1
1 AND it shall come to pass, that if the Gentiles shall hearken unto the Lamb of God in that day that he shall manifest himself unto them in word, and also in power, in very deed, unto the taking away of their stumbling blocks--

1 Nephi 14:Verse 2
2 And harden not their hearts against the Lamb of God, they shall be numbered among the seed of thy father; yea, they shall be numbered among the house of Israel; and they shall be a blessed people upon the promised land forever; they shall be no more brought down into captivity; and the house of Israel shall no more be confounded.

---

1 Nephi 22:Verse 6
6 Nevertheless, after they shall be nursed by the Gentiles, and the Lord has lifted up his hand upon the Gentiles and set them up for a standard, and their children have been carried in their arms, and their daughters have been carried upon their shoulders, behold these things of which are spoken are temporal; for thus are the covenants of the Lord with our fathers; and it meaneth us in the days to come, and also all our brethren who are of the house of Israel.

1 Nephi 22:Verse 7

7 And it meaneth that the time cometh that **after all the house of Israel have been scattered and confounded, that the Lord God will raise up a mighty nation among the Gentiles, yea, even upon the face of this land; and by them shall our seed be scattered.**

1 Nephi 22:Verse 8

8 And after our seed is scattered the Lord God will proceed to do a marvelous work among the Gentiles, which shall be of great worth unto our seed; wherefore, it is likened unto their being nourished by the Gentiles and being carried in their arms and upon their shoulders.

1 Nephi 22:Verse 9

9 And it shall also be of worth unto the Gentiles; and not only unto the Gentiles but unto all the house of Israel, unto the making known of the covenants of the Father of heaven unto Abraham, saying: In thy seed shall all the kindreds of the earth be blessed.

---

1 Nephi 22:Verse 12

12 Wherefore, **he will bring them again out of captivity, and they shall be gathered together to the lands of their inheritance; and they shall be brought out of obscurity and out of darkness; and they shall know that the Lord is their Savior and their Redeemer, the Mighty One of Israel.**

---

2 Nephi 29:Verse 1

1 BUT behold, there shall be many--**at that day when I shall proceed to do a marvelous work among them, that I may remember my covenants which I have made unto the children of men, that I may set my hand again the second time to recover my people, which are of the house of Israel;**

2 Nephi 29:Verse 2

2 And also, **that I may remember the promises which I have made** unto thee, Nephi, and also unto thy father, that I would remember your seed; and that the words of your seed should proceed forth out of my mouth unto your seed; and my words shall hiss forth unto the ends of the earth, for a standard unto my people, which are of the house of Israel;

---

2 Nephi 29:Verse 13

13 And it shall come to pass that **the Jews shall have the words of the Nephites, and the Nephites shall have the words of the Jews; and the Nephites and the Jews shall have the words of the lost tribes of Israel; and the lost tribes of Israel shall have the words of the Nephites and the Jews.**

2 Nephi 29:Verse 14

14 And it shall come to pass that **my people, which are of the house of Israel, shall be gathered home unto the lands of their possessions; and my word also shall be gathered in one**. And I will show unto them that fight against my word and against my people, who are of the house of Israel, that I am God, and that I covenanted with Abraham that I would remember his seed forever.

---

3 Nephi 20:Verse 13

13 And then **shall the remnants, which shall be scattered abroad upon the face of the earth, be gathered in from the east and from the west, and from the south and from the north; and they shall be brought to the knowledge of the Lord their God, who hath redeemed them.**

---

3 Nephi 21:Verse 1

1 AND verily I say unto you, **I give unto you a sign, that ye may know the time when these things shall be about to take place--that I shall gather in, from their long dispersion, my people, O house of Israel, and shall establish again among them my Zion;**

3 Nephi 21:Verse 2

2 And behold, this is the thing which I will give unto you for a sign--for verily I say unto you that when these things which I declare unto you, and which I shall declare unto you hereafter of myself, and by the power of the Holy Ghost which shall be given unto you of the Father, shall be made known unto the Gentiles that they may know concerning this people who are a remnant of the house of Jacob, and concerning this my people who shall be scattered by them;

3 Nephi 21:Verse 3

3 Verily, verily, I say unto you, when these things shall be made known unto them of the Father, and shall come forth of the Father, from them unto you;

3 Nephi 21:Verse 4

4 For it is wisdom in the Father that they should be established in this land, and be set up as a free people by the power of the Father, that these things might come forth from them unto a remnant of your seed, that the covenant of the Father may be fulfilled which he hath covenanted with his people, O house of Israel;

3 Nephi 21:Verse 5

5 Therefore, when these works and the works which shall be wrought among you hereafter shall come forth from the Gentiles, unto your seed which shall dwindle in unbelief because of iniquity;

3 Nephi 21:Verse 6

6 For thus it behooveth the Father that it should come forth from the Gentiles, that he may show forth his power unto the Gentiles, for this cause that the Gentiles, if they will not harden their hearts, that they may repent and come unto me and be baptized in my name and know of the true points of my doctrine, that they may be numbered among my people, O house of Israel;

3 Nephi 21:Verse 7

7 And **when these things come to pass that thy seed shall begin to know these things--it shall be a sign unto them, that they may know that the work of the Father hath already commenced unto the fulfilling of the covenant which he hath made unto the people who are of the house of Israel.**

---

3 Nephi 21:Verse 26

26 And **then shall the work of the Father commence at that day, even when this gospel shall be preached among the remnant of this people**. Verily I say unto you, at that day shall the work of the Father commence among all the dispersed of my people, yea, even the tribes which have been lost, which the Father hath led away out of Jerusalem.

3 Nephi 21:Verse 27

27 Yea, **the work shall commence among all the dispersed of my people, with the Father to prepare the way whereby they may come unto me, that they may call on the Father in my name.**

3 Nephi 21:Verse 28

28 Yea, and then shall the work commence, with the Father among all nations in preparing the way whereby his people may be gathered home to the land of their inheritance.

3 Nephi 21:Verse 29

29 And they shall go out from all nations; and they shall not go out in haste, nor go by flight, for I will go before them, saith the Father, and I will be their rearward.

D&C 29:Verse 7

7 And **ye are called to bring to pass the gathering of mine elect**; for mine elect hear my voice and harden not their hearts;

D&C 29:Verse 8

8 Wherefore the decree hath gone forth from the Father that **they shall be gathered in unto one place upon the face of this land, to prepare their hearts and be prepared in all things against the day when tribulation and desolation are sent forth upon the wicked.**

D&C 45:Verse 25

25 But **they shall be gathered again; but they shall remain until the times of the Gentiles be fulfilled.**

D&C 63:Verse 36

36 Wherefore, seeing that I, the Lord, have decreed all these things upon the face of the earth, I will that my saints should be assembled upon the land of Zion;

D&C 87:Verse 7

7 That the cry of the saints, and of the blood of the saints, shall cease to come up into the ears of the Lord of Sabaoth, from the earth, to be avenged of their enemies.

D&C 87:Verse 8

8 Wherefore, stand ye in holy places, and be not moved, until the day of the Lord come; for behold, it cometh quickly, saith the Lord. Amen.

D&C 133:Verse 4

4 Wherefore, prepare ye, prepare ye, O my people; sanctify yourselves; gather ye together, O ye people of my church, upon the land of Zion, all you that have not been commanded to tarry.

D&C 133:Verse 9

9 And behold, and lo, this shall be their cry, and the voice of the Lord unto all people: **Go ye forth unto the land of Zion, that the borders of my people may be enlarged, and that her stakes may be strengthened, and that Zion may go forth unto the regions round about.**

D&C 133:Verse 12

12 **Let them, therefore, who are among the Gentiles flee unto Zion.**

D&C 133:Verse 13

13 And **let them who be of Judah flee unto Jerusalem**, unto the mountains of the Lord's house.

D&C 133:Verse 14

14 Go ye out from among the nations, even from Babylon, from the midst of wickedness, which is spiritual Babylon.

Joseph Smith Matthew 1:Verse 27

27 And now I show unto you a parable. Behold, wheresoever the carcass is, there will the eagles be gathered together; **so likewise shall mine elect be gathered from the four quarters of the earth.**

8

Satan's Influence over the Nations of the Earth

Revelation 13: 1-18:14: 9-11

Revelation Chapter 13 describes the earthly kingdoms, and the control that Satan will have over the nations and people of the earth in the last days. Babylon flourishes as Satan reigns with his false priesthoods upon the earth, in this, the great day of his power. The 'love' or 'desire' for money is the root of all-evil, and has become the god of modern man. With this quest for affluence Satan plays upon the pride of all, as we try to lay up treasures on earth, with a pseudo security acting upon Satan's first article of faith, that 'you can have anything in this world for money'. Herein lies the Babylon: trusting in the arm of flesh to provide and protect, to govern our very actions and activities as we seek for greater security in stocks, bonds, and portfolios that will provide a successful life-style for the well to do in Babylon. You cannot, have one foot in Babylon and the other in Zion, and be righteous, in the eyes of God. As the Lord states: 'I would thou wert cold or hot. So then because thou are lukewarm, and neither cold nor hot, I will spue thee out of my mouth' (Rev. 3:15-16). Many Latter-day Saints, are doing two and a half gainers off the 'iron rod' into the 'river of filthy water' trying to reach the 'great and spacious building,' not knowing that they have left the path to the 'tree of life.' The prophet Jeremiah rebukes Israel, because of their attitude of 'all is well in zion' feeling secure in their wickedness. This attitude led to the destruction of Judah by Babylon, and prompted the exodus of Lehi and his family, under the direction of the Lord:

1 THE word that came to Jeremiah from the LORD, saying,
2 Stand in the gate of the LORD'S house, and proclaim there this word, and say, Hear the word of the LORD, all [ye of] Judah, that enter in at these gates to worship the LORD.
3 Thus saith the LORD of hosts, the God of Israel, Amend your ways and your doings, and I will cause you to dwell in this place.
4 Trust ye not in lying words, saying, The temple of the LORD, The temple of the LORD, The temple of the LORD, [are] these.
5 For if ye throughly amend your ways and your doings; if ye throughly execute judgment between a man and his neighbour;
6 [If] ye oppress not the stranger, the fatherless, and the widow, and shed not innocent blood in this place, neither walk after other gods to your hurt:
7 Then will I cause you to dwell in this place, in the land that I gave to your fathers, for ever and ever.
8 Behold, ye trust in lying words, that cannot profit.

9 Will ye steal, murder, and commit adultery, and swear falsely, and burn incense unto Baal, and walk after other gods whom ye know not;

10 And come and stand before me in this house, which is called by my name, and say, We are delivered to do all these abominations?

11 Is this house, which is called by my name, become a den of robbers in your eyes? Behold, even I have seen [it], saith the LORD.

12 But go ye now unto my place which [was] in Shiloh, where I set my name at the first, and see what I did to it for the wickedness of my people Israel.

13 And now, because ye have done all these works, saith the LORD, and I spake unto you, rising up early and speaking, but ye heard not; and I called you, but ye answered not;

14 Therefore will I do unto [this] house, which is called by my name, wherein ye trust, and unto the place which I gave to you and to your fathers, as I have done to Shiloh.

15 And I will cast you out of my sight, as I have cast out all your brethren, [even] the whole seed of Ephraim.

Jeremiah 7:1-15

Jeremiah, speaking to Israel-- those who have the gospel and know the scriptures, and have been taught correct principles-- states, that they trust in themselves and 'lying words' because they have the temple, (and temple recommends) believing that they are delivered to do wickedness. The chosen people of the Lord, feel secure in being dishonest in their business dealings, and taking advantage of the unsuspecting individual. Declaring 'all is well' in their personal Zion, being active in the church, but inactive in the gospel, feeling no need for repentance as they look down on their spiritual brothers and sisters from their personal rameumptom like residences. Jeremiah then tells Israel to look back to where the temple (the ark and tabernacle) had been, look back at Shiloh, Kirkland, Nauvoo, and Far West.

As Babylon becomes a Aglobal economy@ all the nations of the earth delight in her delicacies, as all the world enjoys the pleasures of the 'great whore'. The judgment of God will come and Babylon will fall.

(See the appendix: 'The False Gods we Worship' the Bicentennial talk by President Kimball)

Revelation 13:Verse 1

1 AND I stood upon the sand of the sea, and **saw a beast** rise up out of the sea, having seven heads and ten horns, and upon his horns ten crowns, and upon his heads the name of blasphemy.

Revelation 13:Verse 2

2 And the beast which I saw was like unto a leopard, and his feet were as [the feet] of a bear, and his mouth as the mouth of a lion: and the dragon gave him his power, and his seat, and great authority.

Revelation 13:Verse 3

3 And I saw **one of his heads as it were wounded to death; and his deadly wound was healed:** and all the world wondered after the beast.

Revelation 13:Verse 4

4 And they worshipped the dragon which gave power unto the beast: and they worshipped the beast, saying, Who [is] like unto the beast? who is able to make war with him?

Revelation 13:Verse 5

5 And there was given unto him a mouth **speaking great things and blasphemies;** and power was given unto him to continue forty [and] two months.

Revelation 13:Verse 6

6 And **he opened his mouth in blasphemy against God**, to blaspheme his name, and his tabernacle, and them that dwell in heaven.

Revelation 13:Verse 7

7 And it was given unto him to make war with the saints, and to overcome them: and power was given him over all kindreds, and tongues, and nations.

Revelation 13:Verse 8

8 And **all that dwell upon the earth shall worship him,** whose names are not written in the book of life of the Lamb slain from the foundation of the world.

Revelation 13:Verse 9

9 If any man have an ear, let him hear.

Revelation 13:Verse 10

10 He that leadeth into captivity shall go into captivity: he that killeth with the sword must be killed with the sword. Here is the patience and the faith of the saints.

Revelation 13:Verse 11

11 And I beheld another beast coming up out of the earth; and he had two horns like a lamb, and he spake as a dragon.

Revelation 13:Verse 12

12 And he exerciseth all the power of the first beast before him, and causeth the earth and them which dwell therein to worship the first beast, whose deadly wound was healed.

Revelation 13:Verse 13

13 And **he doeth great wonders, so that he maketh fire come down from heaven on the earth in the sight of men,**

Revelation 13:Verse 14

14 **And deceiveth them that dwell on the earth by [the means of] those miracles which he had power to do in the sight** of the beast; saying to them that dwell on the earth, that they should make an image to the beast, which had the wound by a sword, and did live.

Revelation 13:Verse 15

15 And he had power to give life unto the image of the beast, that the image of the beast should both speak, and cause that as many as would not worship the image of the beast should be killed.

Revelation 13:Verse 16

16 And he causeth all, both small and great, rich and poor, free and bond, to receive a mark in their right hand, or in their foreheads:

Revelation 14:Verse 9

9 And the third angel followed them, saying with a loud voice, If any man worship the beast and his image, and receive [his] mark in his forehead, or in his hand,

Revelation 14:Verse 10

10 The same shall drink of the wine of the wrath of God, which is poured out without mixture into the cup of his indignation; and he shall be tormented with fire and brimstone in the presence of the holy angels, and in the presence of the Lamb:

Revelation 14:Verse 11

11 And the smoke of their torment ascendeth up for ever and ever: and they have no rest day nor night, who worship the beast and his image, and whosoever receiveth the mark of his name.

Revelation 13:Verse 17

17 **And that no man might buy or sell, save he that had the mark,** or the name of the beast, or the number of his name.

Revelation 13:Verse 18

18 Here is wisdom. Let him that hath understanding count the number of the beast: for it is the number of a man; and his number [is] Six hundred threescore [and] six.

Daniel 7:Verse 1

1 IN the first year of Belshazzar king of Babylon Daniel had a dream and visions of his head upon his bed: then he wrote the dream, [and] told the sum of the matters.

Daniel 7:Verse 2

2 Daniel spake and said, I saw in my vision by night, and, behold, the four winds of the heaven strove upon the great sea.

Daniel 7:Verse 3

3 And four great beasts came up from the sea, diverse one from another.

Daniel 7:Verse 4

4 The first [was] like a lion, and had eagle's wings: I beheld till the wings thereof were plucked, and it was lifted up from the earth, and made stand upon the feet as a man, and a man's heart was given to it.

Daniel 7:Verse 5

5 And behold another beast, a second, like to a bear, and it raised up itself on one side, and [it had] three ribs in the mouth of it between the teeth of it: and they said thus unto it, Arise, devour much flesh.

Daniel 7:Verse 6

6 After this I beheld, and lo another, like a leopard, which had upon the back of it four wings of a fowl; the beast had also four heads; and dominion was given to it.

Daniel 7:Verse 7

7 After this I saw in the night visions, and behold a fourth beast, dreadful and terrible, and strong exceedingly; and it had great iron teeth: it devoured and brake in pieces, and stamped the residue with the feet of it: and it [was] diverse from all the beasts that [were] before it; and it had ten horns.

Daniel 7:Verse 8

8 I considered the horns, and, behold, there came up among them another little horn, before whom there were three of the first horns plucked up by the roots: and, behold, in this horn [were] eyes like the eyes of man, and a mouth speaking great things.

Daniel 7:Verse 11

11 I beheld then because of the voice of the great words which the horn spake: I beheld [even] till the beast was slain, and his body destroyed, and given to the burning flame.

Daniel 7:Verse 12

12 As concerning the rest of the beasts, they had their dominion taken away: yet their lives were prolonged for a season and time.

Daniel 7:Verse 15

15 I Daniel was grieved in my spirit in the midst of [my] body, and the visions of my head troubled me.

Daniel 7:Verse 16

16 I came near unto one of them that stood by, and asked him the truth of all this. So he told me, and made me know the interpretation of the things.

Daniel 7:Verse 17

17 These great beasts, which are four, [are] four kings, [which] shall arise out of the earth.

Daniel 7:Verse 19

19 Then I would know the truth of the fourth beast, which was diverse from all the others, exceeding dreadful, whose teeth [were of] iron, and his nails [of] brass; [which] devoured, brake in pieces, and stamped the residue with his feet;

Daniel 7:Verse 20

20 And of the ten horns that [were] in his head, and [of] the other which came up, and before whom three fell; even [of] that horn that had eyes, and a mouth that spake very great things, whose look [was] more stout than his fellows.

Daniel 7:Verse 21

21 I beheld, and **the same horn made war with the saints, and prevailed against them;**

Daniel 7:Verse 22

22 **Until** the Ancient of days came, and judgment was given to the saints of the most High; and the time came that the saints possessed the kingdom.

Daniel 7:Verse 23

23 Thus he said, The fourth beast shall be the fourth kingdom upon earth, which shall be diverse from all kingdoms, and shall devour the whole earth, and shall tread it down, and break it in pieces.

Daniel 7:Verse 24

24 And the ten horns out of this kingdom [are] ten kings [that] shall arise: and another shall rise after them; and he shall be diverse from the first, and he shall subdue three kings.

Daniel 7:Verse 25

25 And **he shall speak [great] words against the most High, and shall wear out the saints of the most High, and think to change times and laws: and they shall be given into his hand until a time and times and the dividing of time.**

D&C 76:Verse 29

29 Wherefore, **he maketh war with the saints of God, and encompasseth them round about.**

D&C 76:Verse 30
30 And we saw a vision of the sufferings of those with whom he made war and overcame, for thus came the voice of the Lord unto us:

Joseph Smith Matthew 1:Verse 22
22 For in those days **there shall also arise false Christs, and false prophets, and shall show great signs and wonders**, insomuch, that, if possible, they shall deceive the very elect, who are the elect according to the covenant.

Joseph Smith Matthew 1:Verse 23
23 Behold, I speak these things unto you for the elect's sake; and **you also shall hear of wars, and rumors of wars**; see that ye be not troubled, for all I have told you must come to pass; but the end is not yet.

9

Babylon the Great Reigns over the Leaders of the Earth

Revelation 17: 1-18

Babylon, is the scriptural designation of spiritual wickedness, (D&C 133:14) which wickedness is nurtured by the Mother of Harlots and propagated by the nations of the earth. The lack of morals, and religious conviction, in government leaders, in business, and in the culture itself, leads Satan to boast that this is the great day of his power. Satan reigns in the hearts of mankind, as the love of man waxes cold. First Nephi Chapter Twenty Two states that there are four things that signify the goals of the Church of the Devil, and those who belong to Babylon these are: (1) to get gain (2) to get power over the flesh (3) to become popular (4) seek the lusts of the flesh. These four elements of wickedness are described by the prophet Mormon as the very things that lead to the downfall of the Nephite nation. (see 3 Nephi 6:15)

Chapter Seventeen explains the power, and influence of Babylon in the world, both political, and economic, and it appears that this influence is global. Chapter Seventeen should be read in conjunction with Revelation 18; 1 Nephi 13, 14, 22; and Isaiah 13, 14.

It must be remembered that Babylon, the Church of the Devil, or Great and Abominable Church was set up by Satan from the time of our First Father Adam. The God of this world has been trying to destroy the Church, and Kingdom of God from the time that Adam received the gospel of Jesus Christ and the priesthood of God down to the present day. The devil uses the gold and silver, armies, and governments to reign with blood and horror on the earth, as he tries to exercise his false priesthoods, powers, and teaching false doctrines of men salted with scripture. Trying to convince mankind that there is no devil, or hell, no God or Son of God, thus destroying the nature of Deity and the necessity of the atonement.

Revelation 17:Verse 1
1 AND there came one of the seven angels which had the seven vials, and talked with me, saying unto me, Come hither; I will shew unto thee the judgment of the great whore that sitteth upon **many waters:**

Revelation 17:Verse 15

15 And he saith unto me, **The waters which thou sawest, where the whore sitteth, are peoples, and multitudes, and nations, and tongues.**

The Church of the Devil and Babylon

Revelation 17:Verse 18

18 And the woman which thou sawest is that **great city, which reigneth over the kings of the earth.**

Revelation 17:Verse 5

5 And upon her forehead [was] a name written, **MYSTERY, BABYLON THE GREAT, THE MOTHER OF HARLOTS AND ABOMINATIONS OF THE EARTH.**

Satan's Goal is to persecute and control those that are Valiant, and faithful

Revelation 17:Verse 3

3 So he carried me away in the spirit into the wilderness: and I saw a woman sit upon a scarlet coloured beast, full of names of blasphemy, having seven heads and ten horns.

Revelation 17:Verse 6

6 And I saw **the woman drunken with the blood of the saints, and with the blood of the martyrs of Jesus:** and when I saw her, I wondered with great admiration.

Revelation 17:Verse 7

7 And the angel said unto me, Wherefore didst thou marvel? I will tell thee the mystery of the woman, and of the beast that carrieth her, which hath the seven heads and ten horns.

Revelation 17:Verse 8

8 The **beast that thou sawest was, and is not; and shall ascend out of the bottomless pit, and go into perdition:** and they that dwell on the earth shall wonder, whose names were not written in the book of life from the foundation of the world, when they behold the beast that was, and is not, and yet is.

Revelation 17:Verse 9

9 And here [is] the mind which hath wisdom. The seven heads are seven mountains, on which the woman sitteth.

Revelation 17:Verse 10
10 And there are seven kings: five are fallen, and one is, [and] the other is not yet come; and when he cometh, he must continue a short space.

Revelation 17:Verse 11
11 And the beast that was, and is not, even he is the eighth, and is of the seven, and goeth into perdition.

*Satan desires Gold and silver
to purchase kingdoms and priests
to control the nations*

Revelation 17:Verse 4
4 And the **woman was arrayed in purple and scarlet colour, and decked with gold and precious stones and pearls, having a golden cup in her hand full of abominations and filthiness of her fornication:**

Revelation 17:Verse 2
2 With whom the kings of the earth have committed fornication, and the inhabitants of the earth have been made drunk with the wine of her fornication.

*Satan and those in his power declare
spiritual, and physical war against the righteous*

Revelation 17:Verse 12
12 And the ten horns which thou sawest are ten kings, which have received no kingdom as yet; but receive power as kings one hour with the beast.

Revelation 17:Verse 13
13 These have one mind, and shall give their power and strength unto the beast.

Revelation 17:Verse 14a
14 **These shall make war with the Lamb,**

*The faithful are protected
armed with righteousness*

Revelation 17:Verse 14b
and **the Lamb shall overcome them: for he is Lord of lords,** and King of kings: and they that are with him [are] called, and chosen, and faithful.

*The destruction comes
from within, the wicked
destroy themselves*

Revelation 17:Verse 16

16 And the ten horns which thou sawest upon the beast, **these shall hate the whore, and shall make her desolate and naked,** and shall eat her flesh, and burn her with fire.

Revelation 17:Verse 17

17 **For God hath put in their hearts to fulfil his will,** and to agree, and give their kingdom unto the beast, until the words of God shall be fulfilled.

---

1 Nephi 13:Verse 1

1 AND it came to pass that the angel spake unto me, saying: Look! And I looked and **beheld many nations and kingdoms.**

1 Nephi 13:Verse 2

2 And the angel said unto me: What beholdest thou? And I said: I behold many nations and kingdoms.

1 Nephi 13:Verse 3

3 And he said unto me: These are the nations and kingdoms of the Gentiles.

1 Nephi 13:Verse 4

4 And it came to pass that **I saw among the nations of the Gentiles the formation of a great church.**

1 Nephi 13:Verse 5

5 And the angel said unto me: Behold **the formation of a church which is most abominable above all other churches, which slayeth the saints of God,** yea, and tortureth them and bindeth them down, and yoketh them with a yoke of iron, and bringeth them down into captivity.

1 Nephi 13:Verse 6

6 And it came to pass that I beheld **this great and abominable church; and I saw the devil that he was the founder of it.**

1 Nephi 13:Verse 7

7 And I also saw gold, and silver, and silks, and scarlets, and fine-twined linen, and all manner of precious clothing; and I saw many harlots.

1 Nephi 13:Verse 8

8 And the angel spake unto me, saying: Behold **the gold, and the silver, and the silks, and the scarlets, and the fine-twined linen, and the precious clothing, and the harlots, are the desires of this great and abominable church.**

1 Nephi 13:Verse 9

9 **And also for the praise of the world do they destroy the saints of God, and bring them down into captivity.**

1 Nephi 13:Verse 20

20 And it came to pass that I, Nephi, beheld that they did prosper in the land; and I beheld a book, and it was carried forth among them.

1 Nephi 13:Verse 21

21 And the angel said unto me: Knowest thou the meaning of the book?

1 Nephi 13:Verse 22

22 And I said unto him: I know not.

1 Nephi 13:Verse 23

23 And he said: Behold it proceedeth out of the mouth of a Jew. And I, Nephi, beheld it; and he said unto me: The book that thou beholdest is a record of the Jews, which contains the covenants of the Lord, which he hath made unto the house of Israel; and it also containeth many of the prophecies of the holy prophets; and it is a record like unto the engravings which are upon the plates of brass, save there are not so many; nevertheless, they contain the covenants of the Lord, which he hath made unto the house of Israel; wherefore, they are of great worth unto the Gentiles.

1 Nephi 13:Verse 24

24 And the angel of the Lord said unto me: Thou hast beheld that the book proceeded forth from the mouth of a Jew; and when it proceeded forth from the mouth of a Jew it contained the fulness of the gospel of the Lord, of whom the twelve apostles bear record; and they bear record according to the truth which is in the Lamb of God.

1 Nephi 13:Verse 25

25 Wherefore, these things go forth from the Jews in purity unto the Gentiles, according to the truth which is in God.

1 Nephi 13:Verse 26

26 And after they go forth by the hand of the twelve apostles of the Lamb, from the Jews unto the Gentiles, **thou seest the formation of that great and abominable church, which is most abominable above all other churches; for behold, they have taken away from the gospel of the Lamb many parts which are plain and most precious; and also many covenants of the Lord have they taken away.**

1 Nephi 13:Verse 27

27 And all this have they done **that they might pervert the right ways of the Lord,** that they might blind the eyes and harden the hearts of the children of men.

1 Nephi 13:Verse 28

28 Wherefore, thou seest **that after the book hath gone forth through the hands of the great and abominable church, that there are many plain and precious things taken away from the book,** which is the book of the Lamb of God.

29 And after these plain and precious things were taken away it goeth forth unto all the nations of the Gentiles; and after it goeth forth unto all the nations of the Gentiles, yea, even across the many waters which thou hast seen with the Gentiles which have gone forth out of captivity, thou seest--**because of the many plain and precious things which have been taken out of the book, which were plain unto the understanding of the children of men, according to the plainness which is in the Lamb of God--because of these things which are taken away out of the gospel of the Lamb, an exceedingly great many do stumble, yea, insomuch that Satan hath great power over them.**

---

1 Nephi 14:Verse 3

3 And **that great pit, which hath been digged for them by that great and abominable church, which was founded by the devil and his children, that he might lead away the souls of men down to hell--yea, that great pit which hath been digged for the destruction of men shall be filled by those who digged it, unto their utter destruction**, saith the Lamb of God; not the destruction of the soul, save it be the casting of it into that hell which hath no end.

1 Nephi 14:Verse 4

4 For behold, this is according to the captivity of the devil, and also according to the justice of God, upon all those who will work wickedness and abomination before him.

1 Nephi 14:Verse 5

5 And it came to pass that the angel spake unto me, Nephi, saying: Thou hast beheld that if the Gentiles repent it shall be well with them; and thou also knowest concerning the covenants of the Lord unto the house of Israel; and thou also hast heard that whoso repenteth not must perish.

1 Nephi 14:Verse 6

6 Therefore, wo be unto the Gentiles if it so be that they harden their hearts against the Lamb of God.

---

1 Nephi 14:Verse 8

8 And it came to pass that when the angel had spoken these words, he said unto me: Rememberest thou the covenants of the Father unto the house of Israel? I said unto him, Yea.

1 Nephi 14:Verse 9

9 And it came to pass that he said unto me: Look, and **behold that great and abominable church, which is the mother of abominations, whose founder is the devil.**

1 Nephi 14:Verse 10

10 And he said unto me: Behold **there are save two churches only; the one is the church of the Lamb of God, and the other is the church of the devil; wherefore, whoso belongeth not to the church of the Lamb of God belongeth to that great church, which is the mother of abominations; and she is the whore of all the earth.**

1 Nephi 14:Verse 11

11 And it came to pass that I looked and beheld **the whore of all the earth, and she sat upon many waters; and she had dominion over all the earth, among all nations, kindreds, tongues, and people.**

1 Nephi 14:Verse 12

12 And it came to pass that **I beheld the church of the Lamb of God, and its numbers were few, because of the wickedness and abominations of the whore who sat upon many waters**; nevertheless, I beheld that the church of the Lamb, who were the saints of God, were also upon all the face of the earth; and their dominions upon the face of the earth were small, because of the wickedness of the great whore whom I saw.

1 Nephi 14:Verse 13

13 And it came to pass that **I beheld that the great mother of abominations did gather together multitudes upon the face of all the earth, among all the nations of the Gentiles, to fight against the Lamb of God**.

---

1 Nephi 22:Verse 22

22 And the righteous need not fear, for they are those who shall not be confounded. But it is the kingdom of the devil, which shall be built up among the children of men, which kingdom is established among them which are in the flesh--

1 Nephi 22:Verse 23

23 For the **time speedily shall come that all churches which are built up** *to get gain*, **and all those who are built up** *to get power over the flesh*, **and those who are** *built up to become popular* **in the eyes of the world, and those** *who seek the lusts of the flesh* **and the things of the world, and to do all manner of iniquity; yea, in fine, all those who belong to the kingdom of the devil are they who need fear, and tremble, and quake;** they are those who must be brought low in the dust; they are those who must be consumed as stubble; and this is according to the words of the prophet.

---

2 Nephi 27:Verse 1

1 But, behold, in the last days, or in the days of the Gentiles--yea, **behold all the nations of the Gentiles and also the Jews, both those who shall come upon this land and those who shall be upon other lands, yea, even upon all the lands of the earth, behold, they will be drunken with iniquity and all manner of abominations--**

Because of the plain and precious things that have been taken out of the Bible by the great and abominable church, people and churches stumble not knowing the truth.

---

2 Nephi 28:Verse 3

3 For it shall come to pass in that day that **the churches which are built up, and not unto the Lord, when the one shall say unto the other: Behold, I, I am the Lord's; and the others shall**

say: I, I am the Lord's; and thus shall every one say that hath built up churches, and not unto the Lord--

2 Nephi 28:Verse 4

4 And **they shall contend one with another;** and their priests shall contend one with another, and **they shall teach with their learning, and deny the Holy Ghost,** which giveth utterance.

2 Nephi 28:Verse 5

5 And **they deny the power of God**, the Holy One of Israel; and they say unto the people: Hearken unto us, and hear ye our precept; for behold there is no God today, for the Lord and the Redeemer hath done his work, and he hath given his power unto men;

2 Nephi 28:Verse 6

6 Behold, hearken ye unto my precept; if they shall say there is a miracle wrought by the hand of the Lord, believe it not; for this day he is not a God of miracles; he hath done his work.

2 Nephi 28:Verse 7

7 Yea, and there shall be **many which shall say: Eat, drink, and be merry, for tomorrow we die; and it shall be well with us.**

2 Nephi 28:Verse 8

8 And there shall also be **many which shall say: Eat, drink, and be merry; nevertheless, fear God--he will justify in committing a little sin; yea, lie a little, take the advantage of one because of his words, dig a pit for thy neighbor; there is no harm in this; and do all these things, for tomorrow we die; and if it so be that we are guilty, God will beat us with a few stripes, and at last we shall be saved in the kingdom of God.**

2 Nephi 28:Verse 9

9 Yea, and **there shall be many which shall teach after this manner, false and vain and foolish doctrines, and shall be puffed up in their hearts, and shall seek deep to hide their counsels from the Lord; and their works shall be in the dark**.

2 Nephi 28:Verse 10

10 And **the blood of the saints shall cry from the ground against them.**

2 Nephi 28:Verse 11

11 Yea, they have all gone out of the way; they have become corrupted.

2 Nephi 28:Verse 12

12 **Because of pride, and because of false teachers, and false doctrine, their churches have become corrupted, and their churches are lifted up; because of pride they are puffed up.**

2 Nephi 28:Verse 13

13 **They rob the poor because of their fine sanctuaries**; they rob the poor because of their fine clothing; and they **persecute the meek and the poor in heart, because in their pride they are puffed up.**

2 Nephi 28:Verse 14

14 They wear stiff necks and high heads; yea, and because of pride, and wickedness, and abominations, and whoredoms, **they have all gone astray save it be a few, who are the humble followers of Christ; nevertheless, they are led, that in many instances they do err because they are taught by the precepts of men.**

2 Nephi 28:Verse 15

15 O the wise, and the learned, and the rich, that are puffed up in the pride of their hearts, and all those who preach false doctrines, and all those who commit whoredoms, and pervert the right way of the Lord, wo, wo, wo be unto them, saith the Lord God Almighty, for they shall be thrust down to hell!

2 Nephi 28:Verse 16

16 Wo unto them that turn aside the just for a thing of naught and revile against that which is good, and say that it is of no worth! For the day shall come that the Lord God will speedily visit the inhabitants of the earth; and in that day that they are fully ripe in iniquity they shall perish.

2 Nephi 28:Verse 17

17 But behold, if the inhabitants of the earth shall repent of their wickedness and abominations they shall not be destroyed, saith the Lord of Hosts.

---

3 Nephi 16:Verse 10

10 And thus commandeth the Father that I should say unto you: At that day when the Gentiles shall sin against my gospel, and shall reject the fulness of my gospel, and shall be lifted up in the pride of their hearts above all nations, and above all the people of the whole earth, and shall be filled with all manner of lyings, and of deceits, and of mischiefs, and all manner of hypocrisy, and murders, and priestcrafts, and whoredoms, and of secret abominations; and if they shall do all those things, and shall reject the fulness of my gospel, behold, saith the Father, I will bring the fulness of my gospel from among them.

Mormon 8:Verse 26

26 And no one need say they shall not come, for they surely shall, for the Lord hath spoken it; for out of the earth shall they come, by the hand of the Lord, and none can stay it; and **it shall come in a day when it shall be said that miracles are done away; and it shall come even as if one should speak from the dead.**

Mormon 8:Verse 27

27 And it shall come **in a day when the blood of saints shall cry unto the Lord**, because of secret combinations and the works of darkness.

Mormon 8:Verse 28

28 Yea, **it shall come in a day when the power of God shall be denied**, and churches become defiled and be lifted up in the pride of their hearts; yea, even in a day when leaders of churches and teachers shall rise in the pride of their hearts, even to the envying of them who belong to their churches.

Mormon 8:Verse 29

29 Yea, it shall come in a day when there shall be heard of fires, and tempests, and vapors of smoke in foreign lands;

Mormon 8:Verse 30

30 And there shall also be heard of wars, rumors of wars, and earthquakes in divers places.

Mormon 8:Verse 31

31 Yea, **it shall come in a day when there shall be great pollutions upon the face of the earth; there shall be murders, and robbing, and lying, and deceivings, and whoredoms, and all manner of abominations; when there shall be many who will say, Do this, or do that, and it mattereth not, for the Lord will uphold such at the last day**. But wo unto such, for they are in the gall of bitterness and in the bonds of iniquity.

Mormon 8:Verse 32

32 Yea, it **shall come in a day when there shall be churches built up that shall say: Come unto me, and for your money you shall be forgiven of your sins.**

Mormon 8:Verse 33

33 **O ye wicked and perverse and stiffnecked people, why have ye built up churches unto yourselves to get gain? Why have ye transfigured the holy word of God, that ye might bring damnation upon your souls?** Behold, look ye unto the revelations of God; for behold, the time cometh at that day when all these things must be fulfilled.

Mormon 8:Verse 34

34 Behold, the Lord hath shown unto me great and marvelous things concerning that which must shortly come, at that day when these things shall come forth among you.

———————————————

10

The Sixth Seal is Opened

Revelation 6: 12-17

      The Prophet Joseph revealed in the Doctrine and Covenants the meaning of the Seals that were opened: *Q. What are we to understand by the seven seals with which it was sealed?*
    A. We are to understand that the first seal contains the things of the first thousand years, and the second also of the second thousand years, and so on until the seventh. (D&C 77:7). Interpolation would assume that the time period in which we now live is the sixth seal. This may, or may not be correct, however, Chapter Six, Verse Twelve, with the opening of the sixth seal will be the beginning point for the events of the Last Days.
      With the opening of this seal there is seen signs and wonders in the heavens and on the earth signaling that the end is nigh at hand, and there is none to escape, not even the kings, and rich men of the earth. It is at this time that the mighty learn that God is no respecter of persons, and that the Lord esteemeth all flesh in one; he that is righteous is favored of God. (1 Nephi 17:35).

Revelation 6:Verse 12
12 And I beheld when he had opened the sixth seal, and, lo, there was **a great earthquake; and the sun became black as sackcloth of hair, and the moon became as blood;**

Revelation 6:Verse 13
13 And the **stars of heaven fell unto the earth**, even as a fig tree casteth her untimely figs, when she is shaken of a mighty wind.

Revelation 6:Verse 14
14 And the **heaven departed as a scroll when it is rolled together; and every mountain and island were moved out of their places.**

Revelation 6:Verse 15
15 And the kings of the earth, and the great men, and the rich men, and the chief captains, and the mighty men, and every bondman, and every free man, hid themselves in the dens and in the rocks of the mountains;

Revelation 6:Verse 16
16 And said to the mountains and rocks, Fall on us, and hide us from the face of him that sitteth on the throne, and from the wrath of the Lamb:

Revelation 6:Verse 17
17 For the great day of his wrath is come; and who shall be able to stand?

D&C 77:Verse 7
7 Q. What are we to understand by the seven seals with which it was sealed?
 A. We are to understand that the first seal contains the things of the first thousand years, and the second also of the second thousand years, and so on until the seventh.

Isaiah 24:Verse 17
17 Fear, and the pit, and the snare, [are] upon thee, O inhabitant of the earth.

Isaiah 24:Verse 18
18 And it shall come to pass, [that] **he who fleeth from the noise of the fear shall fall into the pit; and he that cometh up out of the midst of the pit shall be taken in the snare: for the windows from on high are open, and the foundations of the earth do shake.**

Isaiah 24:Verse 19
19 **The earth is utterly broken down, the earth is clean dissolved, the earth is moved exceedingly**.

Isaiah 24:Verse 20
20 **The earth shall reel to and fro like a drunkard**, and shall be removed like a cottage; and the transgression thereof shall be heavy upon it; and it shall fall, and not rise again.

Isaiah 24:Verse 21
21 And it shall come to pass in that day, [that] **the LORD shall punish the host of the high ones [that are] on high, and the kings of the earth upon the earth.**

Isaiah 24:Verse 22
22 And they shall be gathered together, [as] prisoners are gathered in the pit, and shall be shut up in the prison, and after many days shall they be visited.

Isaiah 24:Verse 23
23 Then **the moon shall be confounded, and the sun ashamed, when the LORD of hosts shall reign in mount Zion, and in Jerusalem, and before his ancients gloriously.**

Isaiah 34:Verse 1
1 COME near, ye nations, to hear; and hearken, ye people: let the earth hear, and all that is therein; the world, and all things that come forth of it.

Isaiah 34:Verse 2

2 For **the indignation of the LORD [is] upon all nations,** and [his] fury upon all their armies: he hath utterly destroyed them, he hath delivered them to the slaughter.

Isaiah 34:Verse 3

3 Their slain also shall be cast out, and their stink shall come up out of their carcases, and the mountains shall be melted with their blood.

Isaiah 34:Verse 4

4 And **all the host of heaven shall be dissolved, and the heavens shall be rolled together as a scroll: and all their host shall fall down, as the leaf falleth off from the vine, and as a falling [fig] from the fig tree.**

Isaiah 34:Verse 5

5 For my sword shall be bathed in heaven: behold, it shall come down upon Idumea, and upon the people of my curse, to judgment.

Isaiah 34:Verse 6

6 The sword of the LORD is filled with blood, it is made fat with fatness, [and] with the blood of lambs and goats, with the fat of the kidneys of rams: for the LORD hath a sacrifice in Bozrah, and a great slaughter in the land of Idumea.

Isaiah 34:Verse 7

7 And the unicorns shall come down with them, and the bullocks with the bulls; and their land shall be soaked with blood, and their dust made fat with fatness.

Isaiah 34:Verse 8

8 For [it is] the day of the LORD'S vengeance, [and] the year of recompences for the controversy of Zion.

Joel 2:Verse 10

10 **The earth shall quake before them; the heavens shall tremble: the sun and the moon shall be dark, and the stars shall withdraw their shining:**

Joel 2:Verse 30

30 And **I will shew wonders in the heavens and in the earth, blood, and fire, and pillars of smoke.**

Joel 2:Verse 31

31 The **sun shall be turned into darkness, and the moon into blood,** *before* the great and the terrible day of the LORD come.

Joel 3:Verse 15

15 **The sun and the moon shall be darkened, and the stars shall withdraw their shining**.

---

2 Nephi 27:Verse 2

2 And when that day shall come **they shall be visited of the Lord of Hosts, with thunder and with earthquake, and with a great noise, and with storm, and with tempest, and with the flame of devouring fire.**

D&C 29:Verse 14

14 But, behold, I say unto you that *before* this great day shall come **the sun shall be darkened, and the moon shall be turned into blood, and the stars shall fall from heaven, and there shall be greater signs in heaven above and in the earth beneath;**

D&C 45:Verse 42

42 And *before the day of the Lord shall come,* **the sun shall be darkened, and the moon be turned into blood, and the stars fall from heaven.**

D&C 88:Verse 87

87 For not many days hence and **the earth shall tremble and reel to and fro as a drunken man; and the sun shall hide his face, and shall refuse to give light; and the moon shall be bathed in blood; and the stars shall become exceedingly angry, and shall cast themselves down as a fig that falleth from off a fig-tree.**

Joseph Smith Matthew 1:Verse 33

33 And **immediately after the tribulation of those days, the sun shall be darkened, and the moon shall not give her light, and the stars shall fall from heaven, and the powers of heaven shall be shaken.**

Joseph Smith Matthew 1:Verse 34

34 Verily, I say unto you, this generation, in which these things shall be shown forth, shall not pass away until all I have told you shall be fulfilled.

11

The Sealing of the 144,000

Revelation 7: 1-8; 14: 1-5

The sealing of twelve thousand from each of the twelve tribes was explained by the Prophet Joseph, that these are sealed are high priests, ordained unto the holy order of God, to administer the everlasting gospel; for they are they who are ordained out of every nation, kindred, tongue, and people, by the angels to whom is given power over the nations of the earth, to bring as many as will come to the church of the Firstborn. Apparently these high priests are leaders to administer the everlasting gospel and that they will have a part to play in the temple work of as many as will come to the 'church of the Firstborn'. To become a member of the church of the Firstborn, a person must receive the ordinances of the Firstborn, and inherit 'all that the father hath' and become an heir and joint heir with Jesus Christ the Firstborn of the spirit and the only begotten in the flesh. These ordinances can only come in the House of the Lord where one can receive the endowment of power and the blessings of the firstborn. These one hundred and forty-four thousand high priests will be with the savior at the beginning of the millennium when he comes to the Mount of Olives.

For some reason the list of the twelve tribes, unlike the traditional list, adds Joseph, and Levi, and excludes Ephraim, and Dan.

Revelation 7:Verse 1

1 AND after these things **I saw four angels standing on the four corners of the earth, holding the four winds of the earth,** that the wind should not blow on the earth, nor on the sea, nor on any tree.

Revelation 7:Verse 2

2 And I saw another angel ascending from the east, having the seal of the living God: and he cried with a loud voice to the four angels, to whom it was given to hurt the earth and the sea,

Revelation 7:Verse 3

3 Saying, **Hurt not the earth, neither the sea, nor the trees, till we have sealed the servants of our God in their foreheads.**

Revelation 7:Verse 4
4 And I heard the number of them which were sealed: [and there were] **sealed an hundred [and] forty [and] four thousand of all the tribes of the children of Israel**.

Revelation 7:Verse 5
5 Of the tribe of Judah [were] sealed twelve thousand. Of the tribe of Reuben [were] sealed twelve thousand. Of the tribe of Gad [were] sealed twelve thousand.

Revelation 7:Verse 6
6 Of the tribe of Aser [were] sealed twelve thousand. Of the tribe of Nepthalim [were] sealed twelve thousand. Of the tribe of Manasses [were] sealed twelve thousand.

Revelation 7:Verse 7
7 Of the tribe of Simeon [were] sealed twelve thousand. Of the tribe of Levi [were] sealed twelve thousand. Of the tribe of Issachar [were] sealed twelve thousand.

Revelation 7:Verse 8
8 Of the tribe of Zabulon [were] sealed twelve thousand. Of the tribe of Joseph [were] sealed twelve thousand. Of the tribe of Benjamin [were] sealed twelve thousand.

Revelation 14:Verse 1
1 AND I looked, and, lo, a **Lamb stood on the mount Sion, and with him an hundred forty [and] four thousand,** having his Father's name written in their foreheads.

Revelation 14:Verse 2
2 And I heard a voice from heaven, as the voice of many waters, and as the voice of a great thunder: and I heard the voice of harpers harping with their harps:

Revelation 14:Verse 3
3 And they sung as it were a new song before the throne, and before the four beasts, and the elders: and no man could learn that song but the hundred [and] forty [and] four thousand, which were redeemed from the earth.

Revelation 14:Verse 4
4 **These are they which were not defiled with women; for they are virgins. These are they which follow the Lamb whithersoever he goeth. These were redeemed from among men, [being] the firstfruits unto God and to the Lamb.**

Revelation 14:Verse 5
5 And in their mouth was found no guile: for they are without fault before the throne of God.

D&C 77:Verse 8

8 Q. What are we to understand by the **four angels, spoken of in the 7th chapter and 1st verse** of Revelation?

A. We are to understand that they are four angels sent forth from God, to whom is given power over the four parts of the earth, to save life and to destroy; these are they who have the everlasting gospel to commit to every nation, kindred, tongue, and people; having power to shut up the heavens, to seal up unto life, or to cast down to the regions of darkness.

D&C 77:Verse 9

9 Q. What are we to understand by **the angel ascending from the east, Revelation 7th chapter and 2nd verse?**

A. We are to understand that the angel ascending from the east is he to whom is given the seal of the living God over the twelve tribes of Israel; wherefore, he crieth unto the four angels having the everlasting gospel, saying: **Hurt not the earth, neither the sea, nor the trees, till we have sealed the servants of our God in their foreheads.** And, if you will receive it, this is Elias which was to come to gather together the tribes of Israel and restore all things.

D&C 77:Verse 10

10 Q. **What time are the things spoken of in this chapter to be accomplished?**

A. They are **to be accomplished in the sixth thousand years, or the opening of the sixth seal.**

D&C 77:Verse 11

11 Q. What are we to **understand by sealing the one hundred and forty-four thousand**, out of all the tribes of Israel--twelve thousand out of every tribe?

A. We are to understand that those who **are sealed are high priests, ordained unto the holy order of God, to administer the everlasting gospel; for they are they who are ordained out of every nation, kindred, tongue, and people, by the angels to whom is given power over the nations of the earth, to bring as many as will come to the church of the Firstborn.**

D&C 133:Verse 16

16 Hearken and hear, O ye inhabitants of the earth. Listen, ye elders of my church together, and hear the voice of the Lord; for he calleth upon all men, and he commandeth all men everywhere to repent.

D&C 133:Verse 17

17 For behold, the Lord God hath sent forth the angel crying through the midst of heaven, saying: Prepare ye the way of the Lord, and make his paths straight, for the hour of his coming is nigh--

D&C 133:Verse 18

18 **When the Lamb shall stand upon Mount Zion, and with him a hundred and forty-four thousand, having his Father's name written on their foreheads.**

D&C 133:Verse 19

19 Wherefore, prepare ye for the coming of the Bridegroom; go ye, go ye out to meet him.

D&C 133:Verse 20

20 For behold, **he shall stand upon the mount of Olivet**, and upon the mighty ocean, even the great deep, and upon the islands of the sea, and upon the land of Zion.

12

The Seventh Seal is Opened

Revelation 8: 1-13

The seventh thousand years begins with silence and signs in the heavens, as the angels are sounding their trumpets. The natural disasters continue, which affect **one third** of the lives of plants, animals and mankind. The natural disasters in this seal seem to be connected to asteroid impacts or as John calls it "a great mountain burning with fire was cast into the sea" and also there fell a great star from heaven. God works with natural disasters to change mankind, while Satan uses violence. Damnation and Exaltation each have: Motive, Justification, Method, and a Virtue.

	Satan	**God**
1) A Motive.	Personal Gain	Consecration
2) Justification.	Competition	Love
3) The Method.	Violence	Upheavals of Nature
4) The Virtue.	Denial of Guilt	Repentance

War, or violence can be blamed on mankind without the acknowledgment of the interaction of Deity. Someone can be blamed for the war, the pushing of the button that causes death and destruction. However, a natural disaster cannot be attributed to a human action. Third Nephi reports that the natural upheavals of nature at the time of the crucifixion of Christ caused the people to repent and turn to God. While Mormon reports that during the great wars, the sorrow of the Nephites came because their "sorrowing was not unto repentance, because of the goodness of God; but it was rather the sorrowing of the damned, because the Lord would not always suffer them to take happiness in sin." (Mormon 2:13). When studying the Last Days many focus on a great war, or 'third world war' these wars, and rumors of wars are but signs of the times. The upheavals of nature, the great earthquakes, the sun being darkened, stars falling, and the discoloring of the moon, are events spoken of in greater numbers. The greatest changes in the spiritual nature of an individual come when that individual has no control, and cannot point the finger to any other human being as the cause. To this concept, scriptural history testifies.

The natural destruction that comes from land and oceanic impacts of asteroids, or meteors, can be found in the appendix under *The Cosmic Serpent.*

Revelation 8:Verse 1

1 AND when he had opened the seventh seal, there was **silence in heaven about the space of half an hour.**

Revelation 8:Verse 2

2 And I saw the seven angels which stood before God; and to them were given seven trumpets.

Revelation 8:Verse 3

3 And another angel came and stood at the altar, having a golden censer; and there was given unto him much incense, that he should offer [it] with the prayers of all saints upon the golden altar which was before the throne.

Revelation 8:Verse 4

4 And the smoke of the incense, [which came] with the prayers of the saints, ascended up before God out of the angel's hand.

Revelation 8:Verse 5

5 And the angel took the censer, and filled it with fire of the altar, and cast [it] into the earth: and there were voices, and **thunderings, and lightnings, and an earthquake.**

Revelation 8:Verse 6

6 And the seven angels which had the seven trumpets prepared themselves to sound.

Revelation 8:Verse 7

7 The first angel sounded, and there followed **hail and fire mingled with blood,** and they were cast upon the earth: and the ***third part* of trees was burnt up, and all green grass was burnt up.**

Revelation 8:Verse 8

8 And the second angel sounded, and as it were **a great mountain burning with fire was cast into the sea: and *the third part* of the sea became blood;**

Revelation 8:Verse 9

9 And ***the third part* of the creatures which were in the sea, and had life, died;** and the third part of the ships were destroyed.

Revelation 8:Verse 10

10 And the third angel sounded, and there **fell a great star from heaven, burning** as it were a lamp, and it fell upon *the third part* of the rivers, and upon the fountains of waters;

Revelation 8:Verse 11

11 And the name of the star is called Wormwood: and *the third part* **of the waters became wormwood; and many men died** of the waters, because they were made bitter.

Revelation 8:Verse 12

12 And the fourth angel sounded, and *the third part* **of the sun was smitten, and the third part of the moon, and** *the third part* **of the stars; so as** *the third part* **of them was darkened, and the day shone not for a** *third part of it,* **and the night likewise.**

Revelation 8:Verse 13

13 And I beheld, and heard an angel flying through the midst of heaven, saying with a loud voice, Woe, woe, woe, to the inhabiters of the earth by reason of the other voices of the trumpet of the three angels, which are yet to sound!

D&C 77:Verse 12

12 Q. What are we to understand by the sounding of the trumpets, mentioned in the 8th chapter of Revelation?

A. We are to understand that as God made the world in six days, and on the seventh day he finished his work, and sanctified it, and also formed man out of the dust of the earth, even so, **in the beginning of the seventh thousand years will the Lord God sanctify the earth, and complete the salvation of man, and judge all things, and shall redeem all things, except that which he hath not put into his power, when he shall have sealed all things, unto the end of all things; and the sounding of the trumpets of the seven angels are the preparing and finishing of his work, in the beginning of the seventh thousand years--the preparing of the way before the time of his coming.**

---

2 Peter 3:Verse 3

3 Knowing this first, that there shall come in the last days scoffers, walking after their own lusts,

2 Peter 3:Verse 4

4 And saying, Where is the promise of his coming? for since the fathers fell asleep, all things continue as [they were] from the beginning of the creation.

D&C 29:Verse 15

15 And there shall be weeping and wailing among the hosts of men;

D&C 29:Verse 16

16 And **there shall be a great hailstorm sent forth to destroy the crops of the earth.**

D&C 45:Verse 26

26 And in that day shall be heard of wars and rumors of wars, and **the whole earth shall be in commotion**, and men's hearts shall fail them, and they shall say that Christ delayeth his coming until the end of the earth.

D&C 45:Verse 27

27 And the love of men shall wax cold, and iniquity shall abound.

D&C 45:Verse 31

31 And there shall be men standing in that generation, that shall not pass until they shall see **an overflowing scourge; for a desolating sickness shall cover the land.**

D&C 45:Verse 32

32 But my disciples shall stand in holy places, and shall not be moved; but among the wicked, men shall lift up their voices and curse God and die.

D&C 45:Verse 33

33 And **there shall be earthquakes also in divers places, and many desolations;** yet men will harden their hearts against me, and they will take up the sword, one against another, and they will kill one another.

D&C 45:Verse 40

40 And they shall see **signs and wonders, for they shall be shown forth in the heavens above, and in the earth beneath.**

D&C 45:Verse 41

41 And they shall behold **blood, and fire, and vapors of smoke**.

D&C 49:Verse 23

23 Wherefore, be not deceived, but continue in steadfastness, looking forth **for the heavens to be shaken, and the earth to tremble and to reel to and fro as a drunken man, and for the valleys to be exalted, and for the mountains to be made low, and for the rough places to become smooth--and all this when the angel shall sound his trumpet.**

D&C 84:Verse 118

118 For, with you saith the Lord Almighty, I will rend their kingdoms; **I will not only shake the earth, but the starry heavens shall tremble.**

D&C 84:Verse 119

119 For I, the Lord, have put forth my hand to exert the powers of heaven; ye cannot see it now, yet a little while and ye shall see it, and know that I am, and that I will come and reign with my people.

D&C 87:Verse 6

6 And thus, with the sword and **by bloodshed the inhabitants of the earth shall mourn; and with famine, and plague, and earthquake, and the thunder of heaven, and the fierce and vivid lightning also, shall the inhabitants of the earth be made to feel the wrath, and indignation, and chastening hand of an Almighty God**, until the consumption decreed hath made a full end of all nations;

D&C 88:Verse 88

88 And after your testimony cometh wrath and indignation upon the people.

D&C 88:Verse 89

89 For after your testimony cometh **the testimony of earthquakes, that shall cause groanings in the midst of her, and men shall fall upon the ground and shall not be able to stand.**

D&C 88:Verse 90

90 And also cometh **the testimony of the voice of thunderings, and the voice of lightnings, and the voice of tempests, and the voice of the waves of the sea heaving themselves beyond their bounds.**

D&C 88:Verse 91

91 And **all things shall be in commotion**; and surely, men's hearts shall fail them; for fear shall come upon all people.

D&C 88:Verse 92

92 **And angels shall fly through the midst of heaven, crying with a loud voice, sounding the trump of God, saying: Prepare ye, prepare ye, O inhabitants of the earth; for the judgment of our God is come.** Behold, and lo, the Bridegroom cometh; go ye out to meet him.

D&C 88:Verse 93

93 And immediately there **shall appear a great sign in heaven, and all people shall see it together**.

(NOT DARK NOT LIGHT)

D&C 88:Verse 94

94 And another angel shall sound his trump, saying: That great church, the mother of abominations, that made all nations drink of the wine of the wrath of her fornication, that persecuteth the saints of God, that shed their blood--she who sitteth upon many waters, and upon the islands of the sea--behold, she is the tares of the earth; she is bound in bundles; her bands are made strong, no man can loose them; therefore, she is ready to be burned. And he shall sound his trump both long and loud, and all nations shall hear it.

D&C 88:Verse 95

95 And there shall be **silence in heaven for the space of half an hour; and immediately after shall the curtain of heaven be unfolded, as a scroll is unfolded after it is rolled up, and the face of the Lord shall be unveiled;**

D&C 101:Verse 10

10 I have sworn, and the decree hath gone forth by a former commandment which I have given unto you, that I would **let fall the sword of mine indignation** in behalf of my people; and even as I have said, it shall come to pass.

D&C 101:Verse 11

11 Mine indignation is soon to be poured out without measure upon all nations; and this will I do when the cup of their iniquity is full.

D&C 101:Verse 12

12 And in that day all who are found upon the watch-tower, or in other words, all mine Israel, shall be saved.

Joseph Smith Matthew 1:Verse 28

28 And they shall hear of **wars, and rumors of wars**.

Joseph Smith Matthew 1:Verse 29

29 Behold I speak for mine elect's sake; for nation shall rise against nation, and kingdom against kingdom; there shall be **famines, and pestilences, and earthquakes, in divers places.**

Joseph Smith Matthew 1:Verse 30

30 And again, because iniquity shall abound, the love of men shall wax cold; but he that shall not be overcome, the same shall be saved.

13

Wars, and Plagues, and Nature in Commotion

Revelation 9: 1-21

The events of Chapter Nine seem to be a continuation of those in Chapter Eight as all things are in commotion, both on earth and in heaven. In conjunction with the Chapter Eight, these events see the death of mankind in great numbers by natural disasters and perhaps wars across the face of the earth. See the John Taylor Vision in the appendix as this chapter speaks of the loss of one third of the men. It may be, and I stress 'may' that the events of Chapter Eight, Nine, Fifteen and Sixteen are but different descriptions of the same natural disasters, and wars that are going on at the same time, that lead up to the coming of the Savior on the Mount of Olives. The Best commentary on the scriptures is the scriptures and your understanding, not mine or any other authors. This guide is here to help and to offer other scriptures that may or may not be related to the Book of Revelation. The scriptures are the key to the events of the last days; assumption leading to interpretation may be the greatest problem to understanding scripture.

It must be remembered that the prophet who sees a vision does not see it in linear time, but is forced to write down as best he can, those things he has seen. Latter-day readers assume, because of our experience, and habit, that each chapter, and events in a chapter must follow each other in a chronological fashion. This is not so. For example: Could Revelation 8:10-12, be related to Revelation 9:1, 2, 18. Are the stars the same, the smoke, the pit, the same third part of men that are to be killed? Revelation 9:4 speak of those sealed upon their foreheads, are these the same as the 144,000 who are sealed on their foreheads? It seems so. Is Chapter Eight the natural disasters that are happening while Chapter Nine are the wars that are taking place, at the same time? Is the star in Chapter 9:1 referring to the morning star that fell from heaven and took one third the hosts of heaven with him (the war in heaven)? Most of the events of the Last Days spoken about in the scriptures are natural upheavals of nature. Wars, and rumors of wars, are just some of the minor signs of the times.

The third world war is something everyone talks of, and prepares for, yet, nature should be the greater fear. The Book of Mormon has no prophecy of the Second Coming; yet, it is the pattern of the 'last days.' The destruction that came upon the Nephites just before Christ comes is a description of the types of destruction that will take place when he comes again. The darkness, the more part of the righteous spared, the Savior's return, the gospel spreading, mass conversions, and then the millennial reign of peace and righteousness of Fourth Nephi. The falling away because of pride and the influence of Satan, as wickedness becomes so rampant that the great and last battle destroys the Nephites. The Book of Mormon is the pattern of the Last Days, and the Book of Revelation should not be read without keeping in mind and reading the Book of Mormon for that pattern. The best commentary is your commentary.

Revelation 9:Verse 1

1 AND the fifth angel sounded, and I saw a star fall from heaven unto the earth: and to him was given the key of the bottomless pit.

Revelation 9:Verse 2

2 And he opened the bottomless pit; and there arose a smoke out of the pit, as the smoke of a great furnace; and the sun and the air were darkened by reason of the smoke of the pit.

Revelation 9:Verse 3

3 And there came out of the smoke locusts upon the earth: and unto them was given power, as the scorpions of the earth have power.

Revelation 9:Verse 4

4 And it was commanded them that they should not hurt the grass of the earth, neither any green thing, neither any tree; but only those men which have not the seal of God in their foreheads.

Revelation 9:Verse 5

5 And to them it was given that they should not kill them, but that they should be tormented five months: and their torment [was] as the torment of a scorpion, when he striketh a man.

Revelation 9:Verse 6

6 And in those days shall men seek death, and shall not find it; and shall desire to die, and death shall flee from them.

Revelation 9:Verse 7

7 And the shapes of the locusts [were] like unto horses prepared unto battle; and on their heads [were] as it were crowns like gold, and their faces [were] as the faces of men.

Revelation 9:Verse 8

8 And they had hair as the hair of women, and their teeth were as [the teeth] of lions.

Revelation 9:Verse 9

9 And they had breastplates, as it were breastplates of iron; and the sound of their wings [was] as the sound of chariots of many horses running to battle.

Revelation 9:Verse 10

10 And they had tails like unto scorpions, and there were stings in their tails: and their power [was] to hurt men five months.

Revelation 9:Verse 11

11 And they had a king over them, [which is] the angel of the bottomless pit, whose name in the Hebrew tongue [is] Abaddon, but in the Greek tongue hath [his] name Apollyon.

Revelation 9:Verse 12

12 One woe is past; [and], behold, there come two woes more hereafter.

Revelation 9:Verse 13

13 And the sixth angel sounded, and I heard a voice from the four horns of the golden altar which is before God,

Revelation 9:Verse 14

14 Saying to the sixth angel which had the trumpet, Loose the four angels which are bound in the great river Euphrates.

Revelation 9:Verse 15

15 And the four angels were loosed, which were prepared for an hour, and a day, and a month, and a year, for to slay the third part of men.

Revelation 9:Verse 16

16 And the number of the army of the horsemen [were] two hundred thousand thousand: and I heard the number of them.

Revelation 9:Verse 17

17 And thus I saw the horses in the vision, and them that sat on them, having breastplates of fire, and of jacinth, and brimstone: and the heads of the horses [were] as the heads of lions; and out of their mouths issued fire and smoke and brimstone.

Revelation 9:Verse 18

18 By these three was the third part of men killed, by the fire, and by the smoke, and by the brimstone, which issued out of their mouths.

Revelation 9:Verse 19

19 For their power is in their mouth, and in their tails: for their tails [were] like unto serpents, and had heads, and with them they do hurt.

Revelation 9:Verse 20

20 And the rest of the men which were not killed by these plagues yet repented not of the works of their hands, that they should not worship devils, and idols of gold, and silver, and brass, and stone, and of wood: which neither can see, nor hear, nor walk:

Revelation 9:Verse 21

21 Neither repented they of their murders, nor of their sorceries, nor of their fornication, nor of their thefts.

D&C 77:Verse 13

13 Q. When are the things to be accomplished, which are written in the 9th chapter of Revelation?

A. They are to be accomplished after the opening of the seventh seal, **before the coming of Christ**.

D&C 63:Verse 33

33 I have sworn in my wrath, and decreed wars upon the face of the earth, and the wicked shall slay the wicked, and fear shall come upon every man;

14

The Patience of the Saints

Revelation 14: 12-13

The Lord promises the faithful that all will be well for them in life or in death. The Doctrine and Covenants teaches that death to the righteous is sweet: "And it shall come to pass that those that die in me shall not taste of death, for it shall be sweet unto them; And they that die not in me, wo unto them, for their death is bitter" (D&C 42: 46-47). The second coming is, so to speak, when we die, When all must return and report. All the food storage in the world, guns and ammunition mean nothing if we are not prepared spiritually to meet the Savior because, death is an event we live through. This life is but a small moment in the context of eternity. Seventy years is nothing but a short, very short probationary state for man to prepare to meet God. Reality exists only in the realm of the sacred, in an 'a-temporal' existence, a 'time without time.' The world of the sacred, where the Gods reside, and rule in the heavens, all of creation, where there is no death, this is the real world. The Saints who understand the reality of life after death, can and do have patience in the trials and tribulations of this mortal existence, knowing a better life awaits them.

Revelation 14:Verse 12
12 **Here is the patience of the saints:** here [are] they that keep the commandments of God, and the faith of Jesus.

Revelation 14:Verse 13
13 And I heard a voice from heaven saying unto me, Write, **Blessed [are] the dead which die in the Lord** from henceforth: Yea, saith the Spirit, that they may rest from their labours; and their works do follow them.

D&C 101:Verse 38
38 And seek the face of the Lord always, that **in patience ye may possess your souls, and ye shall have eternal life.**

D&C 101:Verse 37
37 Therefore, care not for the body, neither the life of the body; but care for the soul, and for the life of the soul.

D&C 101:Verse 36

36 Wherefore, **fear not even unto death;** for in this world your joy is not full, but in me your joy is full.

D&C 84:Verse 97

97 And plagues shall go forth, and they shall not be taken from the earth until I have completed my work, which shall be cut short in righteousness--

The Prepared Righteous Need not Fear

The Righteous are the ones repenting. In the story the Savior sold of the publican and the Pharisee coming to the temple to pray, teaches a great lesson.

10. Two men went up into the temple to pray; the one a Pharisee, and the other a publican.
11. The Pharisee stood and prayed thus with himself, God, I thank thee, that I am not as other men [are], extortioners, unjust, adulterers, or even as this publican.
12. I fast twice in the week, I give tithes of all that I possess.
13. And the publican, standing afar off, would not lift up so much as [his] eyes unto heaven, but smote upon his breast, saying, God be merciful to me a sinner.
14. I tell you, this man went down to his house justified [rather] than the other: for every one that exalteth himself shall be abased; and he that humbleth himself shall be exalted. (Luke 18:10-14).

This Pharisee was active in the church, he would fast twice a week, he paid a full tithing, attended all his meetings went to the temple on a regular basis. Like the Zoramites in the Book of Mormon, he even stood on his 'rameumptom' thinking himself to be above the heads of the rest of the congregation, on a day of fast telling God (and the congregation) how good he is, and how thankful he is, to be an active member of his church and not like others who sin, or in a false activity or another religion, or church. Yet, the one Justified by the Savior, the righteous one, was the one active in the gospel, the one exercising faith unto repentance and confessing his sins.

One can be active in the church and totally inactive in the gospel, however, you cannot be active in the gospel and then be inactive in the Church. The church is established for two reasons: 1) to participate in the ordinances under the direction, and authority of the priesthood of God, and 2) to provide an opportunity to serve others, and teach the gospel of repentance, and not the pharisaic gospel of socials, and activities. To show our love to God by ordinance and covenant, and love our fellow man.

The righteous are the people repenting, those exercising faith unto repentance, they are active in the gospel. The wicked are those not repenting, no matter how active they are in the church. Scripturally speaking 'Faith' can only be faith if it is in Jesus Christ and the atonement. Every reference that speaks of faith, does so in the context of the Savior and the atonement, because this atonement cannot fail. The atonement, and the Savior was 'prepared from the foundations of the world,' an 'infinite and eternal sacrifice' as described by Amuleck. Faith, cannot be faith if it is place in something that can fail. Traditionally one of the object lessons on faith is to walk over to the light switch, and the teacher would say 'faith is like this light switch' ant then turn the light on or off. However there could be a power outage and the light might not come on. It can fail. The atonement of Christ cannot ever fail, there is nothing more sure in all of eternity. Faith, can only be faith if it is centered in the Atonement of Jesus Christ, and nothing else, not in a light, the engine of a car, nothing but the atonement. The works that make faith alive, is the exercise of the faith, which can only be as Amuleck teaches 'exercise faith unto repentance.' Because of the atonement we can repent, and be 'washed clean through the blood of the Lamb.' Faith without works (repentance) is dead. Therefore, faithful people are the people repenting; the unfaithful person is not repenting. Activity in the gospel is repentance by the exercise of faith, and the participation in the ordinances of baptism and the Gift of the Holy Ghost.

The righteous need not fear because they have been active in the gospel they like the publican are justified by the exercise of faith unto repentance. The second coming is when we die, and the only way to be prepared for the supreme sacrifice of death is by personal repentance. The Lord made the statement in the inspired version of Matthew 24:

> 46. And what I say unto one, I say unto all men; watch, therefore, for you know not at what hour your Lord doth come.
>
> 46. But know this, if the good man of the house had known in what watch the thief would come, he would have watched, and would not have suffered his house to have been broken up, but would have been ready.
>
> 48 Therefore be ye also ready, for in such an hour as ye think not, the Son of Man cometh.
>
> 49 Who, then, is a faithful and wise servant, whom his lord hath made ruler over his household, to give them meat in due season?
>
> 50 Blessed is that servant whom his lord, when he cometh, shall find so doing; and verily I say unto you, he shall make him ruler over all his goods.

The righteous need not fear for the faithful shall be prepared by repentance for 'blessed is that servant whom his lord, when he cometh, shall find so doing.'

---

1 Nephi 22:Verse 19

19 For behold, the righteous shall not perish; for the time surely must come that all they who fight against Zion shall be cut off.

1 Nephi 22:Verse 22

22 And the righteous need not fear, for they are those who shall not be confounded. But it is the kingdom of the devil, which shall be built up among the children of men, which kingdom is established among them which are in the flesh--

2 Nephi 27:Verse 3
3 And all the nations that fight against Zion, and that distress her, shall be as a dream of a night vision; yea, it shall be unto them, even as unto a hungry man which dreameth, and behold he eateth but he awaketh and his soul is empty; or like unto a thirsty man which dreameth, and behold he drinketh but he awaketh and behold he is faint, and his soul hath appetite; yea, even so shall the multitude of all the nations be that fight against Mount Zion.

2 Nephi 27:Verse 4
4 For behold, all ye that doeth iniquity, stay yourselves and wonder, for ye shall cry out, and cry; yea, ye shall be drunken but not with wine, ye shall stagger but not with strong drink.

2 Nephi 27:Verse 5
5 For behold, the Lord hath poured out upon you the spirit of deep sleep. For behold, ye have closed your eyes, and ye have rejected the prophets; and your rulers, and the seers hath he covered because of your iniquity.

D&C 45:Verse 39
39 And it shall come to pass that he that feareth me shall be looking forth for the great day of the Lord to come, even for the signs of the coming of the Son of Man.

D&C 101:Verse 35
35 And all they who suffer persecution for my name, and endure in faith, though they are called to lay down their lives for my sake yet shall they partake of all this glory.

D&C 101:Verse 36
36 Wherefore, fear not even unto death; for in this world your joy is not full, but in me your joy is full.

D&C 101:Verse 37
37 Therefore, care not for the body, neither the life of the body; but care for the soul, and for the life of the soul.

D&C 101:Verse 38
38 And seek the face of the Lord always, that in patience ye may possess your souls, and ye shall have eternal life.

D&C 133:Verse 9
9 And behold, and lo, this shall be their cry, and the voice of the Lord unto all people: Go ye forth unto the land of Zion, that the borders of my people may be enlarged, and that her stakes may be strengthened, and that Zion may go forth unto the regions round about.

15

The Harvest of God, and Judgments of the Earth

Revelation 14: 14-20

A descriptive 'insert' as the angels are sent to reap for the 'harvest of the earth is ripe.' This section speaks of the 'Harvest of God', which seems to be a spiritual, or heavenly description of the earthly events of the wars, plagues, and elements in commotion that precede and follow this chapter. The 'harvest' is the wicked as they are 'cast into the great winepress of the wrath of God' (Rev. 14:19). The Book of Mormon tell us about the great destruction of Third Nephi, and that after the harvest of the wicked in the America's, only the more righteous part of the people were spared, and they needed to repent.

Revelation 14:Verse 14

14 And I looked, and behold a white cloud, and upon the cloud [one] sat like unto the Son of man, having on his head a golden crown, and in his hand a sharp sickle.

Revelation 14:Verse 15

15 And another angel came out of the temple, crying with a loud voice to him that sat on the cloud, Thrust in thy sickle, and reap: for the time is come for thee to reap; for the harvest of the earth is ripe.

Revelation 14:Verse 16

16 And he that sat on the cloud thrust in his sickle on the earth; and the earth was reaped.

Revelation 14:Verse 17

17 And another angel came out of the temple which is in heaven, he also having a sharp sickle.

Revelation 14:Verse 18

18 And another angel came out from the altar, which had power over fire; and cried with a loud cry to him that had the sharp sickle, saying, Thrust in thy sharp sickle, and gather the clusters of the vine of the earth; for her grapes are fully ripe.

Revelation 14:Verse 19

19 And the angel thrust in his sickle into the earth, and gathered the vine of the earth, and cast [it] into the great winepress of the wrath of God.

Revelation 14:Verse 20

20 And the winepress was trodden without the city, and blood came out of the winepress, even unto the horse bridles, by the space of a thousand [and] six hundred furlongs.

Isaiah 24:Verse 1
1 BEHOLD, the LORD maketh the earth empty, and maketh it waste, and turneth it upside down, and scattereth abroad the inhabitants thereof.

Isaiah 24:Verse 2
2 And it shall be, as with the people, so with the priest; as with the servant, so with his master; as with the maid, so with her mistress; as with the buyer, so with the seller; as with the lender, so with the borrower; as with the taker of usury, so with the giver of usury to him.

Isaiah 24:Verse 3
3 The land shall be utterly emptied, and utterly spoiled: for the LORD hath spoken this word.

Isaiah 24:Verse 4
4 The earth mourneth [and] fadeth away, the world languisheth [and] fadeth away, the haughty people of the earth do languish.

Isaiah 24:Verse 5
5 The earth also is defiled under the inhabitants thereof; because they have transgressed the laws, changed the ordinance, broken the everlasting covenant.

Isaiah 24:Verse 6
6 Therefore hath the curse devoured the earth, and they that dwell therein are desolate: therefore the inhabitants of the earth are burned, and few men left.

Isaiah 24:Verse 7
7 The new wine mourneth, the vine languisheth, all the merryhearted do sigh.

Isaiah 24:Verse 8
8 The mirth of tabrets ceaseth, the noise of them that rejoice endeth, the joy of the harp ceaseth.

Isaiah 24:Verse 9
9 They shall not drink wine with a song; strong drink shall be bitter to them that drink it.

Isaiah 24:Verse 10
10 The city of confusion is broken down: every house is shut up, that no man may come in.

Isaiah 24:Verse 11
11 [There is] a crying for wine in the streets; all joy is darkened, the mirth of the land is gone.

Isaiah 24:Verse 12
12 In the city is left desolation, and the gate is smitten with destruction.

Isaiah 24:Verse 13

13   When thus it shall be in the midst of the land among the people, [there shall be] as the shaking of an olive tree, [and] as the gleaning grapes when the vintage is done.

Isaiah 65:Verse 1

1 I am sought of [them that] asked not [for me]; I am found of [them that] sought me not: I said, Behold me, behold me, unto a nation [that] was not called by my name.

Isaiah 65:Verse 2

2 I have spread out my hands all the day unto a rebellious people, which walketh in a way [that was] not good, after their own thoughts;

Isaiah 65:Verse 3

3 A people that provoketh me to anger continually to my face; that sacrificeth in gardens, and burneth incense upon altars of brick;

Isaiah 65:Verse 4

4 Which remain among the graves, and lodge in the monuments, which eat swine's flesh, and broth of abominable [things is in] their vessels;

Isaiah 65:Verse 5

5 Which say, Stand by thyself, come not near to me; for I am holier than thou. These [are] a smoke in my nose, a fire that burneth all the day.

Isaiah 65:Verse 6

6 Behold, [it is] written before me: I will not keep silence, but will recompense, even recompense into their bosom,

Isaiah 65:Verse 7

7 Your iniquities, and the iniquities of your fathers together, saith the LORD, which have burned incense upon the mountains, and blasphemed me upon the hills: therefore will I measure their former work into their bosom.

Isaiah 65:Verse 8

8 Thus saith the LORD, As the new wine is found in the cluster, and [one] saith, Destroy it not; for a blessing [is] in it: so will I do for my servants' sakes, that I may not destroy them all.

Isaiah 65:Verse 9

9 And I will bring forth a seed out of Jacob, and out of Judah an inheritor of my mountains: and mine elect shall inherit it, and my servants shall dwell there.

Isaiah 65:Verse 10

10 And Sharon shall be a fold of flocks, and the valley of Achor a place for the herds to lie down in, for my people that have sought me.

Isaiah 65:Verse 11

11 But ye [are] they that forsake the LORD, that forget my holy mountain, that prepare a table for that troop, and that furnish the drink offering unto that number.

Isaiah 65:Verse 12

12 Therefore will I number you to the sword, and ye shall all bow down to the slaughter: because when I called, ye did not answer; when I spake, ye did not hear; but did evil before mine eyes, and did choose [that] wherein I delighted not.

Isaiah 65:Verse 13

13 Therefore thus saith the Lord GOD, Behold, my servants shall eat, but ye shall be hungry: behold, my servants shall drink, but ye shall be thirsty: behold, my servants shall rejoice, but ye shall be ashamed:

Isaiah 65:Verse 14

14 Behold, my servants shall sing for joy of heart, but ye shall cry for sorrow of heart, and shall howl for vexation of spirit.
Isaiah 65:Verse 15

15 And ye shall leave your name for a curse unto my chosen: for the Lord GOD shall slay thee, and call his servants by another name:

Isaiah 65:Verse 16

16 That he who blesseth himself in the earth shall bless himself in the God of truth; and he that sweareth in the earth shall swear by the God of truth; because the former troubles are forgotten, and because they are hid from mine eyes.

---

2 Nephi 28:Verse 31

31 Cursed is he that putteth his trust in man, or maketh flesh his arm, or shall hearken unto the precepts of men, save their precepts shall be given by the power of the Holy Ghost.

2 Nephi 28:Verse 32

32 Wo be unto the Gentiles, saith the Lord God of Hosts! For notwithstanding I shall lengthen out mine arm unto them from day to day, they will deny me; nevertheless, I will be merciful unto them, saith the Lord God, if they will repent and come unto me; for mine arm is lengthened out all the day long, saith the Lord God of Hosts.

16

The Seven Last Plagues, Angels from the Temple

Revelation 15: 1, 5-8; 16: 1-13

The plagues listed here could be actual and separate events, beyond the destruction, and death outlined in the previous chapters, or 'insert' passages giving the heavenly description of the physical events described before. These Angels that are seen by John, as he states in verse one, are a 'sign in heaven.' Could the events described in these verses be the heavenly view of earthly events, are these angels the ones that make sure that the Lord's wrath is poured out without measure? Have these angles been released to reap the earth, to gather the elect, and destroy the wicked? Could this be the spiritual description of a physical reality? Do the angles cause this destruction or do they remove their protecting power and allow mankind to begin their own devices and destruction?

Revelation 15:Verse 1
1 AND I saw another sign in heaven, great and marvellous, seven angels having the seven last plagues; for in them is filled up the wrath of God.

Revelation 15:Verse 5
5 And after that I looked, and, behold, the temple of the tabernacle of the testimony in heaven was opened:

Revelation 15:Verse 6
6 And the seven angels came out of the temple, having the seven plagues, clothed in pure and white linen, and having their breasts girded with golden girdles.

Revelation 15:Verse 7
7 And one of the four beasts gave unto the seven angels seven golden vials full of the wrath of God, who liveth for ever and ever.

Revelation 15:Verse 8
8 And the temple was filled with smoke from the glory of God, and from his power; and no man was able to enter into the temple, till the seven plagues of the seven angels were fulfilled.

Revelation 16:Verse 1

1 AND I heard a great voice out of the temple saying to the seven angels, Go your ways, and pour out the vials of the wrath of God upon the earth.

Revelation 16:Verse 2

2 And the first went, and poured out his vial upon the earth; and there fell a noisome and grievous sore upon the men which had the mark of the beast, and [upon] them which worshipped his image.

Revelation 16:Verse 3

3 And the second angel poured out his vial upon the sea; and it became as the blood of a dead [man]: and every living soul died in the sea.

Revelation 16:Verse 4

4 And the third angel poured out his vial upon the rivers and fountains of waters; and they became blood.

Revelation 16:Verse 5

5 And I heard the angel of the waters say, Thou art righteous, O Lord, which art, and wast, and shalt be, because thou hast judged thus.

Revelation 16:Verse 6

6 For they have shed the blood of saints and prophets, and thou hast given them blood to drink; for they are worthy.

Revelation 16:Verse 7

7 And I heard another out of the altar say, Even so, Lord God Almighty, true and righteous [are] thy judgments.

Revelation 16:Verse 8

8 And the fourth angel poured out his vial upon the sun; and power was given unto him to scorch men with fire.

Revelation 16:Verse 9

9 And men were scorched with great heat, and blasphemed the name of God, which hath power over these plagues: and they repented not to give him glory.

Revelation 16:Verse 10

10 And the fifth angel poured out his vial upon the seat of the beast; and his kingdom was full of darkness; and they gnawed their tongues for pain,

Revelation 16:Verse 11

11 And blasphemed the God of heaven because of their pains and their sores, and repented not of their deeds.

Revelation 16:Verse 12

12 And the sixth angel poured out his vial upon the great river Euphrates; and the water thereof was dried up, that the way of the kings of the east might be prepared.

Revelation 16:Verse 13

13 And I saw three unclean spirits like frogs [come] out of the mouth of the dragon, and out of the mouth of the beast, and out of the mouth of the false prophet.

Isaiah 64:Verse 1

1 OH that thou wouldest rend the heavens, that thou wouldest come down, that the mountains might flow down at thy presence,

Isaiah 64:Verse 2

2 As [when] the melting fire burneth, the fire causeth the waters to boil, to make thy name known to thine adversaries, [that] the nations may tremble at thy presence!

Isaiah 64:Verse 3

3 When thou didst terrible things [which] we looked not for, thou camest down, the mountains flowed down at thy presence.

Isaiah 64:Verse 4

4 For since the beginning of the world [men] have not heard, nor perceived by the ear, neither hath the eye seen, O God, beside thee, [what] he hath prepared for him that waiteth for him.

Isaiah 66:Verse 15

15 For, behold, the LORD will come with fire, and with his chariots like a whirlwind, to render his anger with fury, and his rebuke with flames of fire.

Isaiah 66:Verse 16

16 For by fire and by his sword will the LORD plead with all flesh: and the slain of the LORD shall be many.

Isaiah 66:Verse 17

17 They that sanctify themselves, and purify themselves in the gardens behind one [tree] in the midst, eating swine's flesh, and the abomination, and the mouse, shall be consumed together, saith the LORD.

Zechariah 14:Verse 12

12 And this shall be the plague wherewith the LORD will smite all the people that have fought against Jerusalem; Their flesh shall consume away while they stand upon their feet, and their eyes shall consume away in their holes, and their tongue shall consume away in their mouth.

D&C 29:Verse 17

17 And it shall come to pass, because of the wickedness of the world, that I will take vengeance upon the wicked, for they will not repent; for the cup of mine indignation is full; for behold, my blood shall not cleanse them if they hear me not.

D&C 29:Verse 18

18 Wherefore, I the Lord God will send forth flies upon the face of the earth, which shall take hold of the inhabitants thereof, and shall eat their flesh, and shall cause maggots to come in upon them;

D&C 29:Verse 19

19 And their tongues shall be stayed that they shall not utter against me; and their flesh shall fall from off their bones, and their eyes from their sockets;

Joseph Smith Matthew 1:Verse 32

32 And again shall the abomination of desolation, spoken of by Daniel the prophet, be fulfilled.

16a

The Coming of the Lord is a Day of Burning

Ezekiel 39:Verse 6

6 And **I will send a fire on Magog,** and among them that dwell carelessly in the isles: and they shall know that I [am] the LORD.

Malachi 4:Verse 1

1 For, behold, **the day cometh, that shall burn as an oven;** and all the proud, yea, and all that do wickedly, shall be stubble: and the day that cometh shall burn them up, saith the LORD of hosts, that it shall leave them neither root nor branch.

---

2 Thessalonians 1:Verse 7

7 And to you who are troubled rest with us, when the Lord Jesus shall be revealed from heaven with his mighty angels,

2 Thessalonians 1:Verse 8

8 **In flaming fire taking vengeance on them that know not God,** and that obey not the gospel of our Lord Jesus Christ:

2 Thessalonians 1:Verse 9

9 Who shall be punished with everlasting destruction from the presence of the Lord, and **from the glory of his power**;

2 Thessalonians 1:Verse 10

10 When he shall come to be glorified in his saints, and to be admired in all them that believe (because our testimony among you was believed) in that day.

---

2 Peter 3:Verse 5

5 For this they willingly are ignorant of, that by the word of God the heavens were of old, and the earth standing out of the water and in the water:

2 Peter 3:Verse 6

6 Whereby the world that then was, being overflowed with water, perished:

2 Peter 3:Verse 7

7 But the heavens and the earth, which are now, by the same word are kept in store, **reserved unto fire** against the day of judgment and perdition of ungodly men.

1 Nephi 22:Verse 17

17 Wherefore, **he will preserve the righteous by his power, even if it so be that the fulness of his wrath must come, and the righteous be preserved, even unto the destruction of their enemies by fire.** Wherefore, the righteous need not fear; for thus saith the prophet, they shall be saved, even if it so be as by fire.

1 Nephi 22:Verse 18

18 Behold, my brethren, I say unto you, that these things must shortly come; yea, **even blood, and fire, and vapor of smoke** must come; and it must needs be upon the face of this earth; and it cometh unto men according to the flesh if it so be that they will harden their hearts against the Holy One of Israel.

D&C 29:Verse 9

9 For the hour is nigh and the day soon at hand when the earth is ripe; and all the proud and they that do wickedly shall be as stubble; and **I will burn them up,** saith the Lord of Hosts, that wickedness shall not be upon the earth;

D&C 29:Verse 10

10 For the hour is nigh, and that which was spoken by mine apostles must be fulfilled; for as they spoke so shall it come to pass;

D&C 64:Verse 23

23 Behold, now it is called today until the coming of the Son of Man, and verily it is a day of sacrifice, and a day for the tithing of my people; for **he that is tithed shall not be burned at his coming**.

D&C 64:Verse 24

24 **For after today cometh the burning**--this is speaking after the manner of the Lord--for verily I say, tomorrow all the proud and they that do wickedly shall be as stubble; and **I will burn them up**, for I am the Lord of Hosts; and I will not spare any that remain in Babylon.

D&C 101:Verse 24

24 And every corruptible thing, both of man, or of the beasts of the field, or of the fowls of the heavens, or of the fish of the sea, that dwells upon all the face of the earth, shall be consumed;

D&C 133:Verse 41

41 And it shall be answered upon their heads; for the presence of the Lord **shall be as the melting fire that burneth, and as the fire which causeth the waters to boil.**

D&C 133:Verse 42

42 O Lord, thou shalt come down to make thy name known to thine adversaries, and all nations shall tremble at thy presence--

D&C 133:Verse 64

 64 And also that which was written by the prophet Malachi: For, behold, **the day cometh that shall burn as an oven**, and all the proud, yea, and all that do wickedly, shall be stubble; and **the day that cometh shall burn them up**, saith the Lord of hosts, that it shall leave them neither root nor branch.

17

Satan's Preparation for Armageddon

Revelation 16: 14-16

Satan prepares for the great battle of Armageddon by convincing the wicked leaders, governments and nations that they must prepare and launch an offensive battle against Israel. In all the land of Israel there is only one valley large enough for a ground war. This valley is the valley of Jezreel, which is sometimes called the valley of Megiddo. Historically, the great battles in the Old Testament took place here. And because this valley is the only place for a land battle the prophetic "name" of the great war against Israel is called the Battle of Armageddon. It was here at Megiddo that Solomon had his fort and stables for his army. One of the most beautiful and fertile valleys in Israel is also the bloodiest. The Mountain of Megiddo, in Hebrew is called 'har-megiddo' which in Greek (the language of the New Testament) is Ar-Mageddon. Although, this valley is the largest in Israel, and the only place that a chariots could participate in a battle anciently, the last days war of Armageddon will be throughout the all the land.

Revelation 16:Verse 14
14 For they are the spirits of devils, working miracles, [which] go forth unto the kings of the earth and of the whole world, to gather them to the battle of that great day of God Almighty.

Revelation 16:Verse 16
16 And he gathered them together into a place called in the Hebrew tongue Armageddon.

Revelation 16:Verse 15
15 Behold, I come as a thief. Blessed [is] he that watcheth, and keepeth his garments, lest he walk naked, and they see his shame

---

Isaiah 29:Verse 1
1 WOE to Ariel, to Ariel, the city [where] David dwelt! add ye year to year; let them kill sacrifices.

Isaiah 29:Verse 2
2 Yet I will distress Ariel, and there shall be heaviness and sorrow: and it shall be unto me as Ariel.

Isaiah 29:Verse 3

3 And I will camp against thee round about, and will lay siege against thee with a mount, and I will raise forts against thee.

Isaiah 29:Verse 4

4 And thou shalt be brought down, [and] shalt speak out of the ground, and thy speech shall be low out of the dust, and thy voice shall be, as of one that hath a familiar spirit, out of the ground, and thy speech shall whisper out of the dust.

Isaiah 29:Verse 5

5 Moreover the multitude of thy strangers shall be like small dust, and the multitude of the terrible ones [shall be] as chaff that passeth away: yea, it shall be at an instant suddenly.

Isaiah 29:Verse 6

6 Thou shalt be visited of the LORD of hosts with thunder, and with earthquake, and great noise, with storm and tempest, and the flame of devouring fire.

Isaiah 29:Verse 7

7 And the multitude of all the nations that fight against Ariel, even all that fight against her and her munition, and that distress her, shall be as a dream of a night vision.

Isaiah 29:Verse 8

8 It shall even be as when an hungry [man] dreameth, and, behold, he eateth; but he awaketh, and his soul is empty: or as when a thirsty man dreameth, and, behold, he drinketh; but he awaketh, and, behold, [he is] faint, and his soul hath appetite: so shall the multitude of all the nations be, that fight against mount Zion.

Joel 3:Verse 1

1 For, behold, in those days, and in that time, when I shall bring again the captivity of Judah and Jerusalem,

Joel 3:Verse 2

2 I will also gather all nations, and will bring them down into the valley of Jehoshaphat, and will plead with them there for my people and [for] my heritage Israel, whom they have scattered among the nations, and parted my land.

Joel 3:Verse 3

3 And they have cast lots for my people; and have given a boy for an harlot, and sold a girl for wine, that they might drink.

Joel 3:Verse 4

4 Yea, and what have ye to do with me, O Tyre, and Zidon, and all the coasts of Palestine? will ye render me a recompence? and if ye recompense me, swiftly [and] speedily will I return your recompence upon your own head;

Joel 3:Verse 5
5 Because ye have taken my silver and my gold, and have carried into your temples my goodly pleasant things:

Joel 3:Verse 6
6 The children also of Judah and the children of Jerusalem have ye sold unto the Grecians, that ye might remove them far from their border.

Joel 3:Verse 7
7 Behold, I will raise them out of the place whither ye have sold them, and will return your recompence upon your own head:

Joel 3:Verse 8
8 And I will sell your sons and your daughters into the hand of the children of Judah, and they shall sell them to the Sabeans, to a people far off: for the LORD hath spoken [it].

Joel 3:Verse 9
9 Proclaim ye this among the Gentiles; Prepare war, wake up the mighty men, let all the men of war draw near; let them come up:

Joel 3:Verse 10
10 Beat your plowshares into swords, and your pruninghooks into spears: let the weak say, I [am] strong.

Joel 3:Verse 11
11 Assemble yourselves, and come, all ye heathen, and gather yourselves together round about: thither cause thy mighty ones to come down, O LORD.

Joel 3:Verse 12
12 Let the heathen be wakened, and come up to the valley of Jehoshaphat: for there will I sit to judge all the heathen round about.

Joel 3:Verse 13
13 Put ye in the sickle, for the harvest is ripe: come, get you down; for the press is full, the fats overflow; for their wickedness [is] great.

Joel 3:Verse 14
14 Multitudes, multitudes in the valley of decision: for the day of the LORD [is] near in the valley of decision.

The Great War, The battle of Armageddon

This war, or battle is the most discussed aspect of the last days, it is because of the prophetic descriptions of this battle that many stock, guns and ammunition in preparation to protect their families and food supplies. This war will signal, not the end, but the closeness of the end. This war ends with Christ descending (like he ascended) to the Mount of Olives as the political, and spiritual Savior of the children of Israel.

There are two battles spoken of in latter-day scripture the battle of Armageddon and the battle of Gog and Magog. Speaking of this battle Elder Bruce R. McConkie has stated:

> **"At the very moment of the Second Coming of our Lord, 'all nations' shall be gathered 'against Jerusalem to battle' (Zech. 11; 12; 13; 14), and the battle of Armageddon** (obviously covering the entire area from Jerusalem to Megiddo, and perhaps more) will be in progress. As John expressed it, 'the kings of the earth and of the whole world' will be gathered 'to the battle of that great day of God Almighty, . . . into a place called in the Hebrew tongue Armageddon.' Then Christ will 'come as a thief,' meaning unexpectedly, and **the dramatic upheavals promised to accompany his return** will take place. (Rev. 16:14-21.) **It is incident to this battle of Armageddon that the Supper of the Great God shall take place (Rev. 19:11-18)**, and **it is the same battle described by Ezekiel as the war with Gog and Magog.** (Ezek. 38; 39; Doctrines of Salvation, vol. 3, p. 45.)" (Mormon Doctrine, 2nd ed., p. 74.) (Doctrinal New Testament Commentary Vol. 3, p 543.)

This battle of Armageddon, or the battle of Gog and Magog seems to be a hinge upon which many things that are mentioned in the Book of Revelation swing. They are, according to Elder McConkie: Armageddon, Gog and Magog, the moment of the Second Coming, physical upheavals, the Supper of the Great God. Thus, these chapters must be read as elements of corresponding time, and not linear as the chapters are laid out by John.

Ezekiel 38:Verse 3

3 And say, Thus saith the Lord GOD; Behold, I [am] against thee, O Gog, the chief prince of Meshech and Tubal:

Ezekiel 38:Verse 4

4 And I will turn thee back, and put hooks into thy jaws, and I will bring thee forth, and all thine army, horses and horsemen, all of them clothed with all sorts [of armour, even] a great company [with] bucklers and shields, all of them handling swords:

Ezekiel 38:Verse 5

5 Persia, Ethiopia, and Libya with them; all of them with shield and helmet:

Ezekiel 38:Verse 6

6 Gomer, and all his bands; the house of Togarmah of the north quarters, and all his bands: [and] many people with thee.

Ezekiel 38:Verse 7

7 Be thou prepared, and prepare for thyself, thou, and all thy company that are assembled unto thee, and be thou a guard unto them.

Ezekiel 38:Verse 8

8 After many days thou shalt be visited: in the latter years thou shalt come into the land [that is] brought back from the sword, [and is] gathered out of many people, against the mountains of Israel, which have been always waste: but it is brought forth out of the nations, and they shall dwell safely all of them.

Ezekiel 38:Verse 9

9 Thou shalt ascend and come like a storm, thou shalt be like a cloud to cover the land, thou, and all thy bands, and many people with thee.

Ezekiel 38:Verse 10

10 Thus saith the Lord GOD; It shall also come to pass, [that] at the same time shall things come into thy mind, and thou shalt think an evil thought:

Ezekiel 38:Verse 11

11 And thou shalt say, I will go up to the land of unwalled villages; I will go to them that are at rest, that dwell safely, all of them dwelling without walls, and having neither bars nor gates,

Ezekiel 38:Verse 12

12 To take a spoil, and to take a prey; to turn thine hand upon the desolate places [that are now] inhabited, and upon the people [that are] gathered out of the nations, which have gotten cattle and goods, that dwell in the midst of the land.

Ezekiel 38:Verse 13

13 Sheba, and Dedan, and the merchants of Tarshish, with all the young lions thereof, shall say unto thee, Art thou come to take a spoil? hast thou gathered thy company to take a prey? to carry away silver and gold, to take away cattle and goods, to take a great spoil?

Ezekiel 38:Verse 14

14 Therefore, son of man, prophesy and say unto Gog, Thus saith the Lord GOD; In that day when my people of Israel dwelleth safely, shalt thou not know [it]?

Ezekiel 38:Verse 15

15 And thou shalt come from thy place out of the north parts, thou, and many people with thee, all of them riding upon horses, a great company, and a mighty army:

Ezekiel 38:Verse 16

16 And thou shalt come up against my people of Israel, as a cloud to cover the land; it shall be in the latter days, and I will bring thee against my land, that the heathen may know me, when I shall be sanctified in thee, O Gog, before their eyes.

Ezekiel 38:Verse 17

17 Thus saith the Lord GOD; [Art] thou he of whom I have spoken in old time by my servants the prophets of Israel, which prophesied in those days [many] years that I would bring thee against them?

Ezekiel 38:Verse 18

18 And it shall come to pass at the same time when Gog shall come against the land of Israel, saith the Lord GOD, [that] my fury shall come up in my face.

Ezekiel 38:Verse 19

19 For in my jealousy [and] in the fire of my wrath have I spoken, Surely in that day there shall be a great shaking in the land of Israel;

Ezekiel 38:Verse 20

20 So that the fishes of the sea, and the fowls of the heaven, and the beasts of the field, and all creeping things that creep upon the earth, and all the men that [are] upon the face of the earth, shall shake at my presence, and the mountains shall be thrown down, and the steep places shall fall, and every wall shall fall to the ground.

Ezekiel 38:Verse 21

21 And I will call for a sword against him throughout all my mountains, saith the Lord GOD: every man's sword shall be against his brother.

Ezekiel 38:Verse 22

22 And I will plead against him with pestilence and with blood; and I will rain upon him, and upon his bands, and upon the many people that [are] with him, an overflowing rain, and great hailstones, fire, and brimstone.

Ezekiel 38:Verse 23

23 Thus will I magnify myself, and sanctify myself; and I will be known in the eyes of many nations, and they shall know that I [am] the LORD.

Ezekiel 39:Verse 1

1 THEREFORE, thou son of man, prophesy against Gog, and say, Thus saith the Lord GOD; Behold, I [am] against thee, O Gog, the chief prince of Meshech and Tubal:

Ezekiel 39:Verse 2
2 And I will turn thee back, and leave but the sixth part of thee, and will cause thee to come up from the north parts, and will bring thee upon the mountains of Israel:

Ezekiel 39:Verse 3
3 And I will smite thy bow out of thy left hand, and will cause thine arrows to fall out of thy right hand.

Joel 2:Verse 1
1 BLOW ye the trumpet in Zion, and sound an alarm in my holy mountain: let all the inhabitants of the land tremble: for the day of the LORD cometh, for [it is] nigh at hand;

Joel 2:Verse 2
2 A day of darkness and of gloominess, a day of clouds and of thick darkness, as the morning spread upon the mountains: a great people and a strong; there hath not been ever the like, neither shall be any more after it, [even] to the years of many generations.

Joel 2:Verse 3
3 A fire devoureth before them; and behind them a flame burneth: the land [is] as the garden of Eden before them, and behind them a desolate wilderness; yea, and nothing shall escape them.

Joel 2:Verse 4
4 The appearance of them [is] as the appearance of horses; and as horsemen, so shall they run.

Joel 2:Verse 5
5 Like the noise of chariots on the tops of mountains shall they leap, like the noise of a flame of fire that devoureth the stubble, as a strong people set in battle array.

Joel 2:Verse 6
6 Before their face the people shall be much pained: all faces shall gather blackness.

Joel 2:Verse 7
7 They shall run like mighty men; they shall climb the wall like men of war; and they shall march every one on his ways, and they shall not break their ranks:

Joel 2:Verse 8
8 Neither shall one thrust another; they shall walk every one in his path: and [when] they fall upon the sword, they shall not be wounded.

Joel 2:Verse 9
9 They shall run to and fro in the city; they shall run upon the wall, they shall climb up upon the houses; they shall enter in at the windows like a thief.

Zechariah 12:Verse 2

2 Behold, I will make Jerusalem a cup of trembling unto all the people round about, when they shall be in the siege both against Judah [and] against Jerusalem.

Zechariah 12:Verse 3

3 And in that day will I make Jerusalem a burdensome stone for all people: all that burden themselves with it shall be cut in pieces, though all the people of the earth be gathered together against it.

Zechariah 12:Verse 4

4 In that day, saith the LORD, I will smite every horse with astonishment, and his rider with madness: and I will open mine eyes upon the house of Judah, and will smite every horse of the people with blindness.

Zechariah 14:Verse 1

1 BEHOLD, the day of the LORD cometh, and thy spoil shall be divided in the midst of thee.

Zechariah 14:Verse 2

2 For I will gather all nations against Jerusalem to battle; and the city shall be taken, and the houses rifled, and the women ravished; and half of the city shall go forth into captivity, and the residue of the people shall not be cut off from the city.

Zechariah 14:Verse 13

13 And it shall come to pass in that day, [that] a great tumult from the LORD shall be among them; and they shall lay hold every one on the hand of his neighbour, and his hand shall rise up against the hand of his neighbour.

Zechariah 14:Verse 14

14 And Judah also shall fight at Jerusalem; and the wealth of all the heathen round about shall be gathered together, gold, and silver, and apparel, in great abundance.

Zechariah 14:Verse 15

15 And so shall be the plague of the horse, of the mule, of the camel, and of the ass, and of all the beasts that shall be in these tents, as this plague.

18

The Two Prophets

Revelation 11: 1-12

The Two Prophets, the Two Olive Trees, or the Two candlesticks, these two prophets will vex the nations that come against Israel during the battle and time of Armageddon. By the divine power they will prophecy, and preform miracles for three and a half years, keeping the nations that come against Israel from completely destroying the Jewish state. Many assume that they will be members of the First Presidency or Quourm of Apostles, however, there are many with a prophetic mantel that are not responsible for the administration of the Gospel. There are four individuals that are prophets that are living today that have no responsibility for the administration of the Gospel and church in Salt Lake City. These are John and the Three Nephites. John and the Three Nephites are given to responsibility to work for the salvation of the children of Israel, and are promised not to die until Christ returns, as do these two prophets rise to meet the Savior after only three days of death.

Revelation 11:Verse 1
1 AND there was given me a reed like unto a rod: and the angel stood, saying, Rise, and measure the temple of God, and the altar, and them that worship therein.

Revelation 11:Verse 2
2 But the court which is without the temple leave out, and measure it not; for it is given unto the Gentiles: and the holy city shall they tread under foot forty [and] two months.

Revelation 11:Verse 3
3 And I will give [power] unto my two witnesses, and they shall prophesy a thousand two hundred [and] threescore days, clothed in sackcloth.

Revelation 11:Verse 4
4 These are the two olive trees, and the two candlesticks standing before the God of the earth.

Revelation 11:Verse 5
5 And if any man will hurt them, fire proceedeth out of their mouth, and devoureth their enemies: and if any man will hurt them, he must in this manner be killed.

Revelation 11:Verse 6
6 These have power to shut heaven, that it rain not in the days of their prophecy: and have power over waters to turn them to blood, and to smite the earth with all plagues, as often as they will.

Revelation 11:Verse 7
7 And when they shall have finished their testimony, the beast that ascendeth out of the bottomless pit shall make war against them, and shall overcome them, and kill them.

Revelation 11:Verse 8
8 And their dead bodies [shall lie] in the street of the great city, which spiritually is called Sodom and Egypt, where also our Lord was crucified.

Revelation 11:Verse 9
9 And they of the people and kindreds and tongues and nations shall see their dead bodies three days and an half, and shall not suffer their dead bodies to be put in graves.

Revelation 11:Verse 10
10 And they that dwell upon the earth shall rejoice over them, and make merry, and shall send gifts one to another; because these two prophets tormented them that dwelt on the earth.

Revelation 11:Verse 11
11 And after three days and an half the Spirit of life from God entered into them, and they stood upon their feet; and great fear fell upon them which saw them.

Revelation 11:Verse 12
12 And they heard a great voice from heaven saying unto them, Come up hither. And they ascended up to heaven in a cloud; and their enemies beheld them.

D&C 77:Verse 15
15 Q. What is to be understood by the two witnesses, in the eleventh chapter of Revelation?

A. **They are two prophets that are to be raised up to the Jewish nation in the last days, at the time of the restoration, and to prophesy to the Jews after they are gathered and have built the city of Jerusalem in the land of their fathers.**

The following scriptures, and references seem to describe the events and the work surrounding the two prophets in the last days. These scriptures prophesy the work of the Lord@s servants in the last days. The patterns and results are the same as those that will be accomplished by these prophets as the battle of Armageddon comes to a close. The nations who fight against the Lord begin to fall, and the full restoration of Israel begins.

---

3 Nephi 20:Verse 16
16 Then shall ye, who are a remnant of the house of Jacob, go forth among them; and ye shall be in the midst of them who shall be many; and ye shall be among them as a lion among the beasts of the forest, and as a young lion among the flocks of sheep, who, if he goeth through both treadeth down and teareth in pieces, and none can deliver.

3 Nephi 20:Verse 17
17 **Thy hand shall be lifted up upon thine adversaries, and all thine enemies shall be cut off.**

3 Nephi 20:Verse 18
18 And I will gather my people together as a man gathereth his sheaves into the floor.

3 Nephi 20:Verse 19
19 For I will make my people with whom the Father hath covenanted, yea, I will make thy horn iron, and I will make thy hoofs brass. And thou shalt beat in pieces many people; and I will consecrate their gain unto the Lord, and their substance unto the Lord of the whole earth. And behold, I am he who doeth it.

3 Nephi 20:Verse 20
20 And it shall come to pass, saith the Father, that the **sword of my justice shall hang over them at that day; and except they repent it shall fall upon them,** saith the Father, yea, even **upon all the nations of the Gentiles**.

3 Nephi 20:Verse 21
21 And it shall come to pass that **I will establish my people, O house of Israel.**

D&C 133:Verse 67
67 When I called again there was none of you to answer; yet **my arm was not shortened** at all that I could not redeem, neither my power to deliver.

D&C 133:Verse 68

68 Behold, at my rebuke I dry up the sea. I make the rivers a wilderness; their fish stink, and die for thirst.

D&C 133:Verse 69

69 I clothe the heavens with blackness, and make sackcloth their covering.

D&C 133:Verse 70

70 And this shall ye have of my hand--**ye shall lie down in sorrow.**

D&C 133:Verse 71

71 Behold, and lo, **there are none to deliver you; for ye obeyed not my voice when I called to you out of the heavens; ye believed not my servants, and when they were sent unto you ye received them not.**

———————————————————

Righteous Dead Ascend into the Cloud, to the Coming Christ

As Christ comes, the righteous saints are redeemed, and worthy dead are resurrected and are caught up to meet Him in the clouds, and descend with Him as he comes to earth in glory, and power. The Savior descends and then stands on the Mount of Olives as the angel revealed when he ascended after his resurrection, stating that 'in like manner' he should return.

D&C 45:Verse 43
43 And the remnant shall be gathered unto this place;

D&C 45:Verse 44
44 And then they shall look for me, and, behold, I will come; and **they shall see me in the clouds of heaven, clothed with power and great glory; with all the holy angels;** and he that watches not for me shall be cut off.

D&C 45:Verse 45
45 But before the arm of the Lord shall fall, an angel shall sound his trump, and **the saints that have slept shall come forth to meet me in the cloud.**

D&C 45:Verse 46
46 Wherefore, if ye have slept in peace blessed are you; for as you now behold me and know that I am, **even so shall ye come unto me and your souls shall live, and your redemption shall be perfected; and the saints shall come forth from the four quarters of the earth.**

D&C 45:Verse 47
47 *Then* **shall the arm of the Lord fall upon the nations.**

D&C 88:Verse 96
96 And **the saints that are upon the earth, who are alive, shall be quickened and be caught up to meet him.**

D&C 88:Verse 97
97 And **they who have slept in their graves shall come forth, for their graves shall be opened; and they also shall be caught up to meet him in the midst of the pillar of heaven--**

D&C 88:Verse 98

98 **They are Christ's, the first fruits, they who shall descend with him first, and they who are on the earth and in their graves, who are first caught up to meet him**; and all this by the voice of the sounding of the trump of the angel of God.

———————————————

D&C 109:Verse 75

75 That when the trump shall sound for the dead, **we shall be caught up in the cloud to meet thee**, that we may ever be with the Lord;

D&C 109:Verse 76

76 That our garments may be pure, that we may be clothed upon with robes of righteousness, with palms in our hands, and crowns of glory upon our heads, and reap eternal joy for all our sufferings.

19

The Great Earthquake

Revelation 11: 13-14, 19;   16: 18-21

As the two prophets are resurrected and caught up to meet the Savior there is the great earthquake that is described as 'such was not since men were upon the earth, so mighty an earthquake, and so great.' (Rev.16:18). This earthquake heralds the coming of the Savior on the Mount of Olives as the mount cleaves in twain with part moving to the north and part to the south. The upheavals of nature, as in the Book of Mormon, create massive destructions. These natural disasters can be blamed on no one but the God of creation. There is nothing more humbling than to know that nature is no respecter of persons, and that affluence, position, and power can buy no favors from nature's God. 'Behold, the Lord esteemeth all flesh in one; he that is righteous is favored of God.' (1 Nephi 17:35). We must realize and understand our relationship, and dependence upon God in order to take the atonement seriously, because of this King Benjamin stated that we must keep in 'remembrance, the greatness of God, and your own nothingness' before God. (Mosiah 4:5, 11). Moses after getting a glimpse of the works of God, and standing in his glory, declares that 'now I know that man is nothing, which thing I never before supposed.' (Moses 1:10).

Revelation 11:Verse 13

13 And the same hour was there a great earthquake, and the tenth part of the city fell, and in the earthquake were slain of men seven thousand: and the remnant were affrighted, and gave glory to the God of heaven.

Revelation 11:Verse 14

14 The second woe is past; [and], behold, the third woe cometh quickly

Revelation 11:Verse 19

19 And the temple of God was opened in heaven, and there was seen in his temple the ark of his testament: and there were lightnings, and voices, and thunderings, and an earthquake, and great hail.

Revelation 16:Verse 18

18 And there were voices, and thunders, and lightnings; and there was a great earthquake, such as was not since men were upon the earth, so mighty an earthquake, [and] so great.

Revelation 16:Verse 19

19 And the great city was divided into three parts, and the cities of the nations fell: and great Babylon came in remembrance before God, to give unto her the cup of the wine of the fierceness of his wrath.

Revelation 16:Verse 20

20 And every island fled away, and the mountains were not found.

Revelation 16:Verse 21

21 And there fell upon men a great hail out of heaven, [every stone] about the weight of a talent: and men blasphemed God because of the plague of the hail; for the plague thereof was exceeding great.

Ezekiel 38:Verse 19

19 For in my jealousy [and] in the fire of my wrath have I spoken, Surely in that day there shall be a **great shaking** in the land of Israel;

Ezekiel 38:Verse 20

20 So that the fishes of the sea, and the fowls of the heaven, and the beasts of the field, and all creeping things that creep upon the earth, and all the men that [are] upon the face of the earth, shall shake at my presence, and **the mountains shall be thrown down, and the steep places shall fall, and every wall shall fall to the ground.**

Joel 3:Verse 16

16 The LORD also shall roar out of Zion, and utter his voice from Jerusalem; **and the heavens and the earth shall shake: but the LORD [will be] the hope of his people, and the strength of the children of Israel.**

Zechariah 12:Verse 8

8 In that day shall the LORD defend the inhabitants of Jerusalem; and he that is feeble among them at that day shall be as David; and the house of David [shall be] as God, as the angel of the LORD before them.

Zechariah 12:Verse 9

9 And it shall come to pass in that day, [that] I will seek to destroy all the nations that come against Jerusalem.

D&C 109:Verse 73

73 That thy church may come forth out of the wilderness of darkness, and shine forth fair as the moon, clear as the sun, and terrible as an army with banners;

D&C 109:Verse 74
74 And be adorned as a bride for that day **when thou shalt unveil the heavens, and cause the mountains to flow down at thy presence, and the valleys to be exalted, the rough places made smooth; that thy glory may fill the earth;**

D&C 133:Verse 1
1 Hearken, O ye people of my church, saith the Lord your God, and hear the word of the Lord concerning you--

D&C 133:Verse 2
2 The Lord who shall suddenly come to his temple; the **Lord who shall come down upon the world with a curse to judgment; yea, upon all the nations that forget God,** and upon all the ungodly among you.

D&C 133:Verse 3
3 For he shall make bare his holy arm in the eyes of all the nations, and all the ends of the earth shall see the salvation of their God.

D&C 133:Verse 22
22 **And it shall be a voice as the voice of many waters, and as the voice of a great thunder, which shall break down the mountains, and the valleys shall not be found.**

D&C 133:Verse 23
23 **He shall command the great deep, and it shall be driven back into the north countries, and the islands shall become one land;**

D&C 133:Verse 24
24 And the land of Jerusalem and the land of Zion shall **be turned back into their own place, and the earth shall be like as it was in the days before it was divided.**

D&C 133:Verse 27
27 **And an highway shall be cast up in the midst of the great deep.**

D&C 133:Verse 40
40 Calling upon the name of the Lord day and night, saying: **O that thou wouldst rend the heavens, that thou wouldst come down, that the mountains might flow down at thy presence.**

D&C 133:Verse 43
43 When thou doest terrible things, things they look not for;

D&C 133:Verse 44

44 Yea, **when thou comest down, and the mountains flow down at thy presence,** thou shalt meet him who rejoiceth and worketh righteousness, who remembereth thee in thy ways.

D&C 133:Verse 45

45 **For since the beginning of the world have not men heard nor perceived by the ear, neither hath any eye seen, O God, besides thee, how great things thou hast prepared for him that waiteth for thee.**

The Coming of the Lord on the Mount of Olives

The Lord comes with the righteous saints to stand on the Mount of Olives. This event signals the beginning of the end with the destruction from the great worldwide earthquake, and the salvation of the Jewish people who flee in the valley left by the upheavals of the earth. Here they learn of the Savior and the wounds in his hands and feet, and how he received them in the house of his friends.

Joel 2:Verse 11
11 And the LORD shall utter his voice before his army: for his camp [is] very great: for [he is] strong that executeth his word: for the day of the LORD [is] great and very terrible; and who can abide it?

Joel 2:Verse 12
12 Therefore also now, saith the LORD, turn ye [even] to me with all your heart, and with fasting, and with weeping, and with mourning:

Joel 2:Verse 13
13 And rend your heart, and not your garments, and turn unto the LORD your God: for he [is] gracious and merciful, slow to anger, and of great kindness, and repenteth him of the evil.

Joel 2:Verse 14
14 Who knoweth [if] he will return and repent, and leave a blessing behind him; [even] a meat offering and a drink offering unto the LORD your God?

Joel 2:Verse 15
15 Blow the trumpet in Zion, sanctify a fast, call a solemn assembly:

Joel 2:Verse 16
16 Gather the people, sanctify the congregation, assemble the elders, gather the children, and those that suck the breasts: **let the bridegroom go forth of his chamber, and the bride out of her closet.**
Joel 2:Verse 17
17 Let the priests, the ministers of the LORD, weep between the porch and the altar, and let them say, Spare thy people, O LORD, and give not thine heritage to reproach, that the heathen should rule over them: wherefore should they say among the people, Where [is] their God?

Zechariah 12:Verse 10
10 And I will pour upon the house of David, and upon the inhabitants of Jerusalem, the spirit of grace and of supplications: and **they shall look upon me whom they have pierced, and they**

shall mourn for him, as one mourneth for [his] only [son], and shall be in bitterness for him, as one that is in bitterness for [his] firstborn.

Zechariah 12:Verse 11

11 In that day shall there be a great mourning in Jerusalem, as the mourning of Hadadrimmon in the valley of Megiddon.

Zechariah 12:Verse 12

12 And the land shall mourn, every family apart; the family of the house of David apart, and their wives apart; the family of the house of Nathan apart, and their wives apart;

Zechariah 12:Verse 13

13 The family of the house of Levi apart, and their wives apart; the family of Shimei apart, and their wives apart;

Zechariah 12:Verse 14

14 All the families that remain, every family apart, and their wives apart.

Zechariah 13:Verse 6

6 And [one] shall say unto him, **What [are] these wounds in thine hands? Then he shall answer, [Those] with which I was wounded [in] the house of my friends.**

Zechariah 14:Verse 3

3 Then shall the LORD go forth, and fight against those nations, as when he fought in the day of battle.

Zechariah 14:Verse 4

4 **And his feet shall stand in that day upon the mount of Olives, which [is] before Jerusalem on the east, and the mount of Olives shall cleave in the midst thereof toward the east and toward the west, [and there shall be] a very great valley; and half of the mountain shall remove toward the north, and half of it toward the south.**

Zechariah 14:Verse 5

5 And ye shall flee [to] the valley of the mountains; for the valley of the mountains shall reach unto Azal: yea, ye shall flee, like as ye fled from before the earthquake in the days of Uzziah king of Judah: and the LORD my God shall come, [and] all the saints with thee.

Jude 1:Verse 14

14 And Enoch also, the seventh from Adam, prophesied of these, saying, **Behold, the Lord cometh with ten thousands of his saints,**

Jude 1:Verse 15

15 To execute judgment upon all, and to convince all that are ungodly among them of all their ungodly deeds which they have ungodly committed, and of all their hard [speeches] which ungodly sinners have spoken against him.

Jude 1:Verse 16

16 These are murmurers, complainers, walking after their own lusts; and their mouth speaketh great swelling [words], having men's persons in admiration because of advantage.

D&C 38:Verse 17

17 And I have made the earth rich, and behold it is my footstool, wherefore, again I will stand upon it.

D&C 45:Verse 48

48 **And then shall the Lord set his foot upon this mount, and it shall cleave in twain, and the earth shall tremble, and reel to and fro, and the heavens also shall shake.**

D&C 45:Verse 49

49 And the Lord shall utter his voice, and **all the ends of the earth shall hear it; and the nations of the earth shall mourn,** and they that have laughed shall see their folly.

D&C 45:Verse 50

50 And calamity shall cover the mocker, and the scorner shall be consumed; and they that have watched for iniquity shall be hewn down and cast into the fire.

D&C 45:Verse 51

51 And then shall the **Jews look upon me and say: What are these wounds in thine hands and in thy feet?**

D&C 45:Verse 52

52 **Then shall they know that I am the Lord; for I will say unto them: These wounds are the wounds with which I was wounded in the house of my friends. I am he who was lifted up. I am Jesus that was crucified. I am the Son of God.**

D&C 45:Verse 53

53 And **then shall they weep because of their iniquities; then shall they lament because they persecuted their king.**

D&C 45:Verse 74

74 For when the Lord shall appear he shall be terrible unto them, that fear may seize upon them, and they shall stand afar off and tremble.

D&C 45:Verse 75

75 And all nations shall be afraid because of the terror of the Lord, and the power of his might. Even so. Amen.

D&C 63:Verse 34

34 And **the saints also shall hardly escape**; nevertheless, I, the Lord, am with them, and will come down in heaven from the presence of my Father and consume the wicked with unquenchable fire.

D&C 124:Verse 8

8 And that I may visit them in the day of visitation, when I shall unveil the face of my covering, to appoint the portion of the oppressor among hypocrites, where there is gnashing of teeth, if they reject my servants and my testimony which I have revealed unto them.

D&C 133:Verse 17

17 For behold, the Lord God hath sent forth the angel crying through the midst of heaven, saying: Prepare ye the way of the Lord, and make his paths straight, for the hour of his coming is nigh--

D&C 133:Verse 18

18 **When the Lamb shall stand upon Mount Zion, and with him a hundred and forty-four thousand, having his Father's name written on their foreheads.**

D&C 133:Verse 19

19 Wherefore, prepare ye for the coming of the Bridegroom; go ye, go ye out to meet him.

D&C 133:Verse 20

20 For behold, **he shall stand upon the mount of Olivet,** and upon the mighty ocean, even the great deep, and upon the islands of the sea, and upon the land of Zion.

The Refiners Fire

The coming of Christ will be a great and terrible day. Great for the righteous and a terrible day for the wicked. At this time the righteous will be proved and blessed as the wicked are destroyed. Now is the time that the parables of the Matthew 25 shall be fulfilled; the wise and foolish virgins, and the parable of the talents. These two parables show the separation of the sheep and goats, and why there is a separation. Verses 35-46 of Matthew Twenty Five teach what the 'Oil' of the virgins represent and the 'talents' that we must increase.

Zechariah 13:Verse 7

7 Awake, O sword, against my shepherd, and against the man [that is] my fellow, saith the LORD of hosts: smite the shepherd, and the sheep shall be scattered: and I will turn mine hand upon the little ones.

Zechariah 13:Verse 8

8 And it shall come to pass, [that] in all the land, saith the LORD, two parts therein shall be cut off [and] die; but the third shall be left therein.

Zechariah 13:Verse 9

9 And **I will bring the third part through the fire, and will refine them as silver is refined, and will try them as gold** is tried: they shall call on my name, and I will hear them: I will say, It [is] my people: and they shall say, The LORD [is] my God.

Malachi 3:Verse 2

2 But who may abide the day of his coming? and who shall stand when he appeareth? for **he [is] like a refiner's fire, and like fullers' soap:**

Malachi 3:Verse 3

3 And **he shall sit [as] a refiner and purifier of silver:** and he shall purify the sons of Levi, and purge them as gold and silver, that they may offer unto the LORD an offering in righteousness.

Malachi 3:Verse 4

4 Then shall the offering of Judah and Jerusalem be pleasant unto the LORD, as in the days of old, and as in former years.

Malachi 3:Verse 5

5 And I will come near to you to judgment; and I will be a swift witness against the sorcerers, and against the adulterers, and against false swearers, and against those that oppress the hireling in [his] wages, the widow, and the fatherless, and that turn aside the stranger [from his right], and fear not me, saith the LORD of hosts.

Malachi 3:Verse 6

6 For I [am] the LORD, I change not; therefore ye sons of Jacob are not consumed.

———————————————————

20

The Fall of Babylon

Revelation 18: 1-3, 6-24

Babylon, the symbol of wickedness, degradation, idolatry, immorality, and the love of wealth. Spiritual Babylon has been on the earth from the time of Adam, as Satan convinced Cain that he could murder and get gain, saying that 'surely the flocks of my brother falleth into my hands' (Moses 5:33). This wickedness has plagued mankind throughout history, and has become as a 'great whore' and sitteth upon the waters of the earth. The progress of Babylon is seen in Revelation Chapter Seventeen as all the 'kings of the earth have committed fornication, and the inhabitants of the earth have been made drunk with the wine of her fornication.' (Rev. 17:2). 'For all nations have drunk of the wine of the wrath of her fornication, and the kings of the earth have committed fornication with her, and the merchants of The earth are waxed rich through the abundance of her delicacies.' (Rev. 18:3).

It is a mistake to declare that Babylon is a particular church or religion. From the scriptures it appears that the wickedness of Babylon is economic, the love of money, and the desire for wealth as the love of man waxes cold throughout the cultures of mankind, or in the words of Cain to 'murder and get gain.'

The restoration of the Gospel is the greatest threat to secret oaths and combinations, and the philosophies of Babylon or 'the church of the devil' the same 'great and Abominable Church' of the Book of Mormon. 'Equality' in temporal things, taking 'no thought of what you shall eat, or drink . . .' knowing that it is easier for a camel to get through the eye of a needle than a rich man into the kingdom of heaven. Living the law of consecration and loving your neighbor as yourself, rather than living the laws of competition, in the strenuous effort to be better than those around you is the threat to spiritual growth. Giving your excess as required by the law of tithing (D&C 119) having all things in common, in the gospel of love, or charity seeking not your own, and not envying others is the foundation of the battle that rages between Zion and Babylon.

With an economic disaster, and a world wide monetary collapse, Babylon will fall. In order for Zion to flourish through the millennium a people must exist 'with one mind and one heart' and have 'no poor among them.' In this chapter we see the merchants of the earth that weep and mourn over the fall of Babylon because they were 'made rich by her.' Third Nephi shows that it took massive natural disasters to destroy both the governmental, and economic systems, in order to introduce the gospel worldwide, and in Fourth Nephi records a millennial type of existence where there existed no sin, and, no 'ites'. Again, it must be remembered that the Book of Mormon is the pattern of the last days.

This chapter should be read in conjunction with chapters: Seventeen of Revelation, Thirteen, Fourteen and Twenty Two of First Nephi, Thirteen and Fourteen of Isaiah, and Fifty and Fifty One of Jeremiah. The symbol and prophecies of the wickedness of spiritual Babylon is one of the most spoken of in scripture.

Revelation 18:Verse 1
1 AND after these things I saw another angel come down from heaven, having great power; and the earth was lightened with his glory.

Revelation 18:Verse 2
2 And he cried mightily with a strong voice, saying, Babylon the great is fallen, is fallen, and is become the habitation of devils, and the hold of every foul spirit, and a cage of every unclean and hateful bird.

Revelation 18:Verse 3
3 For all nations have drunk of the wine of the wrath of her fornication, and the kings of the earth have committed fornication with her, and the merchants of the earth are waxed rich through the abundance of her delicacies.

Revelation 18:Verse 6
6 Reward her even as she rewarded you, and double unto her double according to her works: in the cup which she hath filled fill to her double.

Revelation 18:Verse 7
7 How much she hath glorified herself, and lived deliciously, so much torment and sorrow give her: for she saith in her heart, I sit a queen, and am no widow, and shall see no sorrow.

Revelation 18:Verse 8
8 Therefore shall her plagues come in one day, death, and mourning, and famine; and she shall be utterly burned with fire: for strong [is] the Lord God who judgeth her.

Revelation 18:Verse 9
9 And the kings of the earth, who have committed fornication and lived deliciously with her, shall bewail her, and lament for her, when they shall see the smoke of her burning,

Revelation 18:Verse 10
10 Standing afar off for the fear of her torment, saying, Alas, alas, that great city Babylon, that mighty city! for in one hour is thy judgment come.

Revelation 18:Verse 11

11 And the merchants of the earth shall weep and mourn over her; for no man buyeth their merchandise any more:

Revelation 18:Verse 12

12 The merchandise of gold, and silver, and precious stones, and of pearls, and fine linen, and purple, and silk, and scarlet, and all thyine wood, and all manner vessels of ivory, and all manner vessels of most precious wood, and of brass, and iron, and marble,

Revelation 18:Verse 13

13 And cinnamon, and odours, and ointments, and frankincense, and wine, and oil, and fine flour, and wheat, and beasts, and sheep, and horses, and chariots, and slaves, and souls of men.

Revelation 18:Verse 14

14 And the fruits that thy soul lusted after are departed from thee, and all things which were dainty and goodly are departed from thee, and thou shalt find them no more at all.

Revelation 18:Verse 15

15 The merchants of these things, which were made rich by her, shall stand afar off for the fear of her torment, weeping and wailing,

Revelation 18:Verse 16

16 And saying, Alas, alas, that great city, that was clothed in fine linen, and purple, and scarlet, and decked with gold, and precious stones, and pearls!

Revelation 18:Verse 17

17 For in one hour so great riches is come to nought. And every shipmaster, and all the company in ships, and sailors, and as many as trade by sea, stood afar off,

Revelation 18:Verse 18

18 And cried when they saw the smoke of her burning, saying, What [city is] like unto this great city!

Revelation 18:Verse 19

19 And they cast dust on their heads, and cried, weeping and wailing, saying, Alas, alas, that great city, wherein were made rich all that had ships in the sea by reason of her costliness! for in one hour is she made desolate.

Revelation 18:Verse 20

20 Rejoice over her, [thou] heaven, and [ye] holy apostles and prophets; for God hath avenged you on her.

Revelation 18:Verse 21
21 And a mighty angel took up a stone like a great millstone, and cast [it] into the sea, saying, Thus with violence shall that great city Babylon be thrown down, and shall be found no more at all.

Revelation 18:Verse 22
22 And the voice of harpers, and musicians, and of pipers, and trumpeters, shall be heard no more at all in thee; and no craftsman, of whatsoever craft [he be], shall be found any more in thee; and the sound of a millstone shall be heard no more at all in thee;

Revelation 18:Verse 23
23 And the light of a candle shall shine no more at all in thee; and the voice of the bridegroom and of the bride shall be heard no more at all in thee: for thy merchants were the great men of the earth; for by thy sorceries were all nations deceived.

Revelation 18:Verse 24
24 And in her was found the blood of prophets, and of saints, and of all that were slain upon the earth.

Isaiah 13:Verse 1
1 THE burden of Babylon, which Isaiah the son of Amoz did see.

Isaiah 13:Verse 2
2 Lift ye up a banner upon the high mountain, exalt the voice unto them, shake the hand, that they may go into the gates of the nobles.

Isaiah 13:Verse 3
3 I have commanded my sanctified ones, I have also called my mighty ones for mine anger, [even] them that rejoice in my highness.

Isaiah 13:Verse 4
4 The noise of a multitude in the mountains, like as of a great people; a tumultuous noise of the kingdoms of nations gathered together: the LORD of hosts mustereth the host of the battle.

Isaiah 13:Verse 5
5 They come from a far country, from the end of heaven, [even] the LORD, and the weapons of his indignation, to destroy the whole land.

Isaiah 13:Verse 6
6 Howl ye; for the day of the LORD [is] at hand; it shall come as a destruction from the Almighty.

Isaiah 13:Verse 7
7 Therefore shall all hands be faint, and every man's heart shall melt:

Isaiah 13:Verse 8
8 And they shall be afraid: pangs and sorrows shall take hold of them; they shall be in pain as a woman that travaileth: they shall be amazed one at another; their faces [shall be as] flames.

Isaiah 13:Verse 9
9 Behold, the day of the LORD cometh, cruel both with wrath and fierce anger, to lay the land desolate: and he shall destroy the sinners thereof out of it.

Isaiah 13:Verse 10
10 For the stars of heaven and the constellations thereof shall not give their light: the sun shall be darkened in his going forth, and the moon shall not cause her light to shine.

Isaiah 13:Verse 11
11 And I will punish the world for [their] evil, and the wicked for their iniquity; and I will cause the arrogancy of the proud to cease, and will lay low the haughtiness of the terrible.

Isaiah 13:Verse 12
12 I will make a man more precious than fine gold; even a man than the golden wedge of Ophir.

Isaiah 13:Verse 13
13 Therefore I will shake the heavens, and the earth shall remove out of her place, in the wrath of the LORD of hosts, and in the day of his fierce anger.

Isaiah 13:Verse 14
14 And it shall be as the chased roe, and as a sheep that no man taketh up: they shall every man turn to his own people, and flee every one into his own land.

Isaiah 13:Verse 15
15 Every one that is found shall be thrust through; and every one that is joined [unto them] shall fall by the sword.

Isaiah 13:Verse 16
16 Their children also shall be dashed to pieces before their eyes; their houses shall be spoiled, and their wives ravished.

Isaiah 13:Verse 17
17 Behold, I will stir up the Medes against them, which shall not regard silver; and [as for] gold, they shall not delight in it.

Isaiah 13:Verse 18
18 [Their] bows also shall dash the young men to pieces; and they shall have no pity on the fruit of the womb; their eye shall not spare children.

Isaiah 13:Verse 19
19 And Babylon, the glory of kingdoms, the beauty of the Chaldees' excellency, shall be as when God overthrew Sodom and Gomorrah.

Isaiah 13:Verse 20
20 It shall never be inhabited, neither shall it be dwelt in from generation to generation: neither shall the Arabian pitch tent there; neither shall the shepherds make their fold there.

Isaiah 13:Verse 21
21 But wild beasts of the desert shall lie there; and their houses shall be full of doleful creatures; and owls shall dwell there, and satyrs shall dance there.

Isaiah 13:Verse 22
22 And the wild beasts of the islands shall cry in their desolate houses, and dragons in [their] pleasant palaces: and her time [is] near to come, and her days shall not be prolonged.

Isaiah 14:Verse 1
1 FOR the LORD will have mercy on Jacob, and will yet choose Israel, and set them in their own land: and the strangers shall be joined with them, and they shall cleave to the house of Jacob.

Isaiah 14:Verse 2
2 And the people shall take them, and bring them to their place: and the house of Israel shall possess them in the land of the LORD for servants and handmaids: and they shall take them captives, whose captives they were; and they shall rule over their oppressors.

Isaiah 14:Verse 3
3 And it shall come to pass in the day that the LORD shall give thee rest from thy sorrow, and from thy fear, and from the hard bondage wherein thou wast made to serve,

Isaiah 14:Verse 4
4 That thou shalt take up this proverb against the king of Babylon, and say, How hath the oppressor ceased! the golden city ceased!

Isaiah 14:Verse 5
5 The LORD hath broken the staff of the wicked, [and] the sceptre of the rulers.

Isaiah 14:Verse 6
6 He who smote the people in wrath with a continual stroke, he that ruled the nations in anger, is persecuted, [and] none hindereth.

Isaiah 14:Verse 9
9 Hell from beneath is moved for thee to meet [thee] at thy coming: it stirreth up the dead for thee, [even] all the chief ones of the earth; it hath raised up from their thrones all the kings of the nations.

Isaiah 14:Verse 10
10 All they shall speak and say unto thee, Art thou also become weak as we? art thou become like unto us?

Isaiah 14:Verse 11
11 Thy pomp is brought down to the grave, [and] the noise of thy viols: the worm is spread under thee, and the worms cover thee.

Isaiah 14:Verse 12
12 How art thou fallen from heaven, O Lucifer, son of the morning! [how] art thou cut down to the ground, which didst weaken the nations!

Isaiah 14:Verse 13
13 For thou hast said in thine heart, I will ascend into heaven, I will exalt my throne above the stars of God: I will sit also upon the mount of the congregation, in the sides of the north:

Isaiah 14:Verse 14
14 I will ascend above the heights of the clouds; I will be like the most High.

Isaiah 14:Verse 15
15 Yet thou shalt be brought down to hell, to the sides of the pit.

Isaiah 14:Verse 16
16 They that see thee shall narrowly look upon thee, [and] consider thee, [saying, Is] this the man that made the earth to tremble, that did shake kingdoms;

Isaiah 14:Verse 17
17 [That] made the world as a wilderness, and destroyed the cities thereof; [that] opened not the house of his prisoners?

Isaiah 14:Verse 18
18 All the kings of the nations, [even] all of them, lie in glory, every one in his own house.

Isaiah 14:Verse 19
19 But thou art cast out of thy grave like an abominable branch, [and as] the raiment of those that are slain, thrust through with a sword, that go down to the stones of the pit; as a carcase trodden under feet.

Isaiah 14:Verse 20
20 Thou shalt not be joined with them in burial, because thou hast destroyed thy land, [and] slain thy people: the seed of evildoers shall never be renowned.

Isaiah 14:Verse 21
21 Prepare slaughter for his children for the iniquity of their fathers; that they do not rise, nor possess the land, nor fill the face of the world with cities.

Isaiah 14:Verse 22
22 For I will rise up against them, saith the LORD of hosts, and cut off from Babylon the name, and remnant, and son, and nephew, saith the LORD.

Isaiah 14:Verse 23

23 I will also make it a possession for the bittern, and pools of water: and I will sweep it with the besom of destruction, saith the LORD of hosts.

Isaiah 34:Verse 9

9 And the streams thereof shall be turned into pitch, and the dust thereof into brimstone, and the land thereof shall become burning pitch.

Isaiah 34:Verse 10

10 It shall not be quenched night nor day; the smoke thereof shall go up for ever: from generation to generation it shall lie waste; none shall pass through it for ever and ever.

Isaiah 34:Verse 11

11 But the cormorant and the bittern shall possess it; the owl also and the raven shall dwell in it: and he shall stretch out upon it the line of confusion, and the stones of emptiness.

Isaiah 34:Verse 12

12 They shall call the nobles thereof to the kingdom, but none [shall be] there, and all her princes shall be nothing.

Isaiah 34:Verse 13

13 And thorns shall come up in her palaces, nettles and brambles in the fortresses thereof: and it shall be an habitation of dragons, [and] a court for owls.

Isaiah 34:Verse 14

14 The wild beasts of the desert shall also meet with the wild beasts of the island, and the satyr shall cry to his fellow; the screech owl also shall rest there, and find for herself a place of rest.

Isaiah 34:Verse 15

15 There shall the great owl make her nest, and lay, and hatch, and gather under her shadow: there shall the vultures also be gathered, every one with her mate.

Isaiah 34:Verse 16

16 Seek ye out of the book of the LORD, and read: no one of these shall fail, none shall want her mate: for my mouth it hath commanded, and his spirit it hath gathered them.

Isaiah 34:Verse 17

17 And he hath cast the lot for them, and his hand hath divided it unto them by line: they shall possess it for ever, from generation to generation shall they dwell therein.

Isaiah 47:Verse 1

1 COME down, and sit in the dust, O virgin daughter of Babylon, sit on the ground: [there is] no throne, O daughter of the Chaldeans: for thou shalt no more be called tender and delicate.

Isaiah 47:Verse 2

2 Take the millstones, and grind meal: uncover thy locks, make bare the leg, uncover the thigh, pass over the rivers.

Isaiah 47:Verse 3

3 Thy nakedness shall be uncovered, yea, thy shame shall be seen: I will take vengeance, and I will not meet [thee as] a man.

Isaiah 47:Verse 4

4 [As for] our redeemer, the LORD of hosts [is] his name, the Holy One of Israel.

Isaiah 47:Verse 5

5 Sit thou silent, and get thee into darkness, O daughter of the Chaldeans: for thou shalt no more be called, The lady of kingdoms.

Isaiah 47:Verse 6

6 I was wroth with my people, I have polluted mine inheritance, and given them into thine hand: thou didst shew them no mercy; upon the ancient hast thou very heavily laid thy yoke.

Isaiah 47:Verse 7

7 And thou saidst, I shall be a lady for ever: [so] that thou didst not lay these [things] to thy heart, neither didst remember the latter end of it.

Isaiah 47:Verse 8

8 Therefore hear now this, [thou that art] given to pleasures, that dwellest carelessly, that sayest in thine heart, I [am], and none else beside me; I shall not sit [as] a widow, neither shall I know the loss of children:

Isaiah 47:Verse 9

9 But these two [things] shall come to thee in a moment in one day, the loss of children, and widowhood: they shall come upon thee in their perfection for the multitude of thy sorceries, [and] for the great abundance of thine enchantments.

Isaiah 47:Verse 10

10 For thou hast trusted in thy wickedness: thou hast said, None seeth me. Thy wisdom and thy knowledge, it hath perverted thee; and thou hast said in thine heart, I [am], and none else beside me.

Isaiah 47:Verse 11

11 Therefore shall evil come upon thee; thou shalt not know from whence it riseth: and mischief shall fall upon thee; thou shalt not be able to put it off: and desolation shall come upon thee suddenly, [which] thou shalt not know.

Isaiah 47:Verse 12

12 Stand now with thine enchantments, and with the multitude of thy sorceries, wherein thou hast laboured from thy youth; if so be thou shalt be able to profit, if so be thou mayest prevail.

Isaiah 47:Verse 13

13 Thou art wearied in the multitude of thy counsels. Let now the astrologers, the stargazers, the monthly prognosticators, stand up, and save thee from [these things] that shall come upon thee.

Isaiah 47:Verse 14

14 Behold, they shall be as stubble; the fire shall burn them; they shall not deliver themselves from the power of the flame: [there shall] not [be] a coal to warm at, [nor] fire to sit before it.

Isaiah 47:Verse 15

15 Thus shall they be unto thee with whom thou hast laboured, [even] thy merchants, from thy youth: they shall wander every one to his quarter; none shall save thee.

Jeremiah 50:Verse 1

1 THE word that the LORD spake against Babylon [and] against the land of the Chaldeans by Jeremiah the prophet.

Jeremiah 50:Verse 2

2 Declare ye among the nations, and publish, and set up a standard; publish, [and] conceal not: say, Babylon is taken, Bel is confounded, Merodach is broken in pieces; her idols are confounded, her images are broken in pieces.

Jeremiah 50:Verse 3

3 For out of the north there cometh up a nation against her, which shall make her land desolate, and none shall dwell therein: they shall remove, they shall depart, both man and beast.

Jeremiah 50:Verse 9

9 For, lo, I will raise and cause to come up against Babylon an assembly of great nations from the north country: and they shall set themselves in array against her; from thence she shall be taken: their arrows [shall be] as of a mighty expert man; none shall return in vain.

Jeremiah 50:Verse 10

10 And Chaldea shall be a spoil: all that spoil her shall be satisfied, saith the LORD.

Jeremiah 50:Verse 11

11 Because ye were glad, because ye rejoiced, O ye destroyers of mine heritage, because ye are grown fat as the heifer at grass, and bellow as bulls;

Jeremiah 50:Verse 12

12 Your mother shall be sore confounded; she that bare you shall be ashamed: behold, the hindermost of the nations [shall be] a wilderness, a dry land, and a desert.

Jeremiah 50:Verse 13

13 Because of the wrath of the LORD it shall not be inhabited, but it shall be wholly desolate: every one that goeth by Babylon shall be astonished, and hiss at all her plagues.

Jeremiah 50:Verse 14

14 Put yourselves in array against Babylon round about: all ye that bend the bow, shoot at her, spare no arrows: for she hath sinned against the LORD.

Jeremiah 50:Verse 15

15 Shout against her round about: she hath given her hand: her foundations are fallen, her walls are thrown down: for it [is] the vengeance of the LORD: take vengeance upon her; as she hath done, do unto her.

Jeremiah 50:Verse 16

16 Cut off the sower from Babylon, and him that handleth the sickle in the time of harvest: for fear of the oppressing sword they shall turn every one to his people, and they shall flee every one to his own land.

Jeremiah 50:Verse 17

17 Israel [is] a scattered sheep; the lions have driven [him] away: first the king of Assyria hath devoured him; and last this Nebuchadrezzar king of Babylon hath broken his bones.

Jeremiah 50:Verse 18

18 Therefore thus saith the LORD of hosts, the God of Israel; Behold, I will punish the king of Babylon and his land, as I have punished the king of Assyria.

Jeremiah 50:Verse 21

21 Go up against the land of Merathaim, [even] against it, and against the inhabitants of Pekod: waste and utterly destroy after them, saith the LORD, and do according to all that I have commanded thee.

Jeremiah 50:Verse 22

22 A sound of battle [is] in the land, and of great destruction.

Jeremiah 50:Verse 23

23 How is the hammer of the whole earth cut asunder and broken! how is Babylon become a desolation among the nations!

Jeremiah 50:Verse 24

24 I have laid a snare for thee, and thou art also taken, O Babylon, and thou wast not aware: thou art found, and also caught, because thou hast striven against the LORD.

Jeremiah 50:Verse 25

25 The LORD hath opened his armoury, and hath brought forth the weapons of his indignation: for this [is] the work of the Lord GOD of hosts in the land of the Chaldeans.

Jeremiah 50:Verse 26

26 Come against her from the utmost border, open her storehouses: cast her up as heaps, and destroy her utterly: let nothing of her be left.

Jeremiah 50:Verse 27

27 Slay all her bullocks; let them go down to the slaughter: woe unto them! for their day is come, the time of their visitation.

Jeremiah 50:Verse 28

28 The voice of them that flee and escape out of the land of Babylon, to declare in Zion the vengeance of the LORD our God, the vengeance of his temple.

Jeremiah 50:Verse 29

29 Call together the archers against Babylon: all ye that bend the bow, camp against it round about; let none thereof escape: recompense her according to her work; according to all that she hath done, do unto her: for she hath been proud against the LORD, against the Holy One of Israel.

Jeremiah 50:Verse 30

30 Therefore shall her young men fall in the streets, and all her men of war shall be cut off in that day, saith the LORD.

Jeremiah 50:Verse 31

31 Behold, I [am] against thee, [O thou] most proud, saith the Lord GOD of hosts: for thy day is come, the time [that] I will visit thee.

Jeremiah 50:Verse 32

32 And the most proud shall stumble and fall, and none shall raise him up: and I will kindle a fire in his cities, and it shall devour all round about him.

Jeremiah 50:Verse 33

33 Thus saith the LORD of hosts; The children of Israel and the children of Judah [were] oppressed together: and all that took them captives held them fast; they refused to let them go.

Jeremiah 50:Verse 34

34 Their Redeemer [is] strong; the LORD of hosts [is] his name: he shall throughly plead their cause, that he may give rest to the land, and disquiet the inhabitants of Babylon.

Jeremiah 50:Verse 35

35 A sword [is] upon the Chaldeans, saith the LORD, and upon the inhabitants of Babylon, and upon her princes, and upon her wise [men].

Jeremiah 50:Verse 36

36 A sword [is] upon the liars; and they shall dote: a sword [is] upon her mighty men; and they shall be dismayed.

Jeremiah 50:Verse 37

37 A sword [is] upon their horses, and upon their chariots, and upon all the mingled people that [are] in the midst of her; and they shall become as women: a sword [is] upon her treasures; and they shall be robbed.

Jeremiah 50:Verse 38

38 A drought [is] upon her waters; and they shall be dried up: for it [is] the land of graven images, and they are mad upon [their] idols.

Jeremiah 50:Verse 39

39 Therefore the wild beasts of the desert with the wild beasts of the islands shall dwell [there], and the owls shall dwell therein: and it shall be no more inhabited for ever; neither shall it be dwelt in from generation to generation.

Jeremiah 50:Verse 40

40 As God overthrew Sodom and Gomorrah and the neighbour [cities] thereof, saith the LORD; [so] shall no man abide there, neither shall any son of man dwell therein.

Jeremiah 50:Verse 41

41 Behold, a people shall come from the north, and a great nation, and many kings shall be raised up from the coasts of the earth.

Jeremiah 50:Verse 42

42 They shall hold the bow and the lance: they [are] cruel, and will not shew mercy: their voice shall roar like the sea, and they shall ride upon horses, [every one] put in array, like a man to the battle, against thee, O daughter of Babylon.

Jeremiah 50:Verse 43

43 The king of Babylon hath heard the report of them, and his hands waxed feeble: anguish took hold of him, [and] pangs as of a woman in travail.

Jeremiah 50:Verse 44

44 Behold, he shall come up like a lion from the swelling of Jordan unto the habitation of the strong: but I will make them suddenly run away from her: and who [is] a chosen [man, that] I may appoint over her? for who [is] like me? and who will appoint me the time? and who [is] that shepherd that will stand before me?

Jeremiah 50:Verse 45

45 Therefore hear ye the counsel of the LORD, that he hath taken against Babylon; and his purposes, that he hath purposed against the land of the Chaldeans: Surely the least of the flock shall draw them out: surely he shall make [their] habitation desolate with them.

Jeremiah 50:Verse 46

46 At the noise of the taking of Babylon the earth is moved, and the cry is heard among the nations.

Jeremiah 51:Verse 1

1 THUS saith the LORD; Behold, I will raise up against Babylon, and against them that dwell in the midst of them that rise up against me, a destroying wind;

Jeremiah 51:Verse 2

2 And will send unto Babylon fanners, that shall fan her, and shall empty her land: for in the day of trouble they shall be against her round about.

Jeremiah 51:Verse 3

3 Against [him that] bendeth let the archer bend his bow, and against [him that] lifteth himself up in his brigandine: and spare ye not her young men; destroy ye utterly all her host.

Jeremiah 51:Verse 4

4 Thus the slain shall fall in the land of the Chaldeans, and [they that are] thrust through in her streets.

Jeremiah 51:Verse 5

5 For Israel [hath] not [been] forsaken, nor Judah of his God, of the LORD of hosts; though their land was filled with sin against the Holy One of Israel.

———————————————

Jeremiah 51:Verse 7

7 Babylon [hath been] a golden cup in the LORD'S hand, that made all the earth drunken: the nations have drunken of her wine; therefore the nations are mad.

Jeremiah 51:Verse 8

8 Babylon is suddenly fallen and destroyed: howl for her; take balm for her pain, if so be she may be healed.

Jeremiah 51:Verse 9

9 We would have healed Babylon, but she is not healed: forsake her, and let us go every one into his own country: for her judgment reacheth unto heaven, and is lifted up [even] to the skies.

Jeremiah 51:Verse 10

10 The LORD hath brought forth our righteousness: come, and let us declare in Zion the work of the LORD our God.

Jeremiah 51:Verse 11

11 Make bright the arrows; gather the shields: the LORD hath raised up the spirit of the kings of the Medes: for his device [is] against Babylon, to destroy it; because it [is] the vengeance of the LORD, the vengeance of his temple.

Jeremiah 51:Verse 12

12 Set up the standard upon the walls of Babylon, make the watch strong, set up the watchmen, prepare the ambushes: for the LORD hath both devised and done that which he spake against the inhabitants of Babylon.

Jeremiah 51:Verse 13

13 O thou that dwellest upon many waters, abundant in treasures, thine end is come, [and] the measure of thy covetousness.

Jeremiah 51:Verse 14

14 The LORD of hosts hath sworn by himself, [saying], Surely I will fill thee with men, as with caterpillars; and they shall lift up a shout against thee.

Jeremiah 51:Verse 15
15 He hath made the earth by his power, he hath established the world by his wisdom, and hath stretched out the heaven by his understanding.

Jeremiah 51:Verse 16
16 When he uttereth [his] voice, [there is] a multitude of waters in the heavens; and he causeth the vapours to ascend from the ends of the earth: he maketh lightnings with rain, and bringeth forth the wind out of his treasures.

Jeremiah 51:Verse 17
17 Every man is brutish by [his] knowledge; every founder is confounded by the graven image: for his molten image [is] falsehood, and [there is] no breath in them.

Jeremiah 51:Verse 18
18 They [are] vanity, the work of errors: in the time of their visitation they shall perish.

Jeremiah 51:Verse 19
19 The portion of Jacob [is] not like them; for he [is] the former of all things: and [Israel is] the rod of his inheritance: the LORD of hosts [is] his name.

Jeremiah 51:Verse 20
20 Thou [art] my battle axe [and] weapons of war: for with thee will I break in pieces the nations, and with thee will I destroy kingdoms;

Jeremiah 51:Verse 21
21 And with thee will I break in pieces the horse and his rider; and with thee will I break in pieces the chariot and his rider;

Jeremiah 51:Verse 22
22 With thee also will I break in pieces man and woman; and with thee will I break in pieces old and young; and with thee will I break in pieces the young man and the maid;

Jeremiah 51:Verse 23
23 I will also break in pieces with thee the shepherd and his flock; and with thee will I break in pieces the husbandman and his yoke of oxen; and with thee will I break in pieces captains and rulers.

Jeremiah 51:Verse 24
24 And I will render unto Babylon and to all the inhabitants of Chaldea all their evil that they have done in Zion in your sight, saith the LORD.

Jeremiah 51:Verse 25
25 Behold, I [am] against thee, O destroying mountain, saith the LORD, which destroyest all the earth: and I will stretch out mine hand upon thee, and roll thee down from the rocks, and will make thee a burnt mountain.

Jeremiah 51:Verse 26
26 And they shall not take of thee a stone for a corner, nor a stone for foundations; but thou shalt be desolate forever, saith the LORD.

Jeremiah 51:Verse 27
27 Set ye up a standard in the land, blow the trumpet among the nations, prepare the nations against her, call together against her the kingdoms of Ararat, Minni, and Ashchenaz; appoint a captain against her; cause the horses to come up as the rough caterpillers.

Jeremiah 51:Verse 28
28 Prepare against her the nations with the kings of the Medes, the captains thereof, and all the rulers thereof, and all the land of his dominion.

Jeremiah 51:Verse 29
29 And the land shall tremble and sorrow: for every purpose of the LORD shall be performed against Babylon, to make the land of Babylon a desolation without an inhabitant.

Jeremiah 51:Verse 30
30 The mighty men of Babylon have forborn to fight, they have remained in [their] holds: their might hath failed; they became as women: they have burned her dwellingplaces; her bars are broken.

Jeremiah 51:Verse 31
31 One post shall run to meet another, and one messenger to meet another, to shew the king of Babylon that his city is taken at [one] end,

Jeremiah 51:Verse 32
32 And that the passages are stopped, and the reeds they have burned with fire, and the men of war are affrighted.

Jeremiah 51:Verse 33
33 For thus saith the LORD of hosts, the God of Israel; The daughter of Babylon [is] like a threshingfloor, [it is] time to thresh her: yet a little while, and the time of her harvest shall come.

Jeremiah 51:Verse 34
34 Nebuchadrezzar the king of Babylon hath devoured me, he hath crushed me, he hath made me an empty vessel, he hath swallowed me up like a dragon, he hath filled his belly with my delicates, he hath cast me out.

Jeremiah 51:Verse 35
35 The violence done to me and to my flesh [be] upon Babylon, shall the inhabitant of Zion say; and my blood upon the inhabitants of Chaldea, shall Jerusalem say.

Jeremiah 51:Verse 36
36 Therefore thus saith the LORD; Behold, I will plead thy cause, and take vengeance for thee; and I will dry up her sea, and make her springs dry.

Jeremiah 51:Verse 37
37 And Babylon shall become heaps, a dwellingplace for dragons, an astonishment, and an hissing, without an inhabitant.

Jeremiah 51:Verse 38
38 They shall roar together like lions: they shall yell as lions' whelps.

Jeremiah 51:Verse 39
39 In their heat I will make their feasts, and I will make them drunken, that they may rejoice, and sleep a perpetual sleep, and not wake, saith the LORD.

Jeremiah 51:Verse 40
40 I will bring them down like lambs to the slaughter, like rams with he goats.

Jeremiah 51:Verse 41
41 How is Sheshach taken! and how is the praise of the whole earth surprised! how is Babylon become an astonishment among the nations!

Jeremiah 51:Verse 42
42 The sea is come up upon Babylon: she is covered with the multitude of the waves thereof.

Jeremiah 51:Verse 43
43 Her cities are a desolation, a dry land, and a wilderness, a land wherein no man dwelleth, neither doth [any] son of man pass thereby.

Jeremiah 51:Verse 44
44 And I will punish Bel in Babylon, and I will bring forth out of his mouth that which he hath swallowed up: and the nations shall not flow together any more unto him: yea, the wall of Babylon shall fall.

Jeremiah 51:Verse 46
46 And lest your heart faint, and ye fear for the rumour that shall be heard in the land; a rumour shall both come [one] year, and after that in [another] year [shall come] a rumour, and violence in the land, ruler against ruler.

Jeremiah 51:Verse 47
47 Therefore, behold, the days come, that I will do judgment upon the graven images of Babylon: and her whole land shall be confounded, and all her slain shall fall in the midst of her.

Jeremiah 51:Verse 48
48 Then the heaven and the earth, and all that [is] therein, shall sing for Babylon: for the spoilers shall come unto her from the north, saith the LORD.

Jeremiah 51:Verse 49
49 As Babylon [hath caused] the slain of Israel to fall, so at Babylon shall fall the slain of all the earth.

Jeremiah 51:Verse 50

50 Ye that have escaped the sword, go away, stand not still: remember the LORD afar off, and let Jerusalem come into your mind.

Jeremiah 51:Verse 51

51 We are confounded, because we have heard reproach: shame hath covered our faces: for strangers are come into the sanctuaries of the LORD'S house.

Jeremiah 51:Verse 52

52 Wherefore, behold, the days come, saith the LORD, that I will do judgment upon her graven images: and through all her land the wounded shall groan.

Jeremiah 51:Verse 53

53 Though Babylon should mount up to heaven, and though she should fortify the height of her strength, [yet] from me shall spoilers come unto her, saith the LORD.

Jeremiah 51:Verse 54

54 A sound of a cry [cometh] from Babylon, and great destruction from the land of the Chaldeans:

Jeremiah 51:Verse 55

55 Because the LORD hath spoiled Babylon, and destroyed out of her the great voice; when her waves do roar like great waters, a noise of their voice is uttered:

Jeremiah 51:Verse 56

56 Because the spoiler is come upon her, [even] upon Babylon, and her mighty men are taken, every one of their bows is broken: for the LORD God of recompences shall surely requite.

Jeremiah 51:Verse 57

57 And I will make drunk her princes, and her wise [men], her captains, and her rulers, and her mighty men: and they shall sleep a perpetual sleep, and not wake, saith the King, whose name [is] the LORD of hosts.

Jeremiah 51:Verse 58

58 Thus saith the LORD of hosts; The broad walls of Babylon shall be utterly broken, and her high gates shall be burned with fire; and the people shall labour in vain, and the folk in the fire, and they shall be weary.

Jeremiah 51:Verse 61

61 And Jeremiah said to Seraiah, When thou comest to Babylon, and shalt see, and shalt read all these words;

Jeremiah 51:Verse 62

62 Then shalt thou say, O LORD, thou hast spoken against this place, to cut it off, that none shall remain in it, neither man nor beast, but that it shall be desolate for ever.

Jeremiah 51:Verse 63

63 And it shall be, when thou hast made an end of reading this book, [that] thou shalt bind a stone to it, and cast it into the midst of Euphrates:

Jeremiah 51:Verse 64

64 And thou shalt say, Thus shall Babylon sink, and shall not rise from the evil that I will bring upon her: and they shall be weary. Thus far [are] the words of Jeremiah.

---

1 Nephi 22:Verse 13

13 And the blood of that great and abominable church, which is the whore of all the earth, shall turn upon their own heads; for they shall war among themselves, and the sword of their own hands shall fall upon their own heads, and they shall be drunken with their own blood.

1 Nephi 22:Verse 14

14 And every nation which shall war against thee, O house of Israel, shall be turned one against another, and they shall fall into the pit which they digged to ensnare the people of the Lord. And all that fight against Zion shall be destroyed, and that great whore, who hath perverted the right ways of the Lord, yea, that great and abominable church, shall tumble to the dust and great shall be the fall of it.

1 Nephi 22:Verse 15

15 For behold, saith the prophet, the time cometh speedily that Satan shall have no more power over the hearts of the children of men; for the day soon cometh that all the proud and they who do wickedly shall be as stubble; and the day cometh that they must be burned.

1 Nephi 22:Verse 16

16 For the time soon cometh that the fulness of the wrath of God shall be poured out upon all the children of men; for he will not suffer that the wicked shall destroy the righteous.

---

1 Nephi 22:Verse 23

23 For the time speedily shall come that all churches which are built up to get gain, and all those who are built up to get power over the flesh, and those who are built up to become popular in the eyes of the world, and those who seek the lusts of the flesh and the things of the world, and to do all manner of iniquity; yea, in fine, all those who belong to the kingdom of the devil are they who need fear, and tremble, and quake; they are those who must be brought low in the dust; they are those who must be consumed as stubble; and this is according to the words of the prophet.

---

2 Nephi 28:Verse 18

18 But behold, that great and abominable church, the whore of all the earth, must tumble to the earth, and great must be the fall thereof.

2 Nephi 28:Verse 19

19 For the kingdom of the devil must shake, and they which belong to it must needs be stirred up unto repentance, or the devil will grasp them with his everlasting chains, and they be stirred up to anger, and perish;

2 Nephi 28:Verse 20

20 For behold, at that day shall he rage in the hearts of the children of men, and stir them up to anger against that which is good.

2 Nephi 28:Verse 21

21 And others will he pacify, and lull them away into carnal security, that they will say: All is well in Zion; yea, Zion prospereth, all is well--and thus the devil cheateth their souls, and leadeth them away carefully down to hell.

2 Nephi 28:Verse 22

22 And behold, others he flattereth away, and telleth them there is no hell; and he saith unto them: I am no devil, for there is none--and thus he whispereth in their ears, until he grasps them with his awful chains, from whence there is no deliverance.

2 Nephi 28:Verse 23

23 Yea, they are grasped with death, and hell; and death, and hell, and the devil, and all that have been seized therewith must stand before the throne of God, and be judged according to their works, from whence they must go into the place prepared for them, even a lake of fire and brimstone, which is endless torment.

2 Nephi 28:Verse 24

24 Therefore, wo be unto him that is at ease in Zion!

2 Nephi 28:Verse 25

25 Wo be unto him that crieth: All is well!

2 Nephi 28:Verse 26

26 Yea, wo be unto him that hearkeneth unto the precepts of men, and denieth the power of God, and the gift of the Holy Ghost!

2 Nephi 28:Verse 27

27 Yea, wo be unto him that saith: We have received, and we need no more!

2 Nephi 28:Verse 28

28 And in fine, wo unto all those who tremble, and are angry because of the truth of God! For behold, he that is built upon the rock receiveth it with gladness; and he that is built upon a sandy foundation trembleth lest he shall fall.

2 Nephi 28:Verse 29

29 Wo be unto him that shall say: We have received the word of God, and we need no more of the word of God, for we have enough!

---

3 Nephi 21:Verse 14

14 Yea, wo be unto the Gentiles except they repent; for it shall come to pass in that day, saith the Father, that I will cut off thy horses out of the midst of thee, and I will destroy thy chariots;

3 Nephi 21:Verse 15
15 And I will cut off the cities of thy land, and throw down all thy strongholds;

3 Nephi 21:Verse 16
16 And I will cut off witchcrafts out of thy land, and thou shalt have no more soothsayers;

3 Nephi 21:Verse 17
17 Thy graven images I will also cut off, and thy standing images out of the midst of thee, and thou shalt no more worship the works of thy hands;

3 Nephi 21:Verse 18
18 And I will pluck up thy groves out of the midst of thee; so will I destroy thy cities.

3 Nephi 21:Verse 19
19 And it shall come to pass that all lyings, and deceivings, and envyings, and strifes, and priestcrafts, and whoredoms, shall be done away.

3 Nephi 21:Verse 20
20 For it shall come to pass, saith the Father, that at that day whosoever will not repent and come unto my Beloved Son, them will I cut off from among my people, O house of Israel;

3 Nephi 21:Verse 21
21 And I will execute vengeance and fury upon them, even as upon the heathen, such as they have not heard.

D&C 29:Verse 21
21 And the great and abominable church, which is the whore of all the earth, shall be cast down by devouring fire, according as it is spoken by the mouth of Ezekiel the prophet, who spoke of these things, which have not come to pass but surely must, as I live, for abominations shall not reign.

D&C 88:Verse 105
105 And again, another angel shall sound his trump, which is the sixth angel, saying: She is fallen who made all nations drink of the wine of the wrath of her fornication; she is fallen, is fallen!

D&C 97:Verse 22
22 For behold, and lo, vengeance cometh speedily upon the ungodly as the whirlwind; and who shall escape it?

D&C 97:Verse 23
23 The Lord's scourge shall pass over by night and by day, and the report thereof shall vex all people; yea, it shall not be stayed until the Lord come;

D&C 97:Verse 24
24 For the indignation of the Lord is kindled against their abominations and all their wicked works.

Joseph Smith Matthew 1:Verse 41
41 But as it was in the days of Noah, so it shall be also at the coming of the Son of Man;

Joseph Smith Matthew 1:Verse 42
42 For it shall be with them, as it was in the days which were before the flood; for until the day that Noah entered into the ark they were eating and drinking, marrying and giving in marriage;

Joseph Smith Matthew 1:Verse 43
43 And knew not until the flood came, and took them all away; so shall also the coming of the Son of Man be.

Joseph Smith Matthew 1:Verse 44
44 Then shall be fulfilled that which is written, that in the last days, two shall be in the field, the one shall be taken, and the other left;

Joseph Smith Matthew 1:Verse 45
45 Two shall be grinding at the mill, the one shall be taken, and the other left;

21

The End of Babylon

Revelation 10: 7; 11: 15-19; 14: 8; 16: 17

The end of Babylon is declared by the angel as the upheavals of nature are taking place and the collapse of the economic institutions and the governments that control them. Wickedness is coming to an end as the Judgements of God are poured 'without measure' upon the earth. The prophet Mormon views the attitude of the wicked during their destruction, and makes the statement of their sorrow:

13 But behold this my joy was vain, for their sorrowing was not unto repentance, because of the goodness of God; but it was rather **the sorrowing of the damned, because the Lord would not always suffer them to take happiness in sin.**
14 And they did not come unto Jesus with broken hearts and contrite spirits, but they did curse God, and wish to die. Nevertheless they would struggle with the sword for their lives.

Mormon 2:13-14

As Mormon abridged the plates he would often leave his parting commentary to the historical narrative he just wrote. Mormon's phrase 'and thus we see' is a flag to his conclusion of the whole matter, which often is: 'wickedness never was happiness.'

Revelation 10:Verse 7
7 But in the days of the voice of the seventh angel, when he shall begin to sound, the mystery of God should be finished, as he hath declared to his servants the prophets.

Revelation 11:Verse 15
15 And the seventh angel sounded; and there were great voices in heaven, saying, **The kingdoms of this world are become [the kingdoms] of our Lord, and of his Christ; and he shall reign for ever and ever.**

Revelation 11:Verse 16
16 And the four and twenty elders, which sat before God on their seats, fell upon their faces, and worshipped God,

Revelation 11:Verse 17

17 Saying, We give thee thanks, O Lord God Almighty, which art, and wast, and art to come; because thou hast taken to thee thy great power, and hast reigned.

Revelation 11:Verse 18

18 And the nations were angry, and thy wrath is come, and the time of the dead, that they should be judged, and that thou shouldest give reward unto thy servants the prophets, and to the saints, and them that fear thy name, small and great; and shouldest destroy them which destroy the earth. .

Revelation 11:Verse 19

19 And the temple of God was opened in heaven, and there was seen in his temple the ark of his testament: and there were **lightnings, and voices, and thunderings, and an earthquake, and great hail.**

Revelation 14:Verse 8

8 And there followed another angel, saying, **Babylon is fallen, is fallen**, that great city, because she made all nations drink of the wine of the wrath of her fornication.

Revelation 16:Verse 17

17 And the seventh angel poured out his vial into the air; and there came a great voice out of the temple of heaven, from the throne, saying, **It is done.**

Isaiah 25:Verse 5

5 Thou shalt bring down the noise of strangers, as the heat in a dry place; [even] the heat with the shadow of a cloud: the branch of the terrible ones shall be brought low.

Isaiah 25:Verse 6

6 And in this mountain shall the LORD of hosts make unto all people a feast of fat things, a feast of wines on the lees, of fat things full of marrow, of wines on the lees well refined.

Isaiah 25:Verse 7

7 And he will destroy in this mountain the face of the covering cast over all people, and the vail that is spread over all nations.

Isaiah 25:Verse 8

8 He will swallow up death in victory; and the Lord GOD will wipe away tears from off all faces; and the rebuke of his people shall he take away from off all the earth: for the LORD hath spoken [it].

Isaiah 25:Verse 9

9 And it shall be said in that day, Lo, this [is] our God; we have waited for him, and he will save us: this [is] the LORD; we have waited for him, we will be glad and rejoice in his salvation.

Isaiah 25:Verse 10

10 For in this mountain shall the hand of the LORD rest, and Moab shall be trodden down under him, even as straw is trodden down for the dunghill.

Isaiah 25:Verse 11

11 And he shall spread forth his hands in the midst of them, as he that swimmeth spreadeth forth [his hands] to swim: and he shall bring down their pride together with the spoils of their hands.

Isaiah 25:Verse 12

12 And the fortress of the high fort of thy walls shall he bring down, lay low, [and] bring to the ground, [even] to the dust.

Ezekiel 39:Verse 8

8 Behold, it is come, and it is done, saith the Lord GOD; this [is] the day whereof I have spoken.

D&C 88:Verse 106

106 And again, another angel shall sound his trump, which is the seventh angel, saying: It is finished; it is finished! The Lamb of God hath overcome and trodden the wine-press alone, even the wine-press of the fierceness of the wrath of Almighty God.

Israel Restored Again

With the fall of Babylon, and the enemies of truth destroyed, Israel can now be restored, and learn of the gospel as it is sent throughout the world. With the great conversion process of missionary work, the masses accept the gospel and the righteous gather to Zion. It is the responsibility of the children of Ephraim to gather Israel. Because, of the faithfulness of Ephraim, 'as the servant of the Lord' in the Allegory of the Olive Tree, he is blessed by the children of Israel as saviors on Mount Zion.

Ezekiel 39:Verse 21
21 And I will set my glory among the heathen, and all the heathen shall see my judgment that I have executed, and my hand that I have laid upon them.

Ezekiel 39:Verse 22
22 **So the house of Israel shall know that I [am] the LORD their God from that day and forward.**

Ezekiel 39:Verse 23
23 And the heathen shall know that the house of Israel went into captivity for their iniquity: because they trespassed against me, therefore hid I my face from them, and gave them into the hand of their enemies: so fell they all by the sword.

Ezekiel 39:Verse 24
24 According to their uncleanness and according to their transgressions have I done unto them, and hid my face from them.

Ezekiel 39:Verse 25
25 Therefore thus saith the Lord GOD; **Now will I bring again the captivity of Jacob, and have mercy upon the whole house of Israel, and will be jealous for my holy name;**

Ezekiel 39:Verse 26
26 After that they have borne their shame, and all their trespasses whereby they have trespassed against me, when they dwelt safely in their land, and none made [them] afraid.

Ezekiel 39:Verse 27
27 When **I have brought them again from the people, and gathered them out of their enemies' lands, and am sanctified in them in the sight of many nations;**

Joel 2:Verse 18
18 **Then will the LORD be jealous for his land, and pity his people**.

Joel 2:Verse 19
19 Yea, the LORD will answer and say unto his people, Behold, I will send you corn, and wine, and oil, and ye shall be satisfied therewith: and I will no more make you a reproach among the heathen:

Joel 2:Verse 20
20 But I will remove far off from you the northern [army], and will drive him into a land barren and desolate, with his face toward the east sea, and his hinder part toward the utmost sea, and his stink shall come up, and his ill savour shall come up, because he hath done great things.

D&C 133:Verse 26
26 And they who are in the north countries shall come in remembrance before the Lord; and their prophets shall hear his voice, and shall no longer stay themselves; and they shall smite the rocks, and the ice shall flow down at their presence.

D&C 133:Verse 27
27 And an highway shall be cast up in the midst of the great deep.

D&C 133:Verse 28
28 **Their enemies shall become a prey unto them,**

D&C 133:Verse 29
29 And in the barren deserts there shall come forth pools of living water; and the parched ground shall no longer be a thirsty land.

D&C 133:Verse 30
30 And **they shall bring forth their rich treasures unto the children of Ephraim, my servants.**

D&C 133:Verse 31
31 And the boundaries of the everlasting hills shall tremble at their presence.

D&C 133:Verse 32
32 And **there shall they fall down and be crowned with glory, even in Zion, by the hands of the servants of the Lord, even the children of Ephraim.**

Joseph Smith Matthew 1:Verse 37
37 And whoso treasureth up my word, shall not be deceived, for the Son of Man shall come, and **he shall send his angels before him with the great sound of a trumpet, and they shall gather together the remainder of his elect from the four winds, from one end of heaven to the other.**

22

The Heavens Rejoice

Revelation 19: 1-10

Babylon is destroyed, Christ has come again, only the more righteous part of the people are spared, the Gospel goes forth, and Israel is restored, the reign of peace for a thousand years is beginning. It is no wonder the Heavens Rejoice.

Revelation 19:Verse 1
1 AND after these things I heard a great voice of much people in heaven, saying, Alleluia; Salvation, and glory, and honour, and power, unto the Lord our God:

Revelation 19:Verse 2
2 For true and righteous [are] his judgments: for he hath judged the great whore, which did corrupt the earth with her fornication, and hath avenged the blood of his servants at her hand.

Revelation 19:Verse 3
3 And again they said, Alleluia. And her smoke rose up for ever and ever.

Revelation 19:Verse 4
4 And the four and twenty elders and the four beasts fell down and worshipped God that sat on the throne, saying, Amen; Alleluia.

Revelation 19:Verse 5
5 And a voice came out of the throne, saying, Praise our God, all ye his servants, and ye that fear him, both small and great.

Revelation 19:Verse 6
6 And I heard as it were the voice of a great multitude, and as the voice of many waters, and as the voice of mighty thunderings, saying, Alleluia: for the Lord God omnipotent reigneth.

Revelation 19:Verse 7
7 Let us be glad and rejoice, and give honour to him: for the marriage of the Lamb is come, and his wife hath made herself ready.

Revelation 19:Verse 8

8 And to her was granted that she should be arrayed in fine linen, clean and white: for the fine linen is the righteousness of saints.

Revelation 19:Verse 9

9 And he saith unto me, Write, Blessed [are] they which are called unto the marriage supper of the Lamb. And he saith unto me, These are the true sayings of God.

Revelation 19:Verse 10

10 And I fell at his feet to worship him. And he said unto me, See [thou do it] not: I am thy fellowservant, and of thy brethren that have the testimony of Jesus: worship God: for the testimony of Jesus is the spirit of prophecy.

Isaiah 12:Verse 1

1 AND in that day thou shalt say, O LORD, I will praise thee: though thou wast angry with me, thine anger is turned away, and thou comfortedest me.

Isaiah 12:Verse 2

2 Behold, God [is] my salvation; I will trust, and not be afraid: for **the LORD JEHOVAH [is] my strength and [my] song; he also is become my salvation.**

Isaiah 12:Verse 3

3 Therefore with joy shall ye draw water out of the wells of salvation.

Isaiah 12:Verse 4

4 And in that day shall ye say, Praise the LORD, call upon his name, declare his doings among the people, make mention that his name is exalted.

Isaiah 12:Verse 5

5 Sing unto the LORD; for he hath done excellent things: this [is] known in all the earth.

Isaiah 12:Verse 6

6 Cry out and shout, thou inhabitant of Zion: for great [is] the Holy One of Israel in the midst of thee.

Isaiah 14:Verse 7

7 The whole earth is at rest, [and] is quiet: they break forth into singing.

Isaiah 14:Verse 8

8 Yea, the fir trees rejoice at thee, [and] the cedars of Lebanon, [saying], Since thou art laid down, no feller is come up against us.

Isaiah 24:Verse 14
14 They shall lift up their voice, they shall sing for the majesty of the LORD, they shall cry aloud from the sea.

Isaiah 24:Verse 15
15 Wherefore glorify ye the LORD in the fires, [even] the name of the LORD God of Israel in the isles of the sea.

Isaiah 25:Verse 1
1 O LORD, thou [art] my God; I will exalt thee, I will praise thy name; for thou hast done wonderful [things; thy] counsels of old [are] faithfulness [and] truth.

Isaiah 25:Verse 2
2 For thou hast made of a city an heap; [of] a defenced city a ruin: a palace of strangers to be no city; it shall never be built.

Isaiah 25:Verse 3
3 Therefore shall the strong people glorify thee, the city of the terrible nations shall fear thee.

Isaiah 25:Verse 4
4 For thou hast been a strength to the poor, a strength to the needy in his distress, a refuge from the storm, a shadow from the heat, when the blast of the terrible ones [is] as a storm [against] the wall.

23

The Second Coming

Revelation 19: 11-16

The Second Coming of Jesus Christ is an event, and topic that has topped the lists of gospel discussions, Sunday school classes, sermons, and books. It is the single most important event prophesied in scripture, and an event that the Christian world has been looking for since the time of the original apostles, and early Christian church. The Book of Revelation is often described as the 'Apocalypse' because it deals with the events of the last days, which surround the Second Coming, and the beginning of the millennium. The Savior comes to the Mount of Olives clothed in red apparel symbolizing the blood of the atonement and the death and destruction of mankind during the tribulation period. With Him come the armies of heaven, in contrast, clothed in white garments.

Revelation 19:Verse 11

11 And I saw heaven opened, and behold a white horse; and he that sat upon him [was] called Faithful and True, and in righteousness he doth judge and make war.

Revelation 19:Verse 12

12 His eyes [were] as a flame of fire, and on his head [were] many crowns; and he had a name written, that no man knew, but he himself.

Revelation 19:Verse 13

13 And he [was] **clothed with a vesture dipped in blood:** and his name is called The Word of God.

Revelation 19:Verse 14

14 And the armies [which were] in heaven followed him upon white horses, clothed in fine linen, white and clean.

Revelation 19:Verse 15

15 And out of his mouth goeth a sharp sword, that with it he should smite the nations: and he shall rule them with a rod of iron: and **he treadeth the winepress** of the fierceness and wrath of Almighty God.

Revelation 19:Verse 16

16 And he hath on [his] vesture and on his thigh a name written, KING OF KINGS, AND LORD OF LORDS.

Isaiah 63:Verse 1

1 WHO [is] this that cometh from Edom, with **dyed garments** from Bozrah? this [that is] glorious in his apparel, travelling in the greatness of his strength? I that speak in righteousness, mighty to save.

Isaiah 63:Verse 2

2 Wherefore [art thou] **red in thine apparel,** and thy garments like him that treadeth in the winefat?

Isaiah 63:Verse 3

3 **I have trodden the winepress alone**; and of the people [there was] none with me: for **I will tread them in mine anger, and trample them in my fury; and their blood shall be sprinkled upon my garments, and I will stain all my raiment.**

Isaiah 63:Verse 4

4 For the day of vengeance [is] in mine heart, and the year of my redeemed is come.

Isaiah 63:Verse 5

5 And I looked, and [there was] none to help; and I wondered that [there was] none to uphold: therefore mine own arm brought salvation unto me; and my fury, it upheld me.

Isaiah 63:Verse 6

6 And **I will tread down the people in mine anger, and make them drunk in my fury, and I will bring down their strength to the earth.**

D&C 29:Verse 11

11 For **I will reveal myself from heaven with power and great glory, with all the hosts thereof,** and dwell in righteousness with men on earth a thousand years, and the wicked shall not stand.

D&C 130:Verse 1

1 WHEN the Savior shall appear we shall see him as he is. We shall see that he is a man like ourselves.

D&C 133:Verse 25

25 And the Lord, even the Savior, shall stand in the midst of his people, and shall reign over all flesh.

D&C 133:Verse 46

46 And it shall be said: Who is this **that cometh down from God in heaven with dyed garments**; yea, from the regions which are not known, clothed in his glorious apparel, traveling in the greatness of his strength?

D&C 133:Verse 47

47 And he shall say: I am he who spake in righteousness, mighty to save.

D&C 133:Verse 48

48 And **the Lord shall be red in his apparel, and his garments like him that treadeth in the wine-vat.**

D&C 133:Verse 49

49 And so great shall be the glory of his presence that the sun shall hide his face in shame, and the moon shall withhold its light, and the stars shall be hurled from their places.

D&C 133:Verse 50

50 And his voice shall be heard: **I have trodden the wine-press alone**, and **have brought judgment upon all people**; and none were with me;

D&C 133:Verse 51

51 And I have trampled them in my fury, and I did tread **upon them in mine anger, and their blood have I sprinkled upon my garments, and stained all my raiment;** for this was the day of vengeance which was in my heart.

Joseph Smith Matthew 1:Verse 26

26 For as the light of the morning cometh out of the east, and shineth even unto the west, and covereth the whole earth, so shall also the coming of the Son of Man be.

Joseph Smith Matthew 1:Verse 36

36 And, as I said before, after the tribulation of those days, and the powers of the heavens shall be shaken, then shall appear the sign of the Son of Man in heaven, and then shall all the tribes of the earth mourn; and they shall see **the Son of Man coming the clouds of heaven, with power and great glory;**

24

The Supper of the Great God

Revelation 19: 17-21

The fowls and animals of the earth are invited to feast upon the dead who have died in the great destruction and death that will take place in the battle of Armageddon that leads up to the coming of the Lord. The Supper of the Great God is described in scripture, not only in the Book of Revelation, but also in Isaiah, Ezekiel, and in latter day scripture in the Doctrine & Covenants. This event seems to be real, in the aftermath of the great war, a true abomination of desolation. The scriptures teach that it will take years to bury the dead and clean the destruction that will take place.

Revelation 19:Verse 17
17 And I saw an angel standing in the sun; and he cried with a loud voice, saying to all the fowls that fly in the midst of heaven, Come and gather yourselves together unto the supper of the great God;

Revelation 19:Verse 18
18 That ye may eat the flesh of kings, and the flesh of captains, and the flesh of mighty men, and the flesh of horses, and of them that sit on them, and the flesh of all [men, both] free and bond, both small and great.

Revelation 19:Verse 19
19 And I saw the beast, and the kings of the earth, and their armies, gathered together to make war against him that sat on the horse, and against his army.

Revelation 19:Verse 20
20 And the beast was taken, and with him the false prophet that wrought miracles before him, with which he deceived them that had received the mark of the beast, and them that worshipped his image. These both were cast alive into a lake of fire burning with brimstone.

Revelation 19:Verse 21
21 And the remnant were slain with the sword of him that sat upon the horse, which [sword] proceeded out of his mouth: and all the fowls were filled with their flesh.

Isaiah 66:Verse 24

24 And they shall go forth, and look upon the carcases of the men that have transgressed against me: for their worm shall not die, neither shall their fire be quenched; and they shall be an abhorring unto all flesh.

Ezekiel 39:Verse 4

4 Thou shalt fall upon the mountains of Israel, thou, and all thy bands, and the people that [is] with thee: **I will give thee unto the ravenous birds of every sort, and [to] the beasts of the field to be devoured.**

Ezekiel 39:Verse 5

5 Thou shalt fall upon the open field: for I have spoken [it], saith the Lord GOD.

Ezekiel 39:Verse 9

9 And they that dwell in the cities of Israel shall go forth, and shall set on fire and burn the weapons, both the shields and the bucklers, the bows and the arrows, and the handstaves, and the spears, and they shall burn them with fire seven years:

Ezekiel 39:Verse 10

10 So that they shall take no wood out of the field, neither cut down [any] out of the forests; for they shall burn the weapons with fire: and they shall spoil those that spoiled them, and rob those that robbed them, saith the Lord GOD.

Ezekiel 39:Verse 11

11 And it shall come to pass in that day, [that] I will give unto Gog a place there of graves in Israel, the valley of the passengers on the east of the sea: and it shall stop the [noses] of the passengers: and there shall they bury Gog and all his multitude: and they shall call [it] The valley of Hamongog.

Ezekiel 39:Verse 12

12 And seven months shall the house of Israel be burying of them, that they may cleanse the land.

Ezekiel 39:Verse 13

13 Yea, all the people of the land shall bury [them]; and it shall be to them a renown the day that I shall be glorified, saith the Lord GOD.

Ezekiel 39:Verse 14

14 And they shall sever out men of continual employment, passing through the land to bury with the passengers those that remain upon the face of the earth, to cleanse it: after the end of seven months shall they search.

Ezekiel 39:Verse 15

15 And the passengers [that] pass through the land, when [any] seeth a man's bone, then shall he set up a sign by it, till the buriers have buried it in the valley of Hamongog.

Ezekiel 39:Verse 16

16 And also the name of the city [shall be] Hamonah. Thus shall they cleanse the land.

Ezekiel 39:Verse 17

17 And, thou son of man, thus saith the Lord GOD; **Speak unto every feathered fowl, and to every beast of the field, Assemble yourselves, and come; gather yourselves on every side to my sacrifice that I do sacrifice for you, [even] a great sacrifice upon the mountains of Israel, that ye may eat flesh, and drink blood.**

Ezekiel 39:Verse 18

18 Ye shall **eat the flesh of the mighty, and drink the blood of the princes of the earth,** of rams, of lambs, and of goats, of bullocks, all of them fatlings of Bashan.

Ezekiel 39:Verse 19

19 And **ye shall eat fat till ye be full**, and drink blood till ye be drunken, of my sacrifice which I have sacrificed for you.

Ezekiel 39:Verse 20

20 Thus **ye shall be filled at my table with horses and chariots, with mighty men, and with all men of war, saith the Lord GOD.**

D&C 29:Verse 20

20 And it shall come to pass that **the beasts of the forest and the fowls of the air shall devour them up.**

24a

All Things Revealed

With the coming of the Savior, and only the 'more righteous part of the people spared' the reveled acts of God throughout the ages of the earth will be made manifest to the righteous. Mankind will understand their relationship with their Father in Heaven as they understand the 'why' of creation, and the purpose of life. With this revealed knowledge all will know that the judgments of God are just, and deserved.

D&C 88:Verse 108
108 And then shall the first angel again sound his trump **in the ears of all living, and reveal the secret acts of men**, and the mighty works of God in the first thousand years.

D&C 88:Verse 109
109 And then shall the second angel sound his trump, and **reveal the secret acts of men**, and the thoughts and intents of their hearts, and the mighty works of God in the second thousand years--

D&C 88:Verse 110
110 And so on, until the seventh angel shall sound his trump. . .

D&C 101:Verse 32
32 Yea, verily I say unto you, in that day **when the Lord shall come, he shall reveal all things--**

D&C 101:Verse 33
33 **Things which have passed, and hidden things which no man knew, things of the earth, by which it was made, and the purpose and the end thereof--**

D&C 101:Verse 34
34 **Things most precious, things that are above, and things that are beneath, things that are in the earth, and upon the earth, and in heaven.**

26 God shall give unto you knowledge by his Holy Spirit, yea, by the unspeakable gift of the Holy Ghost, that has not been revealed since the world was until now;
27 Which our forefathers have awaited with anxious expectation to be revealed in the last times, which their minds were pointed to by the angels, as held in reserve for the fulness of their glory;
28 A time to come in the which nothing shall be withheld, whether there be one God or many gods, they shall be manifest.
29 All thrones and dominions, principalities and powers, shall be revealed and set forth upon all who have endured valiantly for the gospel of Jesus Christ.

30 And also, if there be bounds set to the heavens or to the seas, or to the dry land, or to the sun, moon, or stars—

31 All the times of their revolutions, all the appointed days, months, and years, and all the days of their days, months, and years, and all their glories, laws, and set times, shall be revealed in the days of the dispensation of the fulness of times—

32 According to that which was ordained in the midst of the Council of the Eternal God of all other gods before this world was, that should be reserved unto the finishing and the end thereof, when every man shall enter into his eternal presence and into his immortal rest.

D&C 121:26-32

25

Satan Bound for a Thousand Years

Revelation 20: 1-3

Like Fourth Nephi in the Book of Mormon Satan has no influence upon masses of mankind because of the righteousness of every individual. Nephi tells us that because of the righteousness of his people, 'Satan has no power; wherefore, he cannot be loosed for the space of many years; for he hath no power over the hearts of the people, for they dwell in righteousness, and the Holy One of Israel reigneth.' The movement of the masses is always easy to predict, and see, however, the individual cannot be seen because of agency and repentance.

The binding of Satan because of individual righteousness is something that need not wait until the millennium. Every person can bind Satan in their heart as often as one would like. Because, the mind of man can think of only one thing at a time, we have the power to cast Satan out of our life if we choose. This life then becomes a true probationary state because the power is in us to do, and think as we please. A healthy mind and free agency leaves us no excuse for sin, Satan can only have the power over us that we give him. The Book of Mormon teaches that Satan will be bound because of the righteousness of the people. It is not because he is not there, but because of the hearts, character and righteousness of the individuals. If temptations were not present then there could be no righteousness, for there needs be opposition and righteousness is choosing good with the opportunity for evil.

Using the Book of Mormon as a pattern we see that after the destruction and death of the wicked, and the announcing and coming of Christ, the gospel is sent throughout the land. Keep in mind it was not the Church, but, the gospel that went forth. The mistake must not be made in thinking that the 'gospel' and the 'church' are the synonymous. They are not. In the spirit world when the missionary forces teach in the spirit prison they cannot come as missionaries from the 'Church of Jesus Christ of Latter-day Saints,' they come as servants teaching the gospel of Jesus Christ. Perish the thought, but the anti Mormons will be taught the gospel with the rest of Adam's posterity, it is the gospel they must accept that they may baptized by proxy with the baptism of repentance, not as an initiation into the 'Church.' In Third Nephi it is the gospel that is taught and with that acceptance, and the conversion of the masses, then a church is organized. Fourth Nephi is the symbolic millennium, or thousand years of peace, and it was after all people had accepted the gospel, with the church organized (3 Ne. 27) the people could continue 'in fasting and prayer, and in meeting together oft both to pray and to hear the word of the Lord.' Also, it should not be misunderstood that the conversion was over night, it took some time. The gospel must go throughout the earth those that were spared will have to hear and understand, and then repent, accept the gospel of Jesus Christ, and its ordinances. How long will this take? Ten years out of the millennium, fifty, one hundred, two hundred years? What is a hundred and fifty years out of one thousand years. Food for thought: could the coming of the Savior to the prophet and the restoration of the gospel herald the beginning, or opening of the thousand-year period? Or is it when Christ appears on the Mt. of Olive at the Second Coming? The restoration of the gospel will destroy Babylon and prepare the earth to receive her God. Could this be the start? Does the great battle of Armageddon, and the destruction from the upheavals of the earth begin the millennium or is it the return of the Lord? Could the thousand years of peace begin only after the masses that are spared in the destruction, are converted to the gospel?

Will the millennium end when the first person is no longer righteous? Or is it progressive like in the Book of Mormon, does pride silently slip into the hearts of mankind because of the prosperity that exists? If so, will this be in the last two hundred years of the thousand, or last fifty? Don't get caught up into the perfect plan or interpretation. If one should be so 'blessed' or, 'cursed' to live through the tribulation, and see the coming of the Savior, we should not think that we will live a thousand years and then die. Death will came at an old age (age of a tree) and we will be 'twinkled'' but what does that mean? Instantly? If it took a hundred years to be resurrected that would be fast compared to others who have waited thousands of years. One must allow some latitude, no one can out guess God, not even the angels know the time of his coming. Any conversation, discussion or commentary that exceed the information and truths presented in scripture enters through the door that opens into the room of speculation.

Revelation 20:Verse 1
1 AND I saw an angel come down from heaven, having the key of the bottomless pit and a great chain in his hand.

Revelation 20:Verse 2
2 And he laid hold on the dragon, that old serpent, which is the Devil, and Satan, and **bound him a thousand years,**

Revelation 20:Verse 3
3 And cast him into the bottomless pit, and shut him up, and **set a seal upon him, that he should deceive the nations no more, till the thousand years should be fulfilled:** and after that he must be loosed a little season.

Daniel 7:Verse 26
26 But the judgment shall sit, and they shall **take away his dominion**, to consume and to destroy [it] unto the end.

Daniel 7:Verse 27

27 And the kingdom and dominion, and the greatness of the kingdom under the whole heaven, shall be given to the people of the saints of the most High, whose kingdom [is] an everlasting kingdom, and all dominions shall serve and obey him.

Daniel 7:Verse 18

18 But the saints of the most High shall take the kingdom, and possess the kingdom for ever, even for ever and ever.

---

1 Nephi 22:Verse 26

26 And because of the righteousness of his people, **Satan has no power; wherefore, he cannot be loosed for the space of many years;** for he hath no power over the hearts of the people, for they dwell in righteousness, and the Holy One of Israel reigneth.

D&C 45:Verse 55

55 And **Satan shall be bound,** that he shall have no place in the hearts of the children of men.

D&C 88: Verse 110

110 And so on, until the seventh angel shall sound his trump, and he shall stand forth upon the land and upon the sea, and swear in the name of him who sitteth upon the throne, that there shall be time no longer; and **Satan shall be bound, that old serpent, who is called the devil, and shall not be loosed for the space of a thousand years.**

26

The Judgment and the First Resurrection

The judgment and resurrection go hand in hand. To participate in one is to participate in the other. The Doctrine and Covenants teaches that the individual will be resurrected to that glory which he will inherit, which is a partial judgment in itself. D&C 88 teaches:

> 28 **They who are of a celestial spirit shall receive the same body which was a natural body; even ye shall receive your bodies, and your glory shall be that glory by which your bodies are quickened.**
> **29 Ye who are quickened by a portion of the celestial glory shall then receive of the same, even a fulness.**
> 30 And they who are quickened by a portion of the terrestrial glory shall then receive of the same, even a fulness.
> 31 And also they who are quickened by a portion of the telestial glory shall then receive of the same, even a fulness.
> 32 And they who remain shall also be quickened; nevertheless, they shall return again to their own place, **to enjoy that which they are willing to receive**, because they were not willing to enjoy that which they might have received.
> 33 For what doth it profit a man if a gift is bestowed upon him, and he receive not the gift? Behold, he rejoices not in that which is given unto him, neither rejoices in him who is the giver of the gift.
> 34 And again, verily I say unto you, that which is governed by law is also preserved by law and perfected and sanctified by the same.
> 35 That which breaketh a law, and abideth not by law, but seeketh to become a law unto itself, and willeth to abide in sin, and altogether abideth in sin, cannot be sanctified by law, neither by mercy, justice, nor judgment. Therefore, they must remain filthy still. (D&C 88:28-35)

We have choices in this life, and each moral choice can be celestial, terrestrial, or telestial. The Book of Mormon tells us that our 'words, works, and thoughts' will condemn us at the last day. This life is a probationary state in which we prepare to meet God, and our choices, and life style will fall into one of these three glories. The celestial spirit, is the spirit, character and person that has made celestial choices during mortality, and that spirit will receive a celestial body in the resurrection. Resurrection is a judgment, for mankind will 'receive that which they are willing to receive.'

Revelation 20: Verse 4

4 And I saw thrones, and they sat upon them, and judgment was given unto them: and [I saw] the souls of them that were beheaded for the witness of Jesus, and for the word of God, and which had not worshipped the beast, neither his image, neither had received [his] mark upon their foreheads, or in their hands; and they lived and reigned with Christ a thousand years.

Revelation 20:Verse 5

5 But the rest of the dead lived not again until the thousand years were finished. This [is] the first resurrection.

Revelation 20:Verse 6

6 Blessed and holy [is] he that hath part in the first resurrection: on such the second death hath no power, but they shall be priests of God and of Christ, and shall reign with him a thousand years.

Daniel 12:Verse 2

2 And **many of them that sleep in the dust of the earth shall awake, some to everlasting life, and some to shame [and] everlasting contempt.**

Daniel 12:Verse 3

3 And they that be wise shall shine as the brightness of the firmament; and they that turn many to righteousness as the stars for ever and ever.

Alma 42:Verse 23

23 But God ceaseth not to be God, and mercy claimeth the penitent, and mercy cometh because of the atonement; and **the atonement bringeth to pass the resurrection of the dead; and the resurrection of the dead bringeth back men into the presence of God; and thus they are restored into his presence, to be judged according to their works, according to the law and justice.**

Alma 42:Verse 24

24 For behold, justice exerciseth all his demands, and also mercy claimeth all which is her own; and thus, none but the truly penitent are saved.

Mormon 9:Verse 1

1 AND now, I speak also concerning those who do not believe in Christ.

Mormon 9:Verse 2

2 Behold, will ye believe in the day of your visitation--behold, **when the Lord shall come, yea, even that great day when the earth shall be rolled together as a scroll, and the elements**

shall melt with fervent heat, yea, in that great day when ye shall be brought to stand before the Lamb of God--then will ye say that there is no God?

Mormon 9:Verse 3

3 Then will ye longer deny the Christ, or can ye behold the Lamb of God? Do ye suppose that ye shall dwell with him under a consciousness of your guilt? Do ye suppose that ye could be happy to dwell with that holy Being, when your souls are racked with a consciousness of guilt that ye have ever abused his laws?

Mormon 9:Verse 4

4 Behold, I say unto you that ye would be more miserable to dwell with a holy and just God, under a consciousness of your filthiness before him, than ye would to dwell with the damned souls in hell.

Mormon 9:Verse 5

5 For behold, **when ye shall be brought to see your nakedness before God, and also the glory of God, and the holiness of Jesus Christ, it will kindle a flame of unquenchable fire upon you.**

Mormon 9:Verse 12

12 Behold, he created Adam, and by Adam came the fall of man. And because of the fall of man came Jesus Christ, even the Father and the Son; and because of Jesus Christ came the redemption of man.

Mormon 9:Verse 13

13 And because of the redemption of man, which came by Jesus Christ, they are brought back into the presence of the Lord; yea, this is wherein all men are redeemed, because **the death of Christ bringeth to pass the resurrection, which bringeth to pass a redemption from an endless sleep, from which sleep all men shall be awakened by the power of God when the trump shall sound; and they shall come forth, both small and great, and all shall stand before his bar, being redeemed and loosed from this eternal band of death, which death is a temporal death**

.Mormon 9:Verse 14

14 And **then cometh the judgment of the Holy One upon them; and then cometh the time that he that is filthy shall be filthy still; and he that is righteous shall be righteous still; he that is happy shall be happy still; and he that is unhappy shall be unhappy still.**

D&C 29:Verse 12

12 And again, verily, verily, I say unto you, and it hath gone forth in a firm decree, by the will of the Father, that mine apostles, **the Twelve which were with me in my ministry at Jerusalem, shall stand at my right hand at the day of my coming in a pillar of fire, being clothed with robes of righteousness, with crowns upon their heads, in glory even as I am, to judge the whole house of Israel, even as many as have loved me and kept my commandments, and none else.**

D&C 29:Verse 13

13 For a **trump shall sound both long and loud, even as upon Mount Sinai, and all the earth shall quake, and they shall come forth--yea, even the dead which died in me, to receive a crown of righteousness,** and to be clothed upon, even as I am, to be with me, that we may be one.

D&C 29:Verse 26

26 But, behold, verily I say unto you, **before the earth shall pass away, Michael, mine archangel, shall sound his trump, and then shall all the dead awake, for their graves shall be opened, and they shall come forth--yea, even all.**

D&C 29:Verse 27

27 And the righteous shall be gathered on my right hand unto eternal life; and the wicked on my left hand will I be ashamed to own before the Father;

D&C 45:Verse 54

54 And then shall the heathen nations be redeemed, and they that knew no law shall have part in the first resurrection; and it shall be tolerable for them.

D&C 63:Verse 49

49 Yea, and **blessed are the dead that die in the Lord, from henceforth, when the Lord shall come, and old things shall pass away, and all things become new, they shall rise from the dead** and shall not die after, and **shall receive an inheritance before the Lord, in his holy city.**

D&C 76:Verse 39

39 For all the rest shall be brought forth by the resurrection of the dead, through the triumph and the glory of the Lamb, who was slain, who was in the bosom of the Father before the worlds were made.

D&C 88:Verse 28

28 They who are of a celestial spirit *shall receive the same body which was a natural body; even ye shall receive your bodies, and your glory shall be that glory by which your bodies are quickened.*

D&C 88:Verse 29

29 Ye who are quickened by a portion of the celestial glory shall then receive of the same, even a fulness.

D&C 88:Verse 30

30 And they who are quickened by a portion of the terrestrial glory shall then receive of the same, even a fulness.

D&C 88:Verse 31

31 And also they who are quickened by a portion of the telestial glory shall then receive of the same, even a fulness.

D&C 88:Verse 99

99 And **after this another angel shall sound, which is the second trump; and then cometh the redemption of those who are Christ's at his coming; who have received their part in that prison which is prepared for them, that they might receive the gospel, and be judged according to men in the flesh.**

D&C 88:Verse 103

103 And another trump shall sound, which is the fifth trump, which is the fifth angel who committeth the everlasting gospel--flying through the midst of heaven, unto all nations, kindreds, tongues, and people;

D&C 88:Verse 104

104 And this shall be the sound of his trump, saying to all people, both in heaven and in earth, and that are under the earth--for every ear shall hear it, and every knee shall bow, and every tongue shall confess, while they hear the sound of the trump, saying: Fear God, and give glory to him who sitteth upon the throne, forever and ever; for the hour of his judgment is come.

D&C 133:Verse 52

52 And now the year of my redeemed is come; and they shall mention the loving kindness of their Lord, and all that he has bestowed upon them according to his goodness, and according to his loving kindness, forever and ever.

D&C 133:Verse 53

53 In all their afflictions he was afflicted. And the angel of his presence saved them; and in his love, and in his pity, he redeemed them, and bore them, and carried them all the days of old;

D&C 133:Verse 54

54 Yea, and Enoch also, and they who were with him; the prophets who were before him; and Noah also, and they who were before him; and Moses also, and they who were before him;

D&C 133:Verse 55

55 And from Moses to Elijah, and from Elijah to John, who were with Christ in his resurrection, and the holy apostles, with Abraham, Isaac, and Jacob, shall be in the presence of the Lamb.

D&C 133:Verse 56

56 And **the graves of the saints shall be opened; and they shall come forth and stand on the right hand of the Lamb, when he shall stand upon Mount Zion,** and upon the holy city, the New Jerusalem; and they shall sing the song of the Lamb, day and night forever and ever.

26a

Millennial Life

After the great battle that leads to the coming of the Savior and the opening of the thousand year millennial reign of the righteous on the earth, there will be few men. (See the Vision of John Taylor). Life during this time of peace is best described in the opening verses of Fourth Nephi as the millennial lifestyle is discussed. It is a shame so little of this righteous time is spoken of in scripture, as with Enoch and his city. 'Empty are the annals of a happy people' as often our journals and diaries mostly contain our emotions and frustrations during the most trying times.

Isaiah 4:Verse 1

1 AND in that day seven women shall take hold of one man, saying, We will eat our own bread, and wear our own apparel: only let us be called by thy name, to take away our reproach.

Isaiah 4:Verse 2

2 In that day shall the branch of the LORD be beautiful and glorious, and the fruit of the earth [shall be] excellent and comely for them that are escaped of Israel.

Isaiah 4:Verse 3

3 And it shall come to pass, [that he that is] left in Zion, and [he that] remaineth in Jerusalem, shall be called holy, [even] every one that is written among the living in Jerusalem:

Isaiah 4:Verse 4

4 When the Lord shall have washed away the filth of the daughters of Zion, and shall have purged the blood of Jerusalem from the midst thereof by the spirit of judgment, and by the spirit of burning.

Isaiah 4:Verse 5

5 And the LORD will create upon every dwelling place of mount Zion, and upon her assemblies, a cloud and smoke by day, and the shining of a flaming fire by night: for upon all the glory [shall be] a defence.

Isaiah 4:Verse 6

6 And there shall be a tabernacle for a shadow in the daytime from the heat, and for a place of refuge, and for a covert from storm and from rain.

Isaiah 11:Verse 6

6 The wolf also shall dwell with the lamb, and the leopard shall lie down with the kid; and the calf and the young lion and the fatling together; and a little child shall lead them.

Isaiah 11:Verse 7

7 And the cow and the bear shall feed; their young ones shall lie down together: and the lion shall eat straw like the ox.

Isaiah 11:Verse 8

8 And the sucking child shall play on the hole of the asp, and the weaned child shall put his hand on the cockatrice' den.

Isaiah 11:Verse 9

9 They shall not hurt nor destroy in all my holy mountain: for the earth shall be full of the knowledge of the LORD, as the waters cover the sea.

Isaiah 11:Verse 14

14 But they shall fly upon the shoulders of the Philistines toward the west; they shall spoil them of the east together: they shall lay their hand upon Edom and Moab; and the children of Ammon shall obey them.

Isaiah 11:Verse 15

15 And the LORD shall utterly destroy the tongue of the Egyptian sea; and with his mighty wind shall he shake his hand over the river, and shall smite it in the seven streams, and make [men] go over dryshod.

Isaiah 11:Verse 16

16 And there shall be an highway for the remnant of his people, which shall be left, from Assyria; like as it was to Israel in the day that he came up out of the land of Egypt.

––––––––––––––––––––––––

Isaiah 35:Verse 1

1 THE wilderness and the solitary place shall be glad for them; and the desert shall rejoice, and blossom as the rose.

Isaiah 35:Verse 2

2 It shall blossom abundantly, and rejoice even with joy and singing: the glory of Lebanon shall be given unto it, the excellency of Carmel and Sharon, they shall see the glory of the LORD, [and] the excellency of our God.

Isaiah 35:Verse 3

3 Strengthen ye the weak hands, and confirm the feeble knees.

Isaiah 35:Verse 4

4 Say to them [that are] of a fearful heart, Be strong, fear not: behold, your God will come [with] vengeance, [even] God [with] a recompence; he will come and save you.

Isaiah 35:Verse 5

5 Then the eyes of the blind shall be opened, and the ears of the deaf shall be unstopped.

Isaiah 35:Verse 6

6 Then shall the lame [man] leap as an hart, and the tongue of the dumb sing: for in the wilderness shall waters break out, and streams in the desert.

Isaiah 35:Verse 7

7 And the parched ground shall become a pool, and the thirsty land springs of water: in the habitation of dragons, where each lay, [shall be] grass with reeds and rushes.

Isaiah 35:Verse 8

8 And an highway shall be there, and a way, and it shall be called The way of holiness; the unclean shall not pass over it; but it [shall be] for those: the wayfaring men, though fools, shall not err [therein].

Isaiah 35:Verse 9

9 No lion shall be there, nor [any] ravenous beast shall go up thereon, it shall not be found there; but the redeemed shall walk [there]:

Isaiah 35:Verse 10

10 And the ransomed of the LORD shall return, and come to Zion with songs and everlasting joy upon their heads: they shall obtain joy and gladness, and sorrow and sighing shall flee away.

Isaiah 65:Verse 20

20 There shall be no more thence an infant of days, nor an old man that hath not filled his days: for the child shall die an hundred years old; but the sinner [being] an hundred years old shall be accursed.

Isaiah 65:Verse 21

21 And they shall build houses, and inhabit [them]; and they shall plant vineyards, and eat the fruit of them.

Isaiah 65:Verse 22

22 They shall not build, and another inhabit; they shall not plant, and another eat: for as the days of a tree [are] the days of my people, and mine elect shall long enjoy the work of their hands.

Isaiah 65:Verse 23

23 They shall not labour in vain, nor bring forth for trouble; for they [are] the seed of the blessed of the LORD, and their offspring with them.

Isaiah 65:Verse 24

24 And it shall come to pass, that before they call, I will answer; and while they are yet speaking, I will hear.

Isaiah 65:Verse 25

25 The wolf and the lamb shall feed together, and the lion shall eat straw like the bullock: and dust [shall be] the serpent's meat. They shall not hurt nor destroy in all my holy mountain, saith the LORD.

Isaiah 66:Verse 18
18 For I [know] their works and their thoughts: it shall come, that I will gather all nations and tongues; and they shall come, and see my glory.

Isaiah 66:Verse 19
19 And I will set a sign among them, and I will send those that escape of them unto the nations, [to] Tarshish, Pul, and Lud, that draw the bow, [to] Tubal, and Javan, [to] the isles afar off, that have not heard my fame, neither have seen my glory; and they shall declare my glory among the Gentiles.

Isaiah 66:Verse 20
20 And they shall bring all your brethren [for] an offering unto the LORD out of all nations upon horses, and in chariots, and in litters, and upon mules, and upon swift beasts, to my holy mountain Jerusalem, saith the LORD, as the children of Israel bring an offering in a clean vessel into the house of the LORD.

Isaiah 66:Verse 21
21 And I will also take of them for priests [and] for Levites, saith the LORD.

Jeremiah 50:Verse 19
19 And I will bring Israel again to his habitation, and he shall feed on Carmel and Bashan, and his soul shall be satisfied upon mount Ephraim and Gilead.

Jeremiah 50:Verse 20
20 In those days, and in that time, saith the LORD, the iniquity of Israel shall be sought for, and [there shall be] none; and the sins of Judah, and they shall not be found: for I will pardon them whom I reserve.

Ezekiel 37:Verse 21
21 And say unto them, Thus saith the Lord GOD; Behold, I will take the children of Israel from among the heathen, whither they be gone, and will gather them on every side, and bring them into their own land:

Ezekiel 37:Verse 22
22 And I will make them one nation in the land upon the mountains of Israel; and one king shall be king to them all: and they shall be no more two nations, neither shall they be divided into two kingdoms any more at all:

Ezekiel 37:Verse 23
23 Neither shall they defile themselves any more with their idols, nor with their detestable things, nor with any of their transgressions: but I will save them out of all their dwellingplaces, wherein they have sinned, and will cleanse them: so shall they be my people, and I will be their God.

Ezekiel 37:Verse 24
24 And David my servant [shall be] king over them; and they all shall have one shepherd: they shall also walk in my judgments, and observe my statutes, and do them.

Ezekiel 37:Verse 25
25 And they shall dwell in the land that I have given unto Jacob my servant, wherein your fathers have dwelt; and they shall dwell therein, [even] they, and their children, and their children's children for ever: and my servant David [shall be] their prince for ever.

Ezekiel 37:Verse 26
26 Moreover I will make a covenant of peace with them; it shall be an everlasting covenant with them: and I will place them, and multiply them, and will set my sanctuary in the midst of them for evermore.

Ezekiel 37:Verse 27
27 My tabernacle also shall be with them: yea, I will be their God, and they shall be my people.

Ezekiel 37:Verse 28
28 And the heathen shall know that I the LORD do sanctify Israel, when my sanctuary shall be in the midst of them for evermore.

Ezekiel 39:Verse 7
7 So will I make my holy name known in the midst of my people Israel; and I will not [let them] pollute my holy name any more: and the heathen shall know that I [am] the LORD, the Holy One in Israel.

Ezekiel 39:Verse 28
28 Then shall they know that I [am] the LORD their God, which caused them to be led into captivity among the heathen: but I have gathered them unto their own land, and have left none of them any more there.

Ezekiel 39:Verse 29
29 Neither will I hide my face any more from them: for I have poured out my spirit upon the house of Israel, saith the Lord GOD.

Joel 2:Verse 21
21 Fear not, O land; be glad and rejoice: for the LORD will do great things.

Joel 2:Verse 22
22 Be not afraid, ye beasts of the field: for the pastures of the wilderness do spring, for the tree beareth her fruit, the fig tree and the vine do yield their strength.

Joel 2:Verse 23
23 Be glad then, ye children of Zion, and rejoice in the LORD your God: for he hath given you the former rain moderately, and he will cause to come down for you the rain, the former rain, and the latter rain in the first [month].

Joel 2:Verse 24
24 And the floors shall be full of wheat, and the fats shall overflow with wine and oil.

Joel 2:Verse 25
25 And I will restore to you the years that the locust hath eaten, the cankerworm, and the caterpiller, and the palmerworm, my great army which I sent among you.

Joel 2:Verse 26
26 And ye shall eat in plenty, and be satisfied, and praise the name of the LORD your God, that hath dealt wondrously with you: and my people shall never be ashamed.

Joel 2:Verse 27
27 And ye shall know that I [am] in the midst of Israel, and [that] I [am] the LORD your God, and none else: and my people shall never be ashamed.

Joel 2:Verse 28
28 And it shall come to pass afterward, [that] I will pour out my spirit upon all flesh; and your sons and your daughters shall prophesy, your old men shall dream dreams, your young men shall see visions:

Joel 2:Verse 29
29 And also upon the servants and upon the handmaids in those days will I pour out my spirit.

Joel 3:Verse 17
17 So shall ye know that I [am] the LORD your God dwelling in Zion, my holy mountain: then shall Jerusalem be holy, and there shall no strangers pass through her any more.

Joel 3:Verse 18
18 And it shall come to pass in that day, [that] the mountains shall drop down new wine, and the hills shall flow with milk, and all the rivers of Judah shall flow with waters, and a fountain shall come forth of the house of the LORD, and shall water the valley of Shittim.

Joel 3:Verse 19
19 Egypt shall be a desolation, and Edom shall be a desolate wilderness, for the violence [against] the children of Judah, because they have shed innocent blood in their land.

Joel 3:Verse 20
20 But Judah shall dwell for ever, and Jerusalem from generation to generation.

Joel 3:Verse 21
21 For I will cleanse their blood [that] I have not cleansed: for the LORD dwelleth in Zion.

Zechariah 2:Verse 10

10 Sing and rejoice, O daughter of Zion: for, lo, I come, and I will dwell in the midst of thee, saith the LORD.

Zechariah 2:Verse 11

11 And many nations shall be joined to the LORD in that day, and shall be my people: and I will dwell in the midst of thee, and thou shalt know that the LORD of hosts hath sent me unto thee.

Zechariah 2:Verse 12

12 And the LORD shall inherit Judah his portion in the holy land, and shall choose Jerusalem again.

Zechariah 12:Verse 5

5 And the governors of Judah shall say in their heart, The inhabitants of Jerusalem [shall be] my strength in the LORD of hosts their God.

Zechariah 12:Verse 6

6 In that day will I make the governors of Judah like an hearth of fire among the wood, and like a torch of fire in a sheaf; and they shall devour all the people round about, on the right hand and on the left: and Jerusalem shall be inhabited again in her own place, [even] in Jerusalem.

Zechariah 12:Verse 7

7 The LORD also shall save the tents of Judah first, that the glory of the house of David and the glory of the inhabitants of Jerusalem do not magnify [themselves] against Judah.

Zechariah 14:Verse 8

8 And it shall be in that day, [that] living waters shall go out from Jerusalem; half of them toward the former sea, and half of them toward the hinder sea: in summer and in winter shall it be.

Zechariah 14:Verse 9

9 And the LORD shall be king over all the earth: in that day shall there be one LORD, and his name one.

Zechariah 14:Verse 10

10 All the land shall be turned as a plain from Geba to Rimmon south of Jerusalem: and it shall be lifted up, and inhabited in her place, from Benjamin's gate unto the place of the first gate, unto the corner gate, and [from] the tower of Hananeel unto the king's winepresses.

Zechariah 14:Verse 11

11 And [men] shall dwell in it, and there shall be no more utter destruction; but Jerusalem shall be safely inhabited.

Zechariah 14:Verse 16

16 And it shall come to pass, [that] every one that is left of all the nations which came against Jerusalem shall even go up from year to year to worship the King, the LORD of hosts, and to keep the feast of tabernacles.

Zechariah 14:Verse 17

17 And it shall be, [that] whoso will not come up of [all] the families of the earth unto Jerusalem to worship the King, the LORD of hosts, even upon them shall be no rain.

Zechariah 14:Verse 18

18 And if the family of Egypt go not up, and come not, that [have] no [rain]; there shall be the plague, wherewith the LORD will smite the heathen that come not up to keep the feast of tabernacles.

Zechariah 14:Verse 19

19 This shall be the punishment of Egypt, and the punishment of all nations that come not up to keep the feast of tabernacles.

Zechariah 14:Verse 20

20 In that day shall there be upon the bells of the horses, HOLINESS UNTO THE LORD; and the pots in the LORD'S house shall be like the bowls before the altar.

Zechariah 14:Verse 21

21 Yea, every pot in Jerusalem and in Judah shall be holiness unto the LORD of hosts: and all they that sacrifice shall come and take of them, and seethe therein: and in that day there shall be no more the Canaanite in the house of the LORD of hosts.

———————————

Malachi 4:Verse 2

2 But unto you that fear my name shall the Sun of righteousness arise with healing in his wings; and ye shall go forth, and grow up as calves of the stall.

Malachi 4:Verse 3

3 And ye shall tread down the wicked; for they shall be ashes under the soles of your feet in the day that I shall do [this], saith the LORD of hosts.

———————————

D&C 38:Verse 18

18 And I hold forth and deign to give unto you greater riches, even a land of promise, a land flowing with milk and honey, upon which there shall be no curse when the Lord cometh;

D&C 38:Verse 19

19 And I will give it unto you for the land of your inheritance, if you seek it with all your hearts.

D&C 38:Verse 20

20 And this shall be my covenant with you, ye shall have it for the land of your inheritance, and for the inheritance of your children forever, while the earth shall stand, and ye shall possess it again in eternity, no more to pass away.

D&C 38:Verse 21

21 But, verily I say unto you that in time ye shall have no king nor ruler, for I will be your king and watch over you.

D&C 38:Verse 22

22 Wherefore, hear my voice and follow me, and you shall be a free people, and ye shall have no laws but my laws when I come, for I am your lawgiver, and what can stay my hand?

D&C 45:Verse 58

58 And the earth shall be given unto them for an inheritance; and they shall multiply and wax strong, and their children shall grow up without sin unto salvation.

D&C 45:Verse 59

59 For the Lord shall be in their midst, and his glory shall be upon them, and he will be their king and their lawgiver.

D&C 63:Verse 50

50 And he that liveth when the Lord shall come, and hath kept the faith, blessed is he; nevertheless, it is appointed to him to die at the age of man.

D&C 63:Verse 51

51 Wherefore, children shall grow up until they become old; old men shall die; but they shall not sleep in the dust, but they shall be changed in the twinkling of an eye.

D&C 84:Verse 98

98 Until all shall know me, who remain, even from the least unto the greatest, and shall be filled with the knowledge of the Lord, and shall see eye to eye, and shall lift up their voice, and with the voice together sing this new song, saying:

D&C 97:Verse 18

18 And, now, behold, if Zion do these things she shall prosper, and spread herself and become very glorious, very great, and very terrible.

D&C 97:Verse 19

19 And the nations of the earth shall honor her, and shall say: Surely Zion is the city of our God, and surely Zion cannot fall, neither be moved out of her place, for God is there, and the hand of the Lord is there;

D&C 97:Verse 20

20 And he hath sworn by the power of his might to be her salvation and her high tower.

D&C 97:Verse 21

21 Therefore, verily, thus saith the Lord, let Zion rejoice, for this is Zion--THE PURE IN HEART; therefore, let Zion rejoice, while all the wicked shall mourn.

D&C 101:Verse 26

26 And in that day the enmity of man, and the enmity of beasts, yea, the enmity of all flesh, shall cease from before my face.

D&C 101:Verse 27

27 And in that day whatsoever any man shall ask, it shall be given unto him.

D&C 101:Verse 28

28 And in that day Satan shall not have power to tempt any man.

D&C 101:Verse 29

29 And there shall be no sorrow because there is no death.

D&C 101:Verse 30

30 In that day an infant shall not die until he is old; and his life shall be as the age of a tree;

D&C 101:Verse 31

31 And when he dies he shall not sleep, that is to say in the earth, but shall be changed in the twinkling of an eye, and shall be caught up, and his rest shall be glorious.

D&C 133:Verse 33

33 And they shall be filled with songs of everlasting joy.

D&C 133:Verse 34

34 Behold, this is the blessing of the everlasting God upon the tribes of Israel, and the richer blessing upon the head of Ephraim and his fellows.

D&C 133:Verse 35

35 And they also of the tribe of Judah, after their pain, shall be sanctified in holiness before the Lord, to dwell in his presence day and night, forever and ever.

D&C 133:Verse 57

57 And for this cause, that men might be made partakers of the glories which were to be revealed, the Lord sent forth the fulness of his gospel, his everlasting covenant, reasoning in plainness and simplicity--

D&C 133:Verse 58

58 To prepare the weak for those things which are coming on the earth, and for the Lord's errand in the day when the weak shall confound the wise, and the little one become a strong nation, and two shall put their tens of thousands to flight.

D&C 133:Verse 59

59 And by the weak things of the earth the Lord shall thrash the nations by the power of his Spirit.

D&C 133:Verse 60

60 And for this cause these commandments were given; they were commanded to be kept from the world in the day that they were given, but now are to go forth unto all flesh--

D&C 133:Verse 61

61 And this according to the mind and will of the Lord, who ruleth over all flesh.

D&C 133:Verse 62

62 And unto him that repenteth and sanctifieth himself before the Lord shall be given eternal life.

D&C 133:Verse 63

63 And upon them that hearken not to the voice of the Lord shall be fulfilled that which was written by the prophet Moses, that they should be cut off from among the people.

26b

The Blessing and Gathering of the Righteous
To Zion, and Jerusalem

The righteous saints will gather to the 'center stake' of Zion. The two headquarters of administration during the Millennium will be at Zion, and Jerusalem. To these religious centers Israel will gather and be governed, by a perfect theocracy. Often it is taught that Israel will be gathered from the four quarters of the earth before the millennium. However, the scriptures in conjunction with the events of the last days, and pre-millennial events imply that the mass conversion and gathering of the tribes of Israel will be during the thousand years. This is the time the gospel will roll forth and 'fill the whole earth' it is the millennium that opens the door for the full gathering of Israel. When the Savior stands on the Mount of Olives the majority of Judah realize that he is the Messiah, and not before. Again look to the Book of Mormon for the pattern of the last days.

Isaiah 49:Verse 1
1 LISTEN, O isles, unto me; and hearken, ye people, from far; The LORD hath called me from the womb; from the bowels of my mother hath he made mention of my name.

Isaiah 49:Verse 2
2 And he hath made my mouth like a sharp sword; in the shadow of his hand hath he hid me, and made me a polished shaft; in his quiver hath he hid me;

Isaiah 49:Verse 3
3 And said unto me, **Thou [art] my servant, O Israel, in whom I will be glorified**.

Isaiah 49:Verse 4
4 Then I said, I have laboured in vain, I have spent my strength for nought, and in vain: [yet] surely my judgment [is] with the LORD, and my work with my God.

Isaiah 49:Verse 5
5 And now, saith the LORD that formed me from the womb [to be] his servant, to bring Jacob again to him, Though Israel be not gathered, yet shall I be glorious in the eyes of the LORD, and my God shall be my strength.

Isaiah 49:Verse 6
6 And he said, It is a light thing that thou shouldest be my servant to raise up the tribes of Jacob, and to **restore the preserved of Israel: I will also give thee for a light to the Gentiles, that thou mayest be my salvation unto the end of the earth**.

Isaiah 49:Verse 7

7 Thus saith the LORD, the Redeemer of Israel, [and] his Holy One, to him whom man despiseth, to him whom the nation abhorreth, to a servant of rulers, Kings shall see and arise, princes also shall worship, because of the LORD that is faithful, [and] the Holy One of Israel, and he shall choose thee.

Isaiah 49:Verse 8

8 Thus saith the LORD, In an acceptable time have I heard thee, and in a day of salvation have **I helped thee: and I will preserve thee, and give thee for a covenant of the people, to establish the earth, to cause to inherit the desolate heritages;**

Isaiah 49:Verse 9

9 That thou mayest say to the prisoners, Go forth; to them that [are] in darkness, Shew yourselves. They shall feed in the ways, and their pastures [shall be] in all high places.

Isaiah 49:Verse 10

10 **They shall not hunger nor thirst; neither shall the heat nor sun smite them: for he that hath mercy on them shall lead them, even by the springs of water shall he guide them.**

Isaiah 49:Verse 11

11 **And I will make all my mountains a way, and my highways shall be exalted.**

Isaiah 49:Verse 12

12 Behold, these shall come from far: and, lo, these from the north and from the west; and these from the land of Sinim.

Isaiah 49:Verse 13

13 Sing, O heavens; and be joyful, O earth; and break forth into singing, O mountains: for the LORD hath comforted his people, and will have mercy upon his afflicted.

Isaiah 49:Verse 14

14 But Zion said, The LORD hath forsaken me, and my Lord hath forgotten me.

Isaiah 49:Verse 15

15 Can a woman forget her sucking child, that she should not have compassion on the son of her womb? yea, they may forget, yet will I not forget thee.

Isaiah 49:Verse 16

16 Behold, I have graven thee upon the palms of [my] hands; thy walls [are] continually before me.

Isaiah 49:Verse 17

17 Thy children shall make haste; thy destroyers and they that made thee waste shall go forth of thee.

Isaiah 49:Verse 18

18 Lift up thine eyes round about, and behold: all these gather themselves together, [and] come to thee. [As] I live, saith the LORD, thou shalt surely clothe thee with them all, as with an ornament, and bind them [on thee], as a bride [doeth].

Isaiah 49:Verse 19

19 For thy waste and thy desolate places, and the land of thy destruction, shall even now be too narrow by reason of the inhabitants, and they that swallowed thee up shall be far away.

Isaiah 49:Verse 20

20 The children which thou shalt have, after thou hast lost the other, shall say again in thine ears, The place [is] too strait for me: give place to me that I may dwell.

Isaiah 49:Verse 21

21 Then shalt thou say in thine heart, Who hath begotten me these, seeing I have lost my children, and am desolate, a captive, and removing to and fro? and who hath brought up these? Behold, I was left alone; these, where [had] they [been]?

Isaiah 49:Verse 22

22 **Thus saith the Lord GOD, Behold, I will lift up mine hand to the Gentiles, and set up my standard to the people: and they shall bring thy sons in [their] arms, and thy daughters shall be carried upon [their] shoulders**.

Isaiah 49:Verse 23

23 **And kings shall be thy nursing fathers, and their queens thy nursing mothers: they shall bow down to thee with [their] face toward the earth, and lick up the dust of thy feet; and thou shalt know that I [am] the LORD: for they shall not be ashamed that wait for me.**

Isaiah 49:Verse 24

24 Shall the prey be taken from the mighty, or the lawful captive delivered?

Isaiah 49:Verse 25

25 But thus saith the LORD, Even the captives of the mighty shall be taken away, and the prey of the terrible shall be delivered: for I will contend with him that contendeth with thee, and I will save thy children.

Isaiah 49:Verse 26

26 And I will feed them that oppress thee with their own flesh; and they shall be drunken with their own blood, as with sweet wine: and all flesh shall know that I the LORD [am] thy Saviour and thy Redeemer, the mighty One of Jacob.

———————————————————

Isaiah 54:Verse 1

1 SING, O barren, thou [that] didst not bear; break forth into singing, and cry aloud, thou [that] didst not travail with child: for more [are] the children of the desolate than the children of the married wife, saith the LORD.

Isaiah 54:Verse 2

2 Enlarge the place of thy tent, and let them stretch forth the curtains of thine habitations: spare not, lengthen thy cords, and strengthen thy stakes;

Isaiah 54:Verse 3

3 For thou shalt break forth on the right hand and on the left; and thy seed shall inherit the Gentiles, and make the desolate cities to be inhabited.

Isaiah 54:Verse 4

4 Fear not; for thou shalt not be ashamed: neither be thou confounded; for thou shalt not be put to shame: for thou shalt forget the shame of thy youth, and shalt not remember the reproach of thy widowhood any more.

Isaiah 54:Verse 5

5 For thy Maker [is] thine husband; the LORD of hosts [is] his name; and thy Redeemer the Holy One of Israel; The God of the whole earth shall he be called.

Isaiah 54:Verse 6

6 For the LORD hath called thee as a woman forsaken and grieved in spirit, and a wife of youth, when thou wast refused, saith thy God.

Isaiah 54:Verse 7

7 For a small moment have I forsaken thee; but with great mercies will I gather thee.

Isaiah 54:Verse 8

8 In a little wrath I hid my face from thee for a moment; but with everlasting kindness will I have mercy on thee, saith the LORD thy Redeemer.

Isaiah 54:Verse 9

9 For this [is as] the waters of Noah unto me: for [as] I have sworn that the waters of Noah should no more go over the earth; so have I sworn that I would not be wroth with thee, nor rebuke thee.

Isaiah 54:Verse 10

10 For the mountains shall depart, and the hills be removed; but my kindness shall not depart from thee, neither shall the covenant of my peace be removed, saith the LORD that hath mercy on thee.

Isaiah 54:Verse 11

11 O thou afflicted, tossed with tempest, [and] not comforted, behold, I will lay thy stones with fair colours, and lay thy foundations with sapphires.

Isaiah 54:Verse 12

12 And I will make thy windows of agates, and thy gates of carbuncles, and all thy borders of pleasant stones.

Isaiah 54:Verse 13

13 And all thy children [shall be] taught of the LORD; and great [shall be] the peace of thy children.

Isaiah 54:Verse 14

14 In righteousness shalt thou be established: thou shalt be far from oppression; for thou shalt not fear: and from terror; for it shall not come near thee.

Isaiah 54:Verse 15

15 Behold, they shall surely gather together, [but] not by me: whosoever shall gather together against thee shall fall for thy sake.

Isaiah 54:Verse 16

16 Behold, I have created the smith that bloweth the coals in the fire, and that bringeth forth an instrument for his work; and I have created the waster to destroy.

Isaiah 54:Verse 17

17 No weapon that is formed against thee shall prosper; and every tongue [that] shall rise against thee in judgment thou shalt condemn. This [is] the heritage of the servants of the LORD, and their righteousness [is] of me, saith the LORD.

———————————————

Isaiah 66:Verse 10

10 Rejoice ye with Jerusalem, and be glad with her, all ye that love her: rejoice for joy with her, all ye that mourn for her:

Isaiah 66:Verse 11

11 That ye may suck, and be satisfied with the breasts of her consolations; that ye may milk out, and be delighted with the abundance of her glory.

Isaiah 66:Verse 12

12 For thus saith the LORD, Behold, I will extend peace to her like a river, and the glory of the Gentiles like a flowing stream: then shall ye suck, ye shall be borne upon [her] sides, and be dandled upon [her] knees.

Isaiah 66:Verse 13

13 As one whom his mother comforteth, so will I comfort you; and ye shall be comforted in Jerusalem.

Isaiah 66:Verse 14

14 And when ye see [this], your heart shall rejoice, and your bones shall flourish like an herb: and the hand of the LORD shall be known toward his servants, and [his] indignation toward his enemies.

———————————————

Joel 2:Verse 32
32 And it shall come to pass, [that] whosoever shall call on the name of the LORD shall be delivered: **for in mount Zion and in Jerusalem shall be deliverance, as the LORD hath said, and in the remnant whom the LORD shall call.**

----

1 Nephi 22:Verse 24
24 And the time cometh speedily that the righteous must be led up as calves of the stall, and the Holy One of Israel must reign in dominion, and might, and power, and great glory.

1 Nephi 22:Verse 25
25 And **he gathereth his children from the four quarters of the earth; and he numbereth his sheep, and they know him; and there shall be one fold and one shepherd; and he shall feed his sheep, and in him they shall find pasture.**

----

3 Nephi 16:Verse 18
18 Thy watchmen shall lift up the voice; with the voice together shall they sing, **for they shall see eye to eye when the Lord shall bring again Zion.**

3 Nephi 16:Verse 19
19 **Break forth into joy, sing together, ye waste places of Jerusalem; for the Lord hath comforted his people, he hath redeemed Jerusalem.**

3 Nephi 16:Verse 20
20 The Lord hath made bare his holy arm in the eyes of all the nations; and all the ends of the earth shall see the salvation of God.

----

3 Nephi 20:Verse 22
22 And behold, this people will **I establish in this land, unto the fulfilling of the covenant which I made with your father Jacob; and it shall be a New Jerusalem. And the powers of heaven shall be in the midst of this people; yea, even I will be in the midst of you.**

----

3 Nephi 20:Verse 30
30 **And it shall come to pass that the time cometh, when the fulness of my gospel shall be preached unto them;**

3 Nephi 20:Verse 31
31 **And they shall believe in me, that I am Jesus Christ, the Son of God, and shall pray unto the Father in my name.**

3 Nephi 20:Verse 32
32 **Then shall their watchmen lift up their voice, and with the voice together shall they sing; for they shall see eye to eye.**

3 Nephi 20:Verse 33
33 **Then will the Father gather them together again, and give unto them Jerusalem for the land of their inheritance.**

3 Nephi 20:Verse 34
34 **Then shall they break forth into joy--Sing together, ye waste places of Jerusalem; for the Father hath comforted his people, he hath redeemed Jerusalem.**

3 Nephi 20:Verse 35
35 The Father hath made bare his holy arm in the eyes of all the nations; and all the ends of the earth shall see the salvation of the Father; and the Father and I are one.

3 Nephi 20:Verse 36
36 And then shall be brought to pass that which is written: **Awake, awake again, and put on thy strength, O Zion; put on thy beautiful garments, O Jerusalem, the holy city, for henceforth there shall no more come into thee the uncircumcised and the unclean.**

3 Nephi 20:Verse 37
37 Shake thyself from the dust; arise, sit down, O Jerusalem; loose thyself from the bands of thy neck, O captive daughter of Zion.

3 Nephi 20:Verse 38
38 For thus saith the Lord: Ye have sold yourselves for naught, and ye shall be redeemed without money.

3 Nephi 20:Verse 39
39 Verily, verily, I say unto you, **that my people shall know my name; yea, in that day they shall know that I am he that doth speak.**

3 Nephi 20:Verse 40
40 And then shall they say: How beautiful upon the mountains are the feet of him that bringeth good tidings unto them, that publisheth peace; that bringeth good tidings unto them of good, that publisheth salvation; that saith unto Zion: Thy God reigneth!

---

3 Nephi 21:Verse 22
22 **But if they will repent and hearken unto my words, and harden not their hearts, I will establish my church among them, and they shall come in unto the covenant and be numbered among this the remnant of Jacob, unto whom I have given this land for their inheritance;**

3 Nephi 21:Verse 23
23 And they shall assist my people, the remnant of Jacob, and also as many of the house of Israel as shall come, that they may build a city, which shall be called the New Jerusalem.

3 Nephi 21:Verse 24
24 **And then shall they assist my people that they may be gathered in, who are scattered upon all the face of the land, in unto the New Jerusalem.**

3 Nephi 21:Verse 25
25 And **then shall the power of heaven come down among them; and I also will be in the midst.**

Ether 13:Verse 3
3 And that **it was the place of the New Jerusalem, which should come down out of heaven, and the holy sanctuary of the Lord**.

Ether 13:Verse 4
4 Behold, **Ether saw the days of Christ, and he spake concerning a New Jerusalem upon this land.**

Ether 13:Verse 5
5 And he spake also concerning the house of Israel, and the Jerusalem from whence Lehi should come--after it should be destroyed it should be built up again, a holy city unto the Lord; wherefore, it could not be a new Jerusalem for it had been in a time of old; but it should be built up again, and become a holy city of the Lord; and it should be built unto the house of Israel.

Ether 13:Verse 6
6 And **that a New Jerusalem should be built up upon this land, unto the remnant of the seed of Joseph, for which things there has been a type.**

Ether 13:Verse 8
8 Wherefore, **the remnant of the house of Joseph shall be built upon this land; and it shall be a land of their inheritance; and they shall build up a holy city unto the Lord, like unto the Jerusalem of old; and they shall no more be confounded, until the end come when the earth shall pass away.**

Ether 13:Verse 11
11 **And then also cometh the Jerusalem of old; and the inhabitants thereof, blessed are they, for they have been washed in the blood of the Lamb; and they are they who were scattered and gathered in from the four quarters of the earth, and from the north countries, and are partakers of the fulfilling of the covenant which God made with their father, Abraham.**

D&C 45:Verse 66
66 And it shall be called the New Jerusalem, a land of peace, a city of refuge, a place of safety for the saints of the Most High God;

D&C 45:Verse 67

67 And **the glory of the Lord shall be there, and the terror of the Lord also shall be there, insomuch that the wicked will not come unto it, and it shall be called Zion.**

D&C 45:Verse 69

69 And there shall be gathered unto it out of every nation under heaven; and it shall be the only people that shall not be at war one with another.

D&C 45:Verse 70

70 And it shall be said among the wicked: Let us not go up to battle against Zion, for the inhabitants of Zion are terrible; wherefore we cannot stand.

D&C 45:Verse 71

71 And it shall come to pass that **the righteous shall be gathered out from among all nations, and shall come to Zion, singing with songs of everlasting joy.**

D&C 64:Verse 41

41 For, behold, I say unto you that Zion shall flourish, and the glory of the Lord shall be upon her;

D&C 64:Verse 42

42 And she shall be an ensign unto the people, and there shall come unto her out of every nation under heaven.

D&C 64:Verse 43

43 And the day shall come when the nations of the earth shall tremble because of her, and shall fear because of her terrible ones. The Lord hath spoken it. Amen.

D&C 101:Verse 13

13 And they that have been scattered shall be gathered.

D&C 101:Verse 14

14 And all they who have mourned shall be comforted.

D&C 101:Verse 15

15 And all they who have given their lives for my name shall be crowned.

D&C 101:Verse 16

16 Therefore, let your hearts be comforted concerning Zion; for all flesh is in mine hands; be still and know that I am God.

D&C 101:Verse 17

17 Zion shall not be moved out of her place, notwithstanding her children are scattered.

D&C 101:Verse 18

18 They that remain, and are pure in heart, shall return, and come to their inheritances, they and their children, with songs of everlasting joy, to build up the waste places of Zion--

D&C 101:Verse 19

19 And all these things that the prophets might be fulfilled.

D&C 133:Verse 21

21 **And he shall utter his voice out of Zion, and he shall speak from Jerusalem, and his voice shall be heard among all people;**

27

Satan is Loosed a Little Season

Revelation 20: 7-9

The patterns of Fourth Nephi, and Mormon sheds light on the reasons why, and how Satan gains another hold on the hearts of the children of men. Pride, and temporal prosperity lead to the inequality that flourishes in a Telestial society. The Book of Mormon tells of the reason for the total destruction, and fall of the Nephite culture in these words, the prophet Mormon sums up the power of Satan, as it lies in the hearts of man:

> 15 Now the cause of this iniquity of the people was this--Satan had great power, unto the stirring up of the people to do all manner of iniquity, and to the puffing them up with **pride**, tempting them to **seek for power, and authority**, and **riches,** and the **vain things of the world**. (3 Nephi 6:15)

These four things: 1) pride, 2) power and authority, 3) riches, and 4) the vain things of the world, These are the things that lead to the demise of the Nephites. What would 'prime time' television be without these four things? Are not our daily activities consumed with the satisfaction of these temporal and base desires. These are the things that Satan will tempt mankind with to destroy their souls. These things lay at the foundation of Babylon, and the so called Anti-Christ. Perhaps, the philosophies of Babylon is the great Anti-Christ so often spoken of in the discussions of the Last Days. Below in 3 Nephi we see what the spiritual climate was before the Millennium. and then we will look more closely at Mormon's commentary of the little season that follows:

> 10 But it came to pass in the twenty and ninth year **there began to be some disputings among the people**; and **some were lifted up unto pride and boastings because of their exceedingly great riches, yea, even unto great persecutions;**
> 11 For there were **many merchants in the land, and also many lawyers**, and many officers.
> 12 And the **people began to be distinguished by ranks, according to their riches and their chances for learning;** yea, some were ignorant because of their poverty, and others did receive great learning because of their riches.
> 13 **Some were lifted up in pride**, and others were exceedingly humble; some did **return railing for railing,** while others would receive railing and persecution and all manner of afflictions, and would not turn and revile again, but were humble and penitent before God.

14 And thus **there became a great inequality in all the land, insomuch that the church began to be broken up**; yea, insomuch that in the thirtieth year the church was broken up in all the land save it were among a few of the Lamanites who were converted unto the true faith; and they would not depart from it, for they were firm, and steadfast, and immovable, willing with all diligence to keep the commandments of the Lord.

15 Now **the cause of this iniquity of the people was this--Satan had great power, unto the stirring up of the people to do all manner of iniquity, and to the puffing them up with pride, tempting them to seek for power, and authority, and riches, and the vain things of the world.**

16 And **thus Satan did lead away the hearts of the people to do all manner of iniquity**; therefore they had enjoyed peace but a few years.

17 And thus, in the commencement of the thirtieth year--the people having been **delivered up for the space of a long time to be carried about by the temptations of the devil whithersoever he desired to carry them, and to do whatsoever iniquity he desired they should**--and thus in the commencement of this, the thirtieth year, they were in a state of awful wickedness.

18 Now **they did not sin ignorantly, for they knew the will of God concerning them, for it had been taught unto them; therefore they did wilfully rebel against God.** (3 Nephi 6:10-18)

During this 'little season' Satan must gather his forces, and fight the final battle against righteousness. A few questions must be asked. How long is this 'little season' in comparison to the existence of mankind on the earth? In The Book of Mormon it was about three hundred years. When does it begin? The last three hundred years of the millennium? Is it totally outside of the thousand year period? Will it take hundreds of years to go from righteousness to wickedness, or like the Nephites, ninety to one hundred and twenty years? On the outside, there might be any where from fifteen hundred to two thousand years or more, before the final destruction of the wicked, and the sanctification of the earth.

In Fourth Nephi we can see that after the millennial pattern there is a separation between the true followers and those seeking gain. Of course after the ministry of Christ everyone become converted, having all things in common, a time without any "ites," divisions or distinctions. Slowly the "little season" begins to creep in to the religious culture that remained from the visitation of their Savior.

24 And now, in this *two hundred and first year there began to be among them those who were lifted up in pride, such as the wearing of costly apparel, and all manner of fine pearls, and of the fine things of the world.

25 And from that time forth they did have their goods and their substance no more common among them.

26 And they began to be divided into classes; and they began to build up churches unto themselves to get gain, and began to deny the true church of Christ.

27 And it came to pass that when *two hundred and ten years had passed away there were many churches in the land; yea, there were many churches which professed to know the Christ, and yet they did deny the more parts of his gospel, insomuch that they did receive all manner of wickedness, and did administer that which was sacred unto him to whom it had been forbidden because of unworthiness.

28 And this church did multiply exceedingly because of iniquity, and because of the power of Satan who did get hold upon their hearts.

29 And again, there was another church which denied the Christ; and they did persecute the true church of Christ, because of their humility and their belief in Christ; and they did despise them because of the many miracles which were wrought among them.

30 Therefore they did exercise power and authority over the disciples of Jesus who did tarry with them, and they did cast them into prison; but by the power of the word of God, which was in them, the prisons were rent in twain, and they went forth doing mighty miracles among them.

31 Nevertheless, and notwithstanding all these miracles, the people did harden their hearts, and did seek to kill them, even as the Jews at Jerusalem sought to kill Jesus, according to his word.

34 Nevertheless, the people did harden their hearts, for they were led by many priests and false prophets to build up many churches, and to do all manner of iniquity. And they did smite upon the people of Jesus; but the people of Jesus did not smite again. And thus they did dwindle in unbelief and wickedness, from year to year, even until two hundred and thirty years had passed away.

35 And now it came to pass in this year, yea, in the *two hundred and thirty and first year, there was a great division among the people.

36 And it came to pass that in this year there arose a people who were called the Nephites, and they were true believers in Christ; and among them there were those who were called by the Lamanites—Jacobites, and Josephites, and Zoramites;

37 Therefore the true believers in Christ, and the true worshipers of Christ, (among whom were the three disciples of Jesus who should tarry) were called Nephites, and Jacobites, and Josephites, and Zoramites.

38 And it came to pass that they who rejected the gospel were called Lamanites, and Lemuelites, and Ishmaelites; and they did not dwindle in unbelief, but they did wilfully rebel against the gospel of Christ; and they did teach their children that they should not believe, even as their fathers, from the beginning, did dwindle.

39 And it was because of the wickedness and abomination of their fathers, even as it was in the beginning. And they were taught to hate the children of

God, even as the Lamanites were taught to hate the children of Nephi from the beginning. (4 Nephi 1:24-39)

Revelation 20:Verse 7

7 And **when the thousand years are expired, Satan shall be loosed out of his prison**,

Revelation 20:Verse 8

8 And shall go out **to deceive the nations** which are in the four quarters of the earth, Gog and Magog, **to gather them together to battle:** the number of whom [is] as the sand of the sea.

Revelation 20:Verse 9

9 And they went up on the breadth of the earth, **and compassed the camp of the saints about, and the beloved city: and fire came down from God out of heaven, and devoured them.**

D&C 29:Verse 22

22 And again, verily, verily, I say unto you that **when the thousand years are ended, and men again begin to deny their God, then will I spare the earth but for a little season;**

D&C 45:Verse 68

68 And it shall come to pass among the wicked, that every man that will not take his sword against his neighbor must needs flee unto Zion for safety.

D&C 63:Verse 32

32 I, the Lord, am angry with the wicked; I am holding my Spirit from the inhabitants of the earth.

D&C 63:Verse 33

33 I have sworn in my wrath, and decreed wars upon the face of the earth, and the wicked shall slay the wicked, and fear shall come upon every man;

D&C 63:Verse 34

34 And the saints also shall hardly escape; nevertheless, **I, the Lord, am with them, and will come down in heaven from the presence of my Father and consume the wicked with unquenchable fire.**

D&C 63:Verse 35

35 And behold, this is not yet, but by and by.

D&C 88:Verse 111

111 And then **he shall be loosed for a little season,** that he may gather together his armies

---

Daniel 12:Verse 1

1 AND at that time shall Michael stand up, the great prince which standeth for the children of thy people: and there shall be **a time of trouble, such as never was since there was a nation** [even] to that same time: and at that time thy people shall be delivered, every one that shall be found written in the book.

27a

Michael destroys the armies of Satan, and The Ancient of Days returns the Priesthood Authority to Christ

The responsibility of Michael (the Ancient of Days) in scripture is to control, and detect Satan. It is Michael who casts Satan out of the pre-earth life, and Michael who detects Satan when he appeared to Joseph Smith as an angel of light (D&C 128:20). In extra biblical texts Michael detects Satan when he appears to Abraham, also in the Books of Enoch, Michael's responsibilities includes control over Satan.

Michael is a position in the priesthood order of God. This position is filled by another while Michael is on the earth as Adam, the first man. Many ancient texts speak of Adam and his interaction with Michael, as the combat with Satan ensues in mortality.

Adam is Michael, the Ancient of Days, and as the first patriarch is responsible for the temporal and spiritual welfare of his posterity, which is all of humanity, and holds all the keys rights, and authority for that care which is a definition of the term "priesthood." These keys and authorities Adam will return to him whose power and authority it rightly belongs, when the need for that authority is no longer needed. (See the Discourse on Abbaton in the appendix)

Daniel 7:Verse 9
9 I beheld **till the thrones were cast down, and the Ancient of days did sit,** whose garment [was] white as snow, and the hair of his head like the pure wool: his throne [was like] the fiery flame, [and] his wheels [as] burning fire.

Daniel 7:Verse 10
10 A fiery stream issued and came forth from before him: thousand thousands ministered unto him, and ten thousand times ten thousand stood before him: **the judgment was set, and the books were opened.**

Daniel 7:Verse 13
13 I saw in the night visions, and, behold, [one] like **the Son of man came with the clouds of heaven, and came to the Ancient of days, and they brought him near before him.**

Daniel 7:Verse 14
14 And **there was given him dominion, and glory, and a kingdom**, that all people, nations, and languages, should serve him: his dominion [is] an everlasting dominion, which shall not pass away, and his kingdom [that] which shall not be destroyed.

D&C 88:Verse 112

112 And **Michael, the seventh angel, even the archangel, shall gather together his armies, even the hosts of heaven.**

D&C 88:Verse 113

113 And the **devil shall gather together his armies; even the hosts of hell, and shall come up to battle against Michael and his armies.**

D&C 88:Verse 114

114 And **then cometh the battle of the great God; and the devil and his armies shall be cast away into their own place, that they shall not have power over the saints any more at all.**

D&C 88:Verse 115

115 For **Michael shall fight their battles, and shall overcome him who seeketh the throne of him who sitteth upon the throne, even the Lamb.**

D&C 88:Verse 116

116 This is the glory of God, and the sanctified; and they shall not any more see death.

———————————————

D&C 116:Verse 1

1 SPRING Hill is named by the Lord Adam-ondi-Ahman, because, said he, it is the place where **Adam shall come to visit his people, or the Ancient of Days shall sit, as spoken of by Daniel the prophet.**

———————————————

28

Satan Cast into Outer Darkness

Revelation 20: 10

By the authority of the priesthood and in the Name of Jesus Christ, Michael casts Satan into the pit of outer darkness. This event trumpets the destruction of the wicked and the 'end of the world' as Joseph Smith Matthew declares.

Revelation 20:Verse 10

10 And the **devil that deceived them was cast into the lake of fire and brimstone,** where the beast and the false prophet [are], and shall be tormented day and night for ever and ever.

D&C 76:Verse 31

31 Thus saith the Lord concerning all those who know my power, and have been made partakers thereof, and suffered themselves through the power of the devil to be overcome, and to deny the truth and defy my power--

D&C 76:Verse 32

32 They are **they who are the sons of perdition**, of whom I say that it had been better for them never to have been born;

D&C 76:Verse 33

33 For they are vessels of wrath, **doomed to suffer the wrath of God**, with the devil and his angels in eternity;

D&C 76:Verse 34

34 Concerning whom I have said there is **no forgiveness in this world nor in the world to come--**

D&C 76:Verse 35

35 Having denied the Holy Spirit after having received it, and having denied the Only Begotten Son of the Father, having crucified him unto themselves and put him to an open shame.

D&C 76:Verse 36

36 **These are they who shall go away into the lake of fire and brimstone, with the devil and his angels--**

D&C 76:Verse 37
37 And **the only ones on whom the second death shall have any power;**

D&C 76:Verse 38
38 Yea, verily, the only ones who shall not be redeemed in the due time of the Lord, after the sufferings of his wrath. ─────────────

D&C 76:Verse 45
45 And the end thereof, neither the place thereof, nor their torment, no man knows;

D&C 76:Verse 46
46 Neither was it revealed, neither is, neither will be revealed unto man, except to them who are made partakers thereof;

D&C 76:Verse 47
47 Nevertheless, I, the Lord, show it by vision unto many, but straightway shut it up again;

D&C 76:Verse 48
48 Wherefore, the end, the width, the height, the depth, and the misery thereof, they understand not, neither any man except those who are ordained unto this condemnation.

───────────────

D&C 133:Verse 72
72 Wherefore, they sealed up the testimony and bound up the law, and ye were **delivered over unto darkness.**

D&C 133:Verse 73
73 **These shall go away into outer darkness**, where there is weeping, and wailing, and gnashing of teeth.

D&C 133:Verse 74
74 Behold the Lord your God hath spoken it. Amen.

───────────────

29

All are Judged out of the Books, The Second Death

Revelation 20: 11-15; 21: 8

With Satan put in his place the Judgment continues as the dead both great and small are judged from the books that have been written. The judgment is based on the works or character that man has developed during their life here on earth. As John the Revelator states 'according to their works.' not their belief, or church membership, but their 'works,' who they are, their character whither they be good or evil. The wicked will experience the second death, which is an eternal expulsion from the presence of God the Father. For they will "receive that which they are willing to receive."

Revelation 20:Verse 11
11 And I saw a great white throne, and him that sat on it, from whose face the earth and the heaven fled away; and there was found no place for them.

Revelation 20:Verse 12
12 And I saw **the dead, small and great, stand before God; and the books were opened: and another book was opened, which is [the book] of life: and the dead were judged out of those things which were written in the books, according to their works.**

Revelation 20:Verse 13
13 And the sea gave up the dead which were in it; and death and hell delivered up the dead which were in them: and **they were judged every man according to their works.**

Revelation 20:Verse 14
14 And death and hell were cast into the lake of fire. This is the second death.

Revelation 20:Verse 15
15 And whosoever was not found written in the book of life was cast into the lake of fire.

Revelation 21:Verse 8
8 But the fearful, and unbelieving, and the abominable, and murderers, and whoremongers, and sorcerers, and idolaters, and all liars, shall have their part in the lake which burneth with fire and brimstone: which is the second death.

Daniel 12:Verse 1

1 AND at that time shall **Michael stand up, the great prince which standeth for the children of thy people: and there shall be a time of trouble, such as never was since there was a nation [even] to that same time: and at that time thy people shall be delivered, every one that shall be found written in the book**.

Matthew 25:Verse 1

1 THEN shall **the kingdom of heaven be likened unto ten virgins, which took their lamps, and went forth to meet the bridegroom.**

Matthew 25:Verse 2

2 And five of them were wise, and five [were] foolish.

Matthew 25:Verse 3

3 They that [were] **foolish took their lamps, and took no oil with them:**

Matthew 25:Verse 4

4 But the **wise took oil in their vessels with their lamps**.

Matthew 25:Verse 5

5 While the **bridegroom tarried**, they all slumbered and slept.

Matthew 25:Verse 6

6 And at midnight there was a cry made, Behold, the **bridegroom cometh**; go ye out to meet him.

Matthew 25:Verse 7

7 Then all those virgins arose, and trimmed their lamps.

Matthew 25:Verse 8

8 And the foolish said unto the wise, **Give us of your oil;** for our lamps are gone out.

Matthew 25:Verse 9

9 But the wise answered, saying, [Not so]; lest there be not enough for us and you: but go ye rather to them that sell, and buy for yourselves.

Matthew 25:Verse 10

10 And while they went to buy, the bridegroom came; and they that were ready went in with him to the marriage: and the door was shut.

Matthew 25:Verse 11

11 **Afterward came also the other virgins, saying, Lord, Lord, open to us.**

Matthew 25:Verse 12

12 But he answered and said, Verily I say unto you, I know you not.

Matthew 25:Verse 13
13 Watch **therefore, for ye know neither the day nor the hour wherein the Son of man cometh.**

Matthew 25:Verse 14
14 For **[the kingdom of heaven is] as** a man travelling into a far country, [who] called his own servants, and delivered unto them his goods.

Matthew 25:Verse 15
15 And unto one he gave five talents, to another two, and to another one; to every man according to his several ability; and **straightway took his journey.**

Matthew 25:Verse 16
16 Then he that had received the five talents went and traded with the same, and made [them] other five talents.

Matthew 25:Verse 17
17 And likewise he that [had received] two, he also gained other two.

Matthew 25:Verse 18
18 But he that had received one went and digged in the earth, and hid his lord's money.

Matthew 25:Verse 19
19 **After a long time the lord of those servants cometh, and reckoneth with them.**

Matthew 25:Verse 20
20 And so he that had received five talents came and brought other five talents, saying, Lord, thou deliveredst unto me five talents: behold, I have gained beside them five talents more.

Matthew 25:Verse 21
21 **His lord said unto him, Well done, [thou] good and faithful servant: thou hast been faithful over a few things, I will make thee ruler over many things: enter thou into the joy of thy lord.**

Matthew 25:Verse 22
22 He also that had received two talents came and said, Lord, thou deliveredst unto me two talents: behold, I have gained two other talents beside them.

Matthew 25:Verse 23
23 His lord said unto him, **Well done, good and faithful servant; thou hast been faithful over a few things, I will make thee ruler over many things: enter thou into the joy of thy lord.**

Matthew 25:Verse 24
24 Then he which had received the one talent came and said, Lord, **I knew thee that thou art an hard man, reaping where thou hast not sown, and gathering where thou hast not strawed:**

Matthew 25:Verse 25
25 And I was afraid, and went and hid thy talent in the earth: lo, [there] thou hast [that is] thine.

Matthew 25:Verse 26

26 His lord answered and said unto him, **[Thou] wicked and slothful servant, thou knewest that I reap where I sowed not, and gather where I have not strawed**:

Matthew 25:Verse 27

27 Thou oughtest therefore to have put my money to the exchangers, and [then] at my coming I should have received mine own with usury.

Matthew 25:Verse 28

28 **Take therefore the talent from him, and give [it] unto him which hath ten talents.**

Matthew 25:Verse 29

29 **For unto every one that hath shall be given, and he shall have abundance: but from him that hath not shall be taken away even that which he hath.**

Matthew 25:Verse 30

30 **And cast ye the unprofitable servant into outer darkness: there shall be weeping and gnashing of teeth.**

Matthew 25:Verse 31

31 When the Son of man shall come in his glory, and all the holy angels with him, then shall he sit upon the throne of his glory:

Matthew 25:Verse 32

32 **And before him shall be gathered all nations: and he shall separate them one from another, as a shepherd divideth [his] sheep from the goats:**

Matthew 25:Verse 33

33 **And he shall set the sheep on his right hand, but the goats on the left.**

Matthew 25:Verse 34

34 Then shall the King **say unto them on his right hand, Come, ye blessed of my Father, inherit the kingdom prepared for you from the foundation of the world:**

The 'Oil' and the 'Talents' represent the same thing. Good Works. This separates the 'foolish' from the 'wise,' the 'good and faithful' from the 'wicked and slothful' and the 'sheep' from the 'goats' and the 'left hand' from the 'right hand.' This 'OIL' is described below. It is by this 'oil' that we will be judged from the books. As John says 'according to their works.' And as Christ explains 'For inasmuch as ye did it unto one of the least of these, ye did it unto me.'

Matthew 25:Verse 35

35 **For I was an hungred, and ye gave me meat: I was thirsty, and ye gave me drink: I was a stranger, and ye took me in:**

Matthew 25:Verse 36
36 Naked, and ye clothed me: I was sick, and ye visited me: I was in prison, and ye came unto me.

Matthew 25:Verse 37
37 Then shall the righteous answer him, saying, Lord, when saw we thee an hungred, and fed [thee]? or thirsty, and gave [thee] drink?

Matthew 25:Verse 38
38 When saw we thee a stranger, and took [thee] in? or naked, and clothed [thee]?

Matthew 25:Verse 39
39 Or when saw we thee sick, or in prison, and came unto thee?

Matthew 25:Verse 40
40 And the King shall answer and say unto them, Verily I say unto you, Inasmuch as ye have done [it] unto one of the least of these my brethren, ye have done [it] unto me.

Matthew 25:Verse 41
41 Then shall he say also unto them on the left hand, Depart from me, ye cursed, into everlasting fire, prepared for the devil and his angels:

Matthew 25:Verse 42
42 For I was an hungred, and ye gave me no meat: I was thirsty, and ye gave me no drink:

Matthew 25:Verse 43
43 I was a stranger, and ye took me not in: naked, and ye clothed me not: sick, and in prison, and ye visited me not.

Matthew 25:Verse 44
44 Then shall they also answer him, saying, Lord, when saw we thee an hungred, or athirst, or a stranger, or naked, or sick, or in prison, and did not minister unto thee?

Matthew 25:Verse 45
45 Then shall he answer them, saying, Verily I say unto you, Inasmuch as ye did [it] not to one of the least of these, ye did [it] not to me.

Matthew 25:Verse 46
46 And these shall go away into everlasting punishment: but the righteous into life eternal.

D&C 29:Verse 28
28 Wherefore I will say unto them--**Depart from me, ye cursed, into everlasting fire, prepared for the devil and his angels.**

D&C 29:Verse 29
29 And now, behold, I say unto you, **never at any time have I declared from mine own mouth that they should return, for where I am they cannot come, for they have no power.**

D&C 29:Verse 30

30 But **remember that all my judgments are not given unto men;** and as the words have gone forth out of my mouth even so shall they be fulfilled, that the first shall be last, and that the last shall be first in all things whatsoever I have created by the word of my power, which is the power of my Spirit.

D&C 88:Verse 100

100 And again, another trump shall sound, which is the third trump; and then come the spirits of men who are to be judged, and are found under condemnation;

D&C 88:Verse 101

101 And these are the rest of the dead; and they live not again until the thousand years are ended, neither again, until the end of the earth.

D&C 88:Verse 102

102 And another trump shall sound, which is the fourth trump, saying: There are found among those who are to remain until that great and last day, even the end, who shall remain filthy still.

Joseph Smith Matthew 1:Verse 51

51 But if that evil servant shall say in his heart: My lord delayeth his coming,

Joseph Smith Matthew 1:Verse 52

52 And shall begin to smite his fellow-servants, and to eat and drink with the drunken,

Joseph Smith Matthew 1:Verse 53

53 The lord of that servant shall come in a day when he looketh not for him, and in an hour that he is not aware of,

Joseph Smith Matthew 1:Verse 54

54 **And shall cut him asunder, and shall appoint him his portion with the hypocrites; there shall be weeping and gnashing of teeth.**

Joseph Smith Matthew 1:Verse 55

55 And **thus cometh the end of the wicked, according to the prophecy of Moses, saying: They shall be cut off from among the people; but the end of the earth is not yet, but by and by.**

30

A New Heaven and a New Earth

Revelation 21: 1

The first chapter in the Book of Genesis begins with the creation of the heaven and earth, and the last book in the Bible, ends with a 'new heaven' and 'new earth.' This is not coincidence. The earth will meet the measure of it's creation, and be sanctified as D&C 88 states. There will be a new heaven and a new earth for the earth will become a 'Urim and Thummim' and a home for those of celestial glory.

Revelation 21:Verse 1

1 AND I saw **a new heaven and a new earth:** for the first heaven and the first earth were passed away; and **there was no more sea.**

Isaiah 65:Verse 17

17 For, behold, **I create new heavens and a new earth:** and the former shall not be remembered, nor come into mind.

Isaiah 66:Verse 22

22 For as **the new heavens and the new earth, which I will make,** shall remain before me, saith the LORD, so shall your seed and your name remain.

Isaiah 66:Verse 23

23 And it shall come to pass, [that] from one new moon to another, and from one sabbath to another, shall all flesh come to worship before me, saith the LORD.

---

2 Peter 3:Verse 10

10 But the day of the Lord will come as a thief in the night; in the which **the heavens shall pass away with a great noise, and the elements shall melt with fervent heat, the earth also and the works that are therein shall be burned up.**

2 Peter 3:Verse 11

11 [Seeing] then [that] **all these things shall be dissolved,** what manner [of persons] ought ye to be in [all] holy conversation and godliness,

2 Peter 3:Verse 12

12 Looking for and hasting unto the coming of the day of God, **wherein the heavens being on fire shall be dissolved, and the elements shall melt with fervent heat?**

2 Peter 3:Verse 13

13 Nevertheless we, according to his promise, **look for new heavens and a new earth,** wherein dwelleth righteousness.

2 Peter 3:Verse 14

14 Wherefore, beloved, seeing that ye look for such things, be diligent that ye may be found of him in peace, without spot, and blameless.

Ether 13:Verse 9

9 And **there shall be a new heaven and a new earth;** and they shall be like unto the old save the old have passed away, and all things have become new.

D&C 29:Verse 23

23 And the end shall come, and **the heaven and the earth shall be consumed and pass away, and there shall be a new heaven and a new earth.**

D&C 29:Verse 24

24 For **all old things shall pass away, and all things shall become new, even the heaven and the earth**, and all the fulness thereof, both men and beasts, the fowls of the air, and the fishes of the sea;

D&C 29:Verse 25

25 And not one hair, neither mote, shall be lost, for it is the workmanship of mine hand.

D&C 63:Verse 20

20 Nevertheless, he that endureth in faith and doeth my will, the same shall overcome, and shall receive an inheritance upon the earth when the day of transfiguration shall come;

D&C 63:Verse 21

21 When **the earth shall be transfigured**, even according to the pattern which was shown unto mine apostles upon the mount; of which account the fulness ye have not yet received.

D&C 88: Verse 17

17 And the redemption of the soul is through him that quickeneth all things, in whose bosom it is decreed that **the poor and the meek of the earth shall inherit it.**

D&C 88:Verse 18

18 Therefore, **it must needs be sanctified from all unrighteousness, that it may be prepared for the celestial glory;**

D&C 88:Verse 19

19 For after **it hath filled the measure of its creation, it shall be crowned with glory, even with the presence of God the Father;**

D&C 88:Verse 20

20 That **bodies who are of the celestial kingdom may possess it forever and ever; for, for this intent was it made and created, and for this intent are they sanctified.**

D&C 88: Verse25

25 And again, verily I say unto you, **the earth abideth the law of a celestial kingdom, for it filleth the measure of its creation, and transgresseth not the law--**

D&C 88:Verse 26

26 Wherefore, **it shall be sanctified**; yea, notwithstanding it shall die, it shall be quickened again, and shall abide the power by which it is quickened, and **the righteous shall inherit it.**

D&C 101:Verse 25

25 And also that of element shall melt with fervent heat; and **all things shall become new,** that my knowledge and glory may dwell upon all the earth.

D&C 130:Verse 8

8 The place where God resides is a great Urim and Thummim.

D&C 130:Verse 9

9 **This earth, in its sanctified and immortal state, will be made like unto crystal and will be a Urim and Thummim** to the inhabitants who dwell thereon, whereby all things pertaining to an inferior kingdom, or all kingdoms of a lower order, will be manifest to those who dwell on it; and this earth will be Christ's.

D&C 130:Verse 10

10 Then the white stone mentioned in Revelation 2:17, will become a Urim and Thummim to each individual who receives one, whereby things pertaining to a higher order of kingdoms will be made known;

31

The New Jerusalem, The Holy City

Revelation 21: 2, 9-27

Jerusalem, the Holy City, sacred to Muslims, Christians, and Jews, is considered in myth the center of the earth or 'axis mundi' the beginning place of creation and the closest point between heaven and earth for communication with deity. The prophet Either speaks of the 'New Jerusalem' in the Book of Mormon at greater lengths than anywhere else in scripture. The Dead Sea Scrolls contain a long text called the 'Temple Scroll.' This text comprises a description of the heavenly city or the new Jerusalem as it will exist in glory and exaltation. The scroll not only is an expanded version of Ezekiel vision, but describes the Temple, and the ordinances preformed there.

It must be kept in mind that many scriptures that speak of the New Jerusalem do so with the idea that the New Jerusalem is on the American Continent, and is the Zion that will exist during the Millennium. However, this section in revelation is the 'Holy City of God' that will exist on the sanctified earth and be the celestial kingdom. The scriptures below will include those that speak of the 'New Jerusalem' both during the millennium and in the eternal worlds. This chapter of Revelation is the Holy City after the end of the world.

Revelation 21:Verse 2
2 And I John saw the holy city, new Jerusalem, coming down from God out of heaven, prepared as a bride adorned for her husband.

Revelation 21:Verse 9
9 And there came unto me one of the seven angels which had the seven vials full of the seven last plagues, and talked with me, saying, Come hither, **I will shew thee the bride, the Lamb's wife.**

Revelation 21:Verse 10
10 And he carried me away in the spirit to a great and high mountain, and **shewed me that great city, the holy Jerusalem, descending out of heaven from God,**

Revelation 21:Verse 11
11 Having the glory of God: and her light [was] like unto a stone most precious, even like a jasper stone, clear as crystal;

Revelation 21:Verse 12

12 And had a wall great and high, [and] had twelve gates, and at the gates twelve angels, and names written thereon, which are [the names] of the twelve tribes of the children of Israel:

Revelation 21:Verse 13

13 On the east three gates; on the north three gates; on the south three gates; and on the west three gates.

Revelation 21:Verse 14

14 And the wall of the city had twelve foundations, and in them the names of the twelve apostles of the Lamb.

Revelation 21:Verse 15

15 And he that talked with me had a golden reed to measure the city, and the gates thereof, and the wall thereof.

Revelation 21:Verse 16

16 And the city lieth foursquare, and the length is as large as the breadth: and he measured the city with the reed, twelve thousand furlongs. The length and the breadth and the height of it are equal.

Revelation 21:Verse 17

17 And he measured the wall thereof, an hundred [and] forty [and] four cubits, [according to] the measure of a man, that is, of the angel.

Revelation 21:Verse 18

18 And the building of the wall of it was [of] jasper: and the city [was] pure gold, like unto clear glass.

Revelation 21:Verse 19

19 And the foundations of the wall of the city [were] garnished with all manner of precious stones. The first foundation [was] jasper; the second, sapphire; the third, a chalcedony; the fourth, an emerald;

Revelation 21:Verse 20

20 The fifth, sardonyx; the sixth, sardius; the seventh, chrysolite; the eighth, beryl; the ninth, a topaz; the tenth, a chrysoprasus; the eleventh, a jacinth; the twelfth, an amethyst.

Revelation 21:Verse 21

21 And the twelve gates [were] twelve pearls; every several gate was of one pearl: and the street of the city [was] pure gold, as it were transparent glass.

Revelation 21:Verse 22

22 And I saw no temple therein: for the Lord God Almighty and the Lamb are the temple of it.

Revelation 21:Verse 23

23 And the city had no need of the sun, neither of the moon, to shine in it: for the glory of God did lighten it, and the Lamb [is] the light thereof.

Revelation 21:Verse 24

24 And the nations of them which are saved shall walk in the light of it: and the kings of the earth do bring their glory and honour into it.

Revelation 21:Verse 25

25 And the gates of it shall not be shut at all by day: for there shall be no night there.

Revelation 21:Verse 26

26 And they shall bring the glory and honour of the nations into it.

Revelation 21:Verse 27

27 And there shall in no wise enter into it any thing that defileth, neither [whatsoever] worketh abomination, or [maketh] a lie: but they which are written in the Lamb's book of life.

Isaiah 65:Verse 18

18 But be ye glad and rejoice for ever [in that] which I create: for, behold, **I create Jerusalem a rejoicing, and her people a joy.**

Isaiah 65:Verse 19

19 And I will rejoice in Jerusalem, and joy in my people: and the voice of weeping shall be no more heard in her, nor the voice of crying.

Zechariah 2:Verse 1

1 I lifted up mine eyes again, and looked, and behold a man with a measuring line in his hand.

Zechariah 2:Verse 2

2 Then said I, Whither goest thou? And he said unto me, To measure Jerusalem, to see what [is] the breadth thereof, and what [is] the length thereof.

Zechariah 2:Verse 3

3 And, behold, the angel that talked with me went forth, and another angel went out to meet him,

Zechariah 2:Verse 4

4 And said unto him, Run, speak to this young man, saying, Jerusalem shall be inhabited [as] towns without walls for the multitude of men and cattle therein:

Zechariah 2:Verse 5

5 For I, saith the LORD, will be unto her a wall of fire round about, and will be the glory in the midst of her.

---

3 Nephi 20:Verse 20

20 And it shall come to pass, saith the Father, that the sword of my justice shall hang over them at that day; and except they repent it shall fall upon them, saith the Father, yea, even upon all the nations of the Gentiles.

3 Nephi 20:Verse 21

21 And it shall come to pass that **I will establish my people, O house of Israel.**

3 Nephi 20:Verse 22

22 And behold, this people will I establish in this land, unto the fulfilling of the covenant which I made with your father Jacob; and **it shall be a New Jerusalem. And the powers of heaven shall be in the midst of this people; yea, even I will be in the midst of you.**

---

3 Nephi 21:Verse 22

22 But if they will repent and hearken unto my words, and harden not their hearts, I will establish my church among them, and they shall come in unto the covenant and be numbered among this the remnant of Jacob, unto whom I have given this land for their inheritance;

3 Nephi 21:Verse 23

23 And they shall assist my people, the remnant of Jacob, **and also as many of the house of Israel as shall come, that they may build a city, which shall be called the New Jerusalem.**

3 Nephi 21:Verse 24

24 And **then shall they assist my people that they may be gathered in, who are scattered upon all the face of the land, in unto the New Jerusalem.**

3 Nephi 21:Verse 25

25 And then shall the power of heaven come down among them; and I also will be in the midst.

Ether 13:Verse 2

2 For behold, they rejected all the words of Ether; for he truly told them of all things, from the beginning of man; and that after the waters had receded from off the face of this land it became a choice land above all other lands, a chosen land of the Lord; wherefore the Lord would have that all men should serve him who dwell upon the face thereof;

Ether 13:Verse 3

3 And that **it was the place of the New Jerusalem, which should come down out of heaven, and the holy sanctuary of the Lord.**

Ether 13:Verse 4

4 Behold, Ether saw the days of Christ, and he spake concerning a New Jerusalem upon this land.

Ether 13:Verse 5

5 And he spake also concerning the house of Israel, and the Jerusalem from whence Lehi should come--after it should be destroyed it should be built up again, a holy city unto the Lord; wherefore, it could not be a new Jerusalem for it had been in a time of old; but it should be built up again, and become a holy city of the Lord; and it should be built unto the house of Israel.

Ether 13:Verse 6

6 And that a New Jerusalem should be built up upon this land, unto the remnant of the seed of Joseph, for which things there has been a type.

Ether 13:Verse 7

7 For as Joseph brought his father down into the land of Egypt, even so he died there; wherefore, the Lord brought a remnant of the seed of Joseph out of the land of Jerusalem, that he might be merciful unto the seed of Joseph that they should perish not, even as he was merciful unto the father of Joseph that he should perish not.

Ether 13:Verse 8

8 Wherefore, the remnant of **the house of Joseph shall be built upon this land; and it shall be a land of their inheritance; and they shall build up a holy city unto the Lord, like unto the Jerusalem of old; and they shall no more be confounded, until the end come when the earth shall pass away.**

Ether 13:Verse 9

9 And *there shall be a new heaven and a new earth; and they shall be like unto the old save the old have passed away, and all things have become new.*

Ether 13:Verse 10

10 And then cometh the New Jerusalem; **and blessed are they who dwell therein, for it is they whose garments are white through the blood of the Lamb; and they are they who are numbered among the remnant of the seed of Joseph, who were of the house of Israel.**

Ether 13:Verse 11

11 And then also cometh the Jerusalem of old; and the inhabitants thereof, blessed are they, for they have been washed in the blood of the Lamb; and they are they who were scattered and gathered in from the four quarters of the earth, and from the north countries, and are partakers of the fulfilling of the covenant which God made with their father, Abraham.

Ether 13:Verse 12

12 And when these things come, bringeth to pass the scripture which saith, there are they who were first, who shall be last; and there are they who were last, who shall be first.

Ether 13:Verse 10

10 And **then cometh the New Jerusalem; and blessed are they who dwell therein, for it is they whose garments are white through the blood of the Lamb; and they are they who are numbered among the remnant of the seed of Joseph, who were of the house of Israel.**

D&C 42:Verse 8

8 And from this place ye shall go forth into the regions westward; and inasmuch as ye shall find them that will receive you ye shall build up my church in every region--

D&C 42:Verse 9

9 Until the time shall come when it shall be revealed unto you from on high, **when the city of the New Jerusalem shall be prepared, that ye may be gathered in one, that ye may be my people and I will be your God.**

D&C 42:Verse 35

35 And for the purpose of purchasing lands for the public benefit of the church, and building houses of worship, and building up of the New Jerusalem which is hereafter to be revealed--

D&C 42:Verse 36

36 That my covenant people may be gathered in one in that day when I shall come to my temple. And this I do for the salvation of my people.

D&C 45:Verse 66

66 And it shall be called **the New Jerusalem, a land of peace, a city of refuge, a place of safety for the saints of the Most High God;**

D&C 45:Verse 67

67 And the **glory of the Lord shall be there, and the terror of the Lord also shall be there,** insomuch that the wicked will not come unto it, and it shall be called Zion.

D&C 84:Verse 2

2 Yea, the word of the Lord concerning his church, established in the last days for the restoration of his people, as he has spoken by the mouth of his prophets, and for **the gathering of his saints to stand upon Mount Zion, which shall be the city of New Jerusalem.**

D&C 84:Verse 3

3 Which city shall be built, beginning at the temple lot, which is appointed by the finger of the Lord, in the western boundaries of the State of Missouri, and dedicated by the hand of Joseph Smith, Jun., and others with whom the Lord was well pleased.

D&C 84:Verse 4

4 Verily this is the word of the Lord, **that the city New Jerusalem shall be built by the gathering of the saints,** beginning at this place, even the place of the temple, which temple shall be reared in this generation.

D&C 84:Verse 5

5 For verily this generation shall not all pass away until an house shall be built unto the Lord, and a cloud shall rest upon it, which cloud shall be even the glory of the Lord, which shall fill the house.

D&C 133:Verse 56

56 And the graves of the saints shall be opened; and they shall come forth and stand on the right hand of the Lamb, when he shall stand upon Mount Zion, and upon the holy city, the New Jerusalem; and they shall sing the song of the Lamb, day and night forever and ever.

Moses 7:Verse 62

62 And righteousness will I send down out of heaven; and truth will I send forth out of the earth, to bear testimony of mine Only Begotten; his resurrection from the dead; yea, and also the resurrection of all men; and righteousness and truth will I cause to sweep the earth as with a flood, to gather out mine elect from the four quarters of the earth, unto a place which I shall prepare, an Holy City, that my people may gird up their loins, and be looking forth for the time of my coming; for there shall be my tabernacle, and it shall be called Zion, a New Jerusalem.

Moses 7:Verse 63

63 And the Lord said unto Enoch: Then shalt thou and all thy city meet them there, and we will receive them into our bosom, and they shall see us; and we will fall upon their necks, and they shall fall upon our necks, and we will kiss each other;

Moses 7:Verse 64

64 And there shall be mine abode, and it shall be Zion, which shall come forth out of all the creations which I have made; and for the space of a thousand years the earth shall rest.

32

Exaltation in the Presence of God

Revelation
15: 2-3
7: 9-17
14: 1-5
21: 3-7

The doctrine of exaltation is centered in, and lies at the foundation of all scripture. The three-fold mission of the church has only one goal and that is to provide the ordinances of exaltation. We proclaim the gospel' for temple work. 'Perfect the saints' to be worthy for the reality of the blessings of the temple, and we 'redeem the dead' by doing their temple work. Thus, the three-fold mission is to provide the ordinances of exaltation received in the temple to every individual that has ever lived upon this earth. This concept and doctrine is the foundation of all scripture, and is the civilizing factor of mankind. All scripture has as it's goal, to direct mankind to exaltation. Moses teaches that the work and glory of the Father is to bring to pass immortality and eternal life of mankind. The immortality will come unconditionally by the power of the resurrection of Jesus Christ. However, eternal life is conditional and can come only by virtue of the atonement, choice, and ordinance. God's 'work' is salvation through Jesus Christ; His glory on the other hand, is our exaltation.

This exaltation, is to become an "heir, and joint heir with Jesus Christ" which, is to have the blessings, glory, and a life like the Savior has. The D&C makes the statement: And he that receiveth my Father receiveth my Father's kingdom; *therefore all that my Father hath shall be given unto him*. (D&C 84: Verse 38; italics added). To stand in the presence of God is to endure his glory, and to endure his glory we must be like him, to be encircled about eternally in the arms of his love, as we are embraced by our Eternal Father, and be given the power, and glory that makes God, God. All scripture teaches of exaltation, and all ordinances prepare for exaltation. The ordinances of the temple, are the ordinances of the Afirst born@ and all must become as a first born unto God to inherit all that the Father hath in glory and exaltation, thus, becoming a joint heir with Jesus Christ.

––––––––––––––

Revelation 15:Verse 2
2 And I saw as it were **a sea of glass mingled with fire: and them that had gotten the victory over the beast, and over his image, and over his mark, [and] over the number of his name, stand on the sea of glass, having the harps of God.**

Revelation 15:Verse 3

3 And they sing the song of Moses the servant of God, and the song of the Lamb, saying, Great and marvellous [are] thy works, Lord God Almighty; just and true [are] thy ways, thou King of saints.

Revelation 7:Verse 9

9 After this I beheld, and, lo, a great multitude, which no man could number, of all nations, and kindreds, and people, and tongues, stood before the throne, and before the Lamb, clothed with white robes, and palms in their hands;

Revelation 7:Verse 10

10 And cried with a loud voice, saying, Salvation to our God which sitteth upon the throne, and unto the Lamb.

Revelation 7:Verse 11

11 And all the angels stood round about the throne, and [about] the elders and the four beasts, and fell before the throne on their faces, and worshipped God,

Revelation 7:Verse 12

12 Saying, Amen: Blessing, and glory, and wisdom, and thanksgiving, and honour, and power, and might, [be] unto our God for ever and ever. Amen.

Revelation 7:Verse 13

13 And one of the elders answered, saying unto me, What are these which are arrayed in white robes? and whence came they?

Revelation 7:Verse 14

14 And I said unto him, Sir, thou knowest. And he said to me, **These are they which came out of great tribulation, and have washed their robes, and made them white in the blood of the Lamb.**

Revelation 7:Verse 15

15 Therefore are they before the throne of God, and serve him day and night in his temple: and he that sitteth on the throne shall dwell among them.

Revelation 7:Verse 16

16 They shall hunger no more, neither thirst any more; neither shall the sun light on them, nor any heat.

Revelation 7:Verse 17

17 For the Lamb which is in the midst of the throne shall feed them, and shall lead them unto living fountains of waters: and God shall wipe away all tears from their eyes.

Revelation 14:Verse 1

1 AND I looked, and, lo, a Lamb stood on the mount Sion, and with him an hundred forty [and] four thousand, having his Father's name written in their foreheads.

Revelation 14:Verse 2

2 And I heard a voice from heaven, as the voice of many waters, and as the voice of a great thunder: and I heard the voice of harpers harping with their harps:

Revelation 14:Verse 3

3 And they sung as it were a new song before the throne, and before the four beasts, and the elders: and no man could learn that song but the hundred [and] forty [and] four thousand, which were redeemed from the earth.

Revelation 14:Verse 4

4 These are they which were not defiled with women; for they are virgins. These are they which follow the Lamb whithersoever he goeth. These were redeemed from among men, [being] the firstfruits unto God and to the Lamb.

Revelation 14:Verse 5

5 And in their mouth was found no guile: for they are without fault before the throne of God.

Revelation 21:Verse 3

3 And I heard a great voice out of heaven saying, Behold, the tabernacle of God [is] with men, and he will dwell with them, and they shall be his people, and God himself shall be with them, [and be] their God.

Revelation 21:Verse 4

4 And God shall wipe away all tears from their eyes; and there shall be no more death, neither sorrow, nor crying, neither shall there be any more pain: for the former things are passed away.

Revelation 21:Verse 5

5 And he that sat upon the throne said, Behold, I make all things new. And he said unto me, Write: for these words are true and faithful.

Revelation 21:Verse 6

6 And he said unto me, It is done. I am Alpha and Omega, the beginning and the end. I will give unto him that is athirst of the fountain of the water of life freely.

Revelation 21:Verse 7

7 He that overcometh shall inherit all things; and I will be his God, and he shall be my son.

D&C 77:Verse 1

1 Q. What is the sea of glass spoken of by John, 4th chapter, and 6th verse of the Revelation?
A. It is the earth, in its sanctified, immortal, and eternal state.

D&C 88:Verse 17

17 And the redemption of the soul is through him that quickeneth all things, in whose bosom it is decreed that the poor and the meek of the earth shall inherit it.

D&C 88:Verse 18

18 Therefore, it must needs be sanctified from all unrighteousness, that it may be prepared for the celestial glory;

D&C 88:Verse 19

19 For after it hath filled the measure of its creation, it shall be crowned with glory, even with the presence of God the Father;

D&C 88:Verse 20

20 That bodies who are of the celestial kingdom may possess it forever and ever; for, for this intent was it made and created, and for this intent are they sanctified.

D&C 88:Verse 25

25 And again, verily I say unto you, the earth abideth the law of a celestial kingdom, for it filleth the measure of its creation, and transgresseth not the law--

D&C 88:Verse 26

26 Wherefore, it shall be sanctified; yea, notwithstanding it shall die, it shall be quickened again, and shall abide the power by which it is quickened, and the righteous shall inherit it.

D&C 88:Verse 107

107 And then shall the angels be crowned with the glory of his might, and the saints shall be filled with his glory, and receive their inheritance and be made equal with him.

D&C 130:Verse 2

2 And that same sociality which exists among us here will exist among us there, only it will be coupled with eternal glory, which glory we do not now enjoy.

D&C 130:Verse 7

7 But they reside in the presence of God, on a globe like a sea of glass and fire, where all things for their glory are manifest, past, present, and future, and are continually before the Lord.

D&C 130:Verse 8

8 The place where God resides is a great Urim and Thummim.

D&C 130:Verse 9

9 This earth, in its sanctified and immortal state, will be made like unto crystal and will be a Urim and Thummim to the inhabitants who dwell thereon, whereby all things pertaining to an inferior kingdom, or all kingdoms of a lower order, will be manifest to those who dwell on it; and this earth will be Christ's.

_____

33

Life in the Celestial City

Revelation 22: 1-5

What will be doing in the eternities? It was Martin Luther who made the statement when asked; 'what was God doing before he created the world?' Luther responded, 'creating a hell for people who asked that question.' There will be no shortage of things to do in the eternities for the exalted. The Apostle John here describes the worship of the righteous as they give glory to the Father and Son.

Revelation 22:Verse 1

1 AND he shewed me a pure river of water of life, clear as crystal, proceeding out of the throne of God and of the Lamb.

Revelation 22:Verse 2

2 In the midst of the street of it, and on either side of the river, [was there] the tree of life, which bare twelve [manner of] fruits, [and] yielded her fruit every month: and the leaves of the tree [were] for the healing of the nations.

Revelation 22:Verse 3

3 And there shall be no more curse: but the throne of God and of the Lamb shall be in it; and his servants shall serve him:

Revelation 22:Verse 4

4 And they shall see his face; and his name [shall be] in their foreheads.

Revelation 22:Verse 5

5 And there shall be no night there; and they need no candle, neither light of the sun; for the Lord God giveth them light: and they shall reign for ever and ever.

D&C 132:Verse 19

19 And again, verily I say unto you, if a man marry a wife by my word, which is my law, and by the new and everlasting covenant, and it is sealed unto them by the Holy Spirit of promise, by him who is anointed, unto whom I have appointed this power and the keys of this priesthood; and it shall be said unto them--Ye shall come forth in the first resurrection; and if it be after the first resurrection, in the next resurrection; and shall inherit thrones, kingdoms, principalities, and powers, dominions, all heights and depths--then shall it be written in the Lamb's Book of Life,

that he shall commit no murder whereby to shed innocent blood, and if ye abide in my covenant, and commit no murder whereby to shed innocent blood, it shall be done unto them in all things whatsoever my servant hath put upon them, in time, and through all eternity; and shall be of full force when they are out of the world; and they shall pass by the angels, and the gods, which are set there, to their exaltation and glory in all things, as hath been sealed upon their heads, which glory shall be a fulness and a continuation of the seeds forever and ever.

D&C 132:Verse 20
 20 Then shall they be gods, because they have no end; therefore shall they be from everlasting to everlasting, because they continue; then shall they be above all, because all things are subject unto them. Then shall they be gods, because they have all power, and the angels are subject unto them.

D&C 132:Verse 21
 21 Verily, verily, I say unto you, except ye abide my law ye cannot attain to this glory.

34

These Sayings are Faithful and True

Revelation 22: 6-7, 18-19

These few verses contain the testimony of John the Revelator as well as that of Jesus Christ the Son of the Living God. The things written in the Book of Revelation are true without excuse or understanding. This testimony puts the ball in our court we must prove it, and try to understand it by using the voices of the prophets who speak from the dust in the standard of scripture, and the modern day prophets.

Revelation 22:Verse 6

6 And he said unto me, These sayings [are] faithful and true: and the Lord God of the holy prophets sent his angel to shew unto his servants the things which must shortly be done.

Revelation 22:Verse 7

7 Behold, I come quickly: blessed [is] he that keepeth the sayings of the prophecy of this book.

Revelation 22:Verse 18

18 For I testify unto every man that heareth the words of the prophecy of this book, If any man shall add unto these things, God shall add unto him the plagues that are written in this book:

Revelation 22:Verse 19

19 And if any man shall take away from the words of the book of this prophecy, God shall take away his part out of the book of life, and out of the holy city, and [from] the things which are written in this book.

Isaiah 14:Verse 24
24 The LORD of hosts hath sworn, saying, **Surely as I have thought, so shall it come to pass; and as I have purposed, [so] shall it stand:**

Isaiah 14:Verse 26
26 This [is] the purpose that is purposed upon the whole earth: and this [is] the hand that is stretched out upon all the nations.

Isaiah 14:Verse 27

27 **For the LORD of hosts hath purposed, and who shall disannul [it]? and his hand [is] stretched out, and who shall turn it back?**

D&C 1: Verse 37

37 **Search these commandments, for they are true and faithful, and the prophecies and promises which are in them shall all be fulfilled.**

D&C 1:Verse 38

38 **What I the Lord have spoken, I have spoken, and I excuse not myself; and though the heavens and the earth pass away, my word shall not pass away, but shall all be fulfilled, whether by mine own voice or by the voice of my servants, it is the same.**

D&C 1:Verse 39

39 For behold, and lo, the Lord is God, and the Spirit beareth record, **and the record is true, and the truth abideth forever and ever. Amen.**

35

Instructions to John

Revelation 22: 8-11

Like Nephi, John is given instruction about the vision that he has seen and the record that is to be kept. This book is not to be sealed like parts of the Book of Mormon for the 'time is at hand' and the sayings are true. In the Inspired Version of Mathew Chapter Twenty Four below, the Lord gives the clues, that we should be looking for.

Revelation 22:Verse 8
8 And I John saw these things, and heard [them]. And when I had heard and seen, I fell down to worship before the feet of the angel which shewed me these things.

Revelation 22:Verse 9
9 Then saith he unto me, See [thou do it] not: for I am thy fellowservant, and of thy brethren the prophets, and of them which keep the sayings of this book: worship God.

Revelation 22:Verse 10
10 And he saith unto me, Seal not the sayings of the prophecy of this book: for the time is at hand.

Revelation 22:Verse 11
11 He that is unjust, let him be unjust still: and he which is filthy, let him be filthy still: and he that is righteous, let him be righteous still: and he that is holy, let him be holy still.

---

1 Nephi 14:Verse 20
20 And the angel said unto me: **Behold one of the twelve apostles of the Lamb.**

1 Nephi 14:Verse 21
21 Behold, **he shall see and write the remainder of these things; yea, and also many things which have been.**

1 Nephi 14:Verse 22
22 And **he shall also write concerning the end of the world.**

1 Nephi 14:Verse 23

23 Wherefore, **the things which he shall write are just and true; and behold they are written in the book which thou beheld proceeding out of the mouth of the Jew; and at the time they proceeded out of the mouth of the Jew, or, at the time the book proceeded out of the mouth of the Jew, the things which were written were plain and pure, and most precious** *and easy to the understanding of all men.*

1 Nephi 14:Verse 24

24 And behold, **the things which this apostle of the Lamb shall write are many things which thou hast seen; and behold, the remainder shalt thou see.**

1 Nephi 14:Verse 25

25 But the things which thou shalt see hereafter thou shalt not write; for the Lord God hath ordained the apostle of the Lamb of God that he should write them.

1 Nephi 14:Verse 26

26 And also others who have been, to them hath he shown all things, and they have written them; and they are sealed up to come forth in their purity, according to the truth which is in the Lamb, in the own due time of the Lord, unto the house of Israel.

1 Nephi 14:Verse 27

27 And I, Nephi, heard and bear record, that the name of the apostle of the Lamb was John, according to the word of the angel.

1 Nephi 14:Verse 28

28 And behold, I, Nephi, am forbidden that I should write the remainder of the things which I saw and heard; wherefore the things which I have written sufficeth me; and I have written but a small part of the things which I saw.

Joseph Smith Matthew 1:Verse 36

36 And, as I said before, after the tribulation of those days, and the powers of the heavens shall be shaken, then shall appear the sign of the Son of Man in heaven, and then shall all the tribes of the earth mourn; and they shall see the Son of Man coming the clouds of heaven, with power and great glory;

Joseph Smith Matthew 1:Verse 37

37 And **whoso treasureth up my word, shall not be deceived, for the Son of Man shall come**, and he shall send his angels before him with the great sound of a trumpet, and they shall gather together the remainder of his elect from the four winds, from one end of heaven to the other.

Joseph Smith Matthew 1:Verse 38

38 Now **learn a parable of the fig-tree--When its branches are yet tender, and it begins to put forth leaves, you know that summer is nigh at hand;**

Joseph Smith Matthew 1:Verse 39

39 So likewise, mine elect, **when they shall see all these things, they shall know that he is near**, even at the doors;

Joseph Smith Matthew 1:Verse 40

40 **But of that day, and hour, no one knoweth; no, not the angels of God in heaven, but my Father only.**

Joseph Smith Matthew 1:Verse 41

41 But as it was in the days of Noah, so it shall be also at the coming of the Son of Man;

Joseph Smith Matthew 1:Verse 42

42 For it shall be with them, as it was in the days which were before the flood; for until the day that Noah entered into the ark they were eating and drinking, marrying and giving in marriage;

Business as usual.

Joseph Smith Matthew 1:Verse 43

43 And knew not until the flood came, and took them all away; so shall also the coming of the Son of Man be.

Joseph Smith Matthew 1:Verse 44

44 Then shall be fulfilled that which is written, that in the last days, two shall be in the field, the one shall be taken, and the other left;

Joseph Smith Matthew 1:Verse 45

45 Two shall be grinding at the mill, the one shall be taken, and the other left;

Joseph Smith Matthew 1:Verse 46

46 And what I say unto one, I say unto all men; **watch, therefore, for you know not at what hour your Lord doth come.**

Joseph Smith Matthew 1:Verse 47

47 But know this, if the good man of the house had known in what watch the thief would come, he would have watched, and would not have suffered his house to have been broken up, but would have been ready.

Joseph Smith Matthew 1: Verse 48

48 **Therefore be ye also ready, for in such an hour as ye think not, the Son of Man cometh.**

Joseph Smith Matthew 1:Verse 49

49 Who, then, is a faithful and wise servant, whom his lord hath made ruler over his household, to give them meat in due season?

Joseph Smith Matthew 1:Verse 50
50 Blessed is that servant whom his lord, when he cometh, shall find so doing; and verily I say unto you, he shall make him ruler over all his goods.

Joseph Smith Matthew 1:Verse 51
51 But if that evil servant shall say in his heart: My lord delayeth his coming,

Joseph Smith Matthew 1:Verse 52
52 And shall begin to smite his fellow-servants, and to eat and drink with the drunken,

Joseph Smith Matthew 1:Verse 53
53 The lord of that servant shall come in a day when he looketh not for him, and in an hour that he is not aware of,

Joseph Smith Matthew 1:Verse 54
54 And shall cut him asunder, and shall appoint him his portion with the hypocrites; there shall be weeping and gnashing of teeth.

Joseph Smith Matthew 1:Verse 55
55 And thus cometh the end of the wicked, according to the prophecy of Moses, saying: They shall be cut off from among the people; but the end of the earth is not yet, but by and by.

———————————————

36

I Come Quickly

Revelation 22: 12-21

Revelation 22:12-21

12 And, behold, I come quickly; and my reward [is] with me, to give every man according as his work shall be.

13 I am Alpha and Omega, the beginning and the end, the first and the last.

14 Blessed [are] they that do his commandments, that they may have right to the tree of life, and may enter in through the gates into the city.

15 For without [are] dogs, and sorcerers, and whoremongers, and murderers, and idolaters, and whosoever loveth and maketh a lie.

16 I Jesus have sent mine angel to testify unto you these things in the churches. I am the root and the offspring of David, [and] the bright and morning star.

17 And the Spirit and the bride say, Come. And let him that heareth say, Come. And let him that is athirst come. And whosoever will, let him take the water of life freely.

20 He which testifieth these things saith, Surely I come quickly. Amen. Even so, come, Lord Jesus.

21 The grace of our Lord Jesus Christ [be] with you all. Amen.

APPENDIX

1. Vision of John Taylor

2. War in Heaven

3. Discourses on the Abbaton

4. The Cosmic Serpent

5. The False Gods We Worship

1- Vision of John Taylor

A Vision given to President John Taylor at Salt Lake City, on the evening of December 16, 1877. This was given in response to a questions President Taylor had about the scriptures and last days. President Taylor received this vision a few months after he was set apart as Prophet, Seer and Revelator of the Church of Jesus Christ of latter-day Saints.

I went to bed at my usual hour half past nine o=clock. I had been reading the revelations in the French Language. My mind was calm, more so than usual if possible to be so. I composed myself for sleep but could not sleep.

I felt a strange stupor come over me and apparently became partially unconscious, still I was not asleep, nor awake with a strange far away dreamy feeling.

The first thing I recognized was that I was in the Tabernacle at Ogden sitting on the back seat in the corner for fear they would call upon me to preach, which, after singing the second time, they did by calling me to the stand.

I arose to speak and said I did not know that I had anything special to say except to bear my testimony to the truth of the latter-day work.

When all at once it seemed as though I was lifted out of myself, and I said 'Yes I have something to say, it is this: some of my brethren present have been asking me what is coming to pass, what is the wind blowing up. I will answer you right here what is coming to pass shortly.'

I was immediately in Salt Lake City wandering about the streets in all parts of the city, and on the door of every house I found a badge of mourning, and I could not find a house but what was in mourning.

I passed by my own house and saw the same signs there and asked, 'Is that me that is dead?'

Something gave me an answer 'No you'll live through it all.'

It seemed strange to me that I saw no person on the street in my wandering about through the city.

They seemed to be in their houses with their sick and dead.

I saw no funeral procession, or anything of that kind, but the city looked very still and quiet as though the people were praying, and had control of the disease whatever it was.

I then looked in all directions over the territory, east, west, north and south and I found the same mourning in every place throughout the land.

The next I knew I was just this side of Omaha.

It seemed as though I was above the earth, looking down on it as I passed along on my way east.

I saw the roads full of people, principally women, with just what they could carry in bundles on their backs, traveling to the mountains on foot, and I wondered how the could get there with nothing but a small pack upon their backs.

It was remarkable to me that there were so few men among them.

It did not seem as though the cars were running. The rails looked rusty and the road abandoned and I have no conception how I traveled myself.

As I looked down upon the people I continued eastward through Omaha and Council Bluffs which were full of disease and women everywhere.

The states of Missouri and Illinois were in turmoil and strife, men killing each other, and women joining in the fight, family against family, cutting each other to pieces in the most horrid manner.

The next I saw was Washington and I found the city a desolation. The White House empty, the halls of Congress the same, everything in ruins, the people seemed to have fled from the city and left it to take care of itself.

I was next in the city of Baltimore and in the square where the monument of 1812 stands in front of St. Charles.

And at the hotels I saw the dead piled up so as to fill the square.

I saw mothers cut the throats of their own children for the sake of their blood, which they drank from their veins to quench their thirst and then lie down and die.

The waters of the Chesapeake River and the city were so stagnant and such a stench arose from them on account of the petrification of dead bodies that the very smell caused death.

And that was singular again; I saw no men except they were dead, lying in the streets, and very few women, and they were crazy mad, and in a dying condition.

Everywhere I went I beheld the same all over the city, and it was horrible beyond description to look at.

I thought this must be the end. But no, I was seemingly in Philadelphia and there as in Baltimore everything was still. No living soul was to be seen to greet me, and it seemed as though the whole city was without and inhabitant.

In Arch and Chestnut Street and in fact everywhere I went the petrification of the dead bodies caused such a stench that it was impossible for any creature to exist alive, nor did I see any living thing in the city.

I next found myself in Broadway, New York, and there it seemed the people had done their best to overcome the disease. But in wandering down Broadway I saw the bodies of beautiful women lying stone dead, and others in a dying condition on the sidewalk.

I saw men crawl out of the cellars and rob the dead bodies of the valuables they had on them, and before they could return to their coverts in the cellars, they themselves would roll over a time or two and die in agony.

On some of the back streets I saw mothers kill their own children and eat raw flesh and then in a few minutes die themselves.

Wherever I went I saw the same scenes of horror and desolation, rapine and death. No horses or carriages. No buses or streetcars, but death and destruction everywhere.

I then went to the Grand Central Park and, looking back, I saw a fire start and just at that moment a might east wind sprang up and carried the flames west over the city, and it burned until there was not a single building left standing whole, even down to the wharfs.

And the shipping all seemed to be burned, and swallowed up in the common destruction and left nothing but a desolation where the great city was short time before.

The stench from the bodies that were burning was so great that it was carried a great distance across the Hudson River and Bay, and thus spread disease and death wherever the flames penetrated.

I cannot paint in words the horror that seemed to encompass me around about. It was beyond description or thought of man to conceive.

I supposed this was the end, but I was here given to understand that the same horror was being enacted all over the country, north, south, east and west, that few were left alive, still there were some.

Immediately after, I seemed to be standing on the west bank of the Missouri River opposite the City of Independence, but I saw no city.

I saw the whole states of Missouri and Illinois and part of Iowa were a complete wilderness with no living human being in them.

I then saw a short distance from the river twelve men dressed in the robes of the temple standing in a square or nearly so.

I understood it represented the twelve gates of the New Jerusalem and they were with hands uplifted consecrating the ground and lying the cornerstones.

I saw myriads of angels hovering over them and around about them and also an immense pillar of a cloud hover over them.

And I heard the angels singing the most beautiful music. The words were Anow is established the Kingdom of our God and His Christ and He shall reign forever and ever, and the Kingdom shall never be thrown down, for the Saints have overcome.@

And I saw people coming from the river and from different places a long way off to help build the Temple, and it seemed that the hosts of the angels all helped to get the material to build the Temple.

And I saw some come who wore their temple robes to help build the temple and the city and all the time I saw the great pillar of cloud hovering over the place.

Instantly I found I was in the Tabernacle at Ogden and yet I could see the building going on and I got quite animated in calling to the people in the Tabernacle to listen to the beautiful music that the angels were singing.

I called to them to look at the angels as the house seemed to be full of them and they were singing the same words that I heard before ANow is the kingdom of our God and His Christ established forever and ever.

And then a voice said, ANow shall come to pass that which was spoken by Isaiah the Prophet, that seven women shall take hold of one man saying, &c.@

At this time I seemed to stagger back from the pulpit and F.D. Richards and someone else caught me and prevented me from falling when I requested Brother Richards to apologize tot he audience for me because I stopped so abruptly, and tell them I had not fainted but was exhausted.

I rolled over in my bed and heard the City Hall clock strike twelve o=clock.

*(Wilford Woodruff Journals, June 15, 1878, church Historians office; Also in A*Unpublished Revelation of the Prophets and Presidents of the Church of Jesus Christ of LatterDay Saints*@ Volume 1, compiled by Fred C. Collier, 1979, Collier=s Publishing Co. Salt Lake City, Utah. pp. 119-123.)*

26

2- WAR in HEAVEN

It is evident that there is a common doctrinal thread in many different ancient texts from the Middle East about the 'war in heaven.' This doctrine cannot be ignored, because of its prevalence, and dispersion, in time, space, and culture.

Vita Adae et Evae.

The 'Life of Adam and Eve' contains elements about the War in Heaven doctrine, similar to the 'Discourse' below.

The text will begin after Satan has just appeared as an angel of light to Eve, in order to stop her repentance. Eve, and Satan (as the angel of light) come to Adam, who, immediately recognizes that Satan is not a true messenger from God begins to question Satan.

' . . . Woe unto thee, thou devil. Why dost thou attack us for no cause? What hast thou to do with us? What have we done to thee? For thou pursuest us with craft? Or why doth thy malice assail us? Have we taken away thy glory and caused thee to be without honour? Why dost thou harry us, thou enemy (and persecute us) to the death in wickedness and envy?'

And with a heavy sigh, the devil spake: "O Adam! All my hostility, envy, and sorrow is for thee, since it is for thee that I have been expelled from my glory, which I possessed in the heavens in the midst of the angels and for thee was I cast out in the earth." Adam answered, "What dosst thou tell me? What have I done to thee or what is my fault against thee? Seeing that thou hast received no harm or injury from us, why dost thou pursue us?"

The devil replied, "Adam, what dost thou tell me? It is for thy sake that I have been hurled from that place. When thou wast formed, I was hurled out of the presence of God and banished from the company of the angels. When God blew into thee the breath of life and thy face and likeness was made in the image of God, Michael also brought thee and made (us) worship thee in the sight of God; and God the Lord spake: Here is Adam. I have made thee in our image and likeness."

And Michael went out and called all the angels saying:

"Worship the image of God as the Lord God hath commanded."

And Michael himself worshipped first; then he called me and said: "Worship the image of God the Lord." And I answered, "I have no (need) to worship Adam." And since Michael kept urging me to worship, I said to him, "Why dost thou urge me? I will not worship an inferior and younger being (than I). I am his senior in the creation, before he was made was I already made. It is his duty to worship me."

When the angels, who were under me, heard this, they refused to worship him. And Michael saith, "Worship the image of God, but if thou wilt not worship him, the Lord God will be wrath with thee." And I said, "If He be wrath with me, I will set my seat above the stars of heaven and will be like the Highest."

And God the Lord was wrath with me and banished me and my angels from our glory; and on thy account were we expelled from our abodes into this world and hurled on the earth. And straightway we were overcome with grief, since we had been spoiled of so great glory. And we were grieved when we saw thee in such joy and luxury. And with guile I cheated thy wife and caused thee to be expelled through her (doing) from thy joy and luxury, as I have been driven out of my glory.

When Adam heard the devil say this, he cried out and wept and spake: "O Lord my God, my life is in thy hands. Banish this Adversary far from me, who seeketh to destroy my soul, and give me his glory which he himself hath lost." And at that moment, the devil vanished before him. . . .'
(R. H. Charles, *The Apocrypha and Pseudepigrapha of the Old Testament,* Vol 2, Oxford, 1977, pp.136-137).

2 Enoch

The Enoch Texts are found in: *The Old Testament Pseudepigrapha*, Vol 1, Edited by James H. Charlesworth, Doubleday, Garden City, New York, 1983.

In 2 Enoch 29:4-6, Enoch is viewing the creation with angelic assistance, much like Abraham, and Moses in the *Pearl of Great Price*. Enoch seeing the orders of angels is told, by God, that:

'One from the order of the archangels deviated, together with the division that was under his authority. He thought up the impossible idea, that he might place his throne higher than the clouds which are above the earth, and that he might become equal to my power.
And I hurled him out from the height, together with his angels.' (p.148).

In the *Doctrine and Covenants,* section 76, the prophet Joseph Smith receives a number of visions. The first, a vision of Christ on the right hand of the Father, the second vision, was the fall of Satan. The third vision was the punishments of the wicked. Likewise, in 2 Enoch, the same pattern exists. First the vision of God, and His kingdom, then the punishments of the wicked, followed by a vision of the glories of the righteous. The vision of punishments that Enoch sees, he questions his guide 'Why are these ones being tormented unceasingly?' Enoch is answered that: 'These are those who turned away from the Lord, who did not obey the Lord's commandments, but of their own will plotted together and turned away with their prince . . .' (p.114).

The Koran

The Koran written by Mohammad between 600-650 c.e. (a.d.) is considered for Muslims the infallible Word of God. Mohammad came under the influence of Jewish and Christian scholars, and teachings. Traveling with trading caravans he would have com in contact, and may have collected many ancient documents upon which he based the Koran.

Below are excerpts from different 'surahs' or chapters in the Koran, with their corresponding verse or paragraph numbers.

In surah 2 The satanic angels claim that Adam is not as intelligent as they, wherein God proves that the chosen patriarch is more intelligent than all the angels.

surah 2:34
'And when We said to the angels: "Prostrate yourselves before Adam," they all prostrated themselves except Satan, who in his pride refused and became and unbliever.'

surah 7:11-18
We created you (Adam) and gave you form. Then We said to the angels: "Prostrate yourselves before Adam." They all prostrated themselves except Satan, who refused to prostrate himself.
"Why did you not prostrate yourself when I commanded you?" He asked.
"I am nobler than he,= he replied. >You created me of fire, but You created him of clay"
He said: "Off with you hence! This is no place for you contemptuous pride. Away with you! Henceforth you shall be humble."
He replied: "Reprieve me *(allow me my way)* till the Day of Resurrection."
"You arre reprieved," said He.

"Because You have led me into sin," he declared, "I will waylay Your servants as they walk on Your straight path, and spring upon them from the front and from the rear, from their right and from their left. Then you will find the greater part of them ungrateful."

"Begone!" He said. "A despicable outcast you shall henceforth be. As for those that follow you, I shall fill Hell with you all."

15:22-29

We Created man from dry clay, from black moulded loam, and before him Satan from smokeless fire. Your Lord said to the angels: "I am creating man from dry clay, from black moulded loam. When I have fashioned him and breathed of My spirit into him, kneel down and prostrate yourselves before him."

The angels, one and all, prostrated themselves, except Satan. He refused to prostrate himself with the others.

"Satan," said god, "why do you not prostrate yourself?"

He replied: "I will not bow to a mortal whom You created of dry clay, of black moulded loam."

"Begone," said God, "you are accursed. My curse shall be on you till Judgment day."

"Lord," said Satan, "reprieve me till the Day of Resurrection."

He answered: "You are reprieved till the Appointed Day."

"Lord," said Satan, "since You have thus seduced me, I will tempt mankind on earth: I will seduce them all, except those of them who are your faithful servants."

See also 'surahs' 17:61-63; 18:50; 20:115-124; 38:67-88.

3- DISCOURSE ON ABBATON
By Timothy, Archbishop of Alexandria

This Text was copied by Timothy from the existing document at the library in Jerusalem about 380-385 A.D. The Archbishop seeking information on the origin of Satan and why death and suffering exists in the world, in his words, he was 'wishing to learn concerning this fearful and terrifying being who God made, an who pursueth every soul until it yieldeth up it's spirit.'

This text is described as the Savior's answers to these very questions by the Apostles:
'The Apostles asked the Savior about [Abbaton] so that they might be able to preach about him to all mankind, for they knew that men would ask them questions about everything. And the Saviour, who did not wish to disappoint them about any matter concerning which they asked Him questions, informed them saying 'The day on which my Father created Abbaton . . . He made him king over all creation which he had made, because of the transgression of Adam and Eve'

Timothy requests this text to know why death is in the world, why evil exists, and how Satan became the God of this world. This document speaks of the 'Council in Heaven,' The 'War in Heaven,' the fall of Satan and his angels. These doctrines are some of the 'plain and precious things' that have been taken out of the Bible, as Nephi reveals. There exists other ancient documents and records that teach these things, however, the Discourse on Abbaton is most complete and of a most ancient date, and may have been included in the scriptures at one time.

And it came to pass that when our Saviour, Who is the Root of all good, had finished everything, when the days of his Apocalypse were completed, and he was to ascend up to his Father, he laid His hands upon each one of His holy Apostles, and he prayed over them, and sent them forth into all the world to preach His holy Resurrection to all the heathen, and He filled them with power and with His Holy spirit, and He spake unto them, saying, "The mighty deeds and miracles which I have performed, ye yourselves also shall do. Ye shall lay your hands upon the sick and they shall have rest (or, relief). Ye shall tread upon serpents and scorpions. Ye shall take up serpents in your hands. And when ye drink deadly poisons they shall have no evil effect upon you. Baptize those who believe in Me, and in My Good Father, and the Holy Spirit, and I will forgive them [their sins]. Those who do not believe shall be condemned to the second death. Depart in peace. The peace which is Mine shall be with you. And I will never cease to walk with you even to the end of this world."

Then the Lord answered and said unto Peter, the greatest of the Apostles, the pillar of the Church, the steward of the kingdom which is in the heavens, "Him that thou wishest to take into it, take; and him that thou wishest to reject, reject." [And Peter] said unto the saviour, "My Lord and my God. Behold, Thou hast informed us concerning everything about which we have asked Thee, and Thou hast hidden nothing from us. And now, O my Lord and my God, behold, Thou hast sent us out into the whole world to preach Thy Holy Resurrection to all the nations, and the mighty deeds and miracles which Thou hast done, the which we have seen with our eyes, and concerning which we have heard, and Thou hast explained them all to us, even [the matter of] Thy Mother, and Thy Birth. And, O my Lord, Thou knowest that there are very many contentious and unbelieving people who will ask questions of us concerning everything, and we wish to be able to explain unto them everything. Now therefore, O my Lord, we wish Thee to inform us concerning the day wherein Thou didst establish Abbaton, the Angel of Death, and didst make him to be awful and disturbing, and to pursue all souls until they yield up their spirits, so that we may preach concerning him to all mankind, even as we preach concerning all his fellow angels whom Thou hast created, and whom Thou hast shewn us the days of their establishing, and also that when men hear of [him on] the day of his establishing they may be afraid, and my repent, and may give charities and gifts on the day of his commemoration, just as they do to Michael and Gabriel, so that their souls may find mercy and respite on the day of Thy Holy Resurrection."

And the Saviour, the Storehouse that is filled with mercy and compassion of every kind, who loveth everything which is good in respect of His day, Who wisheth not to cause us disappointment about anything concerning which we are asked, and said unto them, "O ye whom I have chosen from out of the whole world, I will hide nothing from you, but I will inform you how My Father established him (i.e. Abbaton) over all the created things which He had made. For I and My Father are one, according to what Philip said unto me, 'Lord, shew us the Father, and it sufficeth us.' And I said unto him, 'O Philip, in all the time which thou hast been with Me, hast thou not known Me? He who hath seen Me hath seen My Father, Believe thou that I am in My Father, and My Father is in Me. If it be impossible [for thee], believe His works.' And now, O my holy members, whom I have chosen from out of the whole world, I will hide nothing from you.

This is the creation and the council in heaven, which each and every world created by our Father must have. The spiritual offspring must all have a chance to approve of the plan or reject it. 'Without agency there is no existence.'

It came to pass that when My Father was creating the heavens, and the earth, and the things which are therein, He spake the word, and they all came into being, angel, and Archangel, and cherubim, and Seraphim, and Thrones, and divine Governors, and Dominions, and all the Powers that are in the heavens, and all the army of heaven. And he made the earth also, [and] the wild animals, and the reptiles, and the cattle, and the birds, and everything which moveth upon it. And He planted also a paradise in the eastern part of the earth. And My Father saw that the whole world was a desert, and that there was no one to work it. And My Father said, 'Let us make a man in Our image and likeness, that he may continue to praise us by day and by night, and that [every one] may know that it is the hand of the Lord that hath made all these things; for I existed before these things were.' And My Father commanded and angel saying, 'By My wish and by My command get thee to the land of Edem (i.e. *'kerem,'* the East land), and bring to Me some virgin earth in order that I may make a man in Our image

and likeness therewith, so that he may ascribe blessing unto Us by day and by night.'

Abraham 3:24-26; states that the Gods created this earth to see if we will be obedient, and show our love to our Father in Heaven, by this obedience with the promise that if we keep our first estate we will be added upon in the second estate, which if we are obedient here on this earth (the second estate) we will receive glory upon our 'heads for ever and ever.'

"And the angel went to the land of Edem, according to My Father's command. And he stood upon the earth, and he reached out his hand to gather together some of it and take it to My Father. And straightway the earth cried out with a loud voice, saying, 'I swear unto thee by Him Who sent thee to Me, that if thou takest me to Him, He will mold me into a form, and I shall become a man, and a living soul. And very many sins shall come forth from my heart (or, body), and many fornications, and slanderous abuse, and jealousy, and hatred and contention shall come forth from his hand, and many murders and sheddings of blood shall come froth from his hand. And they shall cast me out to the dogs, and to the cats, and into pits and holes in the ground, and into streams of water before my time, and after all these things they will finally cast me into punishment, and they will punish me by day and by night. Let me stay here, and go back to the ground and be quiet.'

"And when the Angel of God had heard these things he was afraid of My father's name, and he returned and came to My Father, and said, 'My Lord, when I heard Thy awful Name I did not wish to bring the earth unto Thee.' And straightway My Father commanded an angel a second time to go to it, and then a third angel, and so on even unto seven angels, and not one of them wished to approach the earth because it took awful oaths by mighty [names]. And when My Father saw that none of the angels wished to bring the earth to him, He sent the angel Mouriel to the earth, saying unto him, 'Go thou by My command to the land of Edem, and bring unto me some virgin earth so that I may fashion a man therefrom, after Mine own image and likeness, that he may ascribe blessing unto Us by day and by night.'

"And when the Angel of God had departed to the earth he stood upon it in great power and might, and in the commandment of God. And he reached out his hand to take some of it, and straightway the dust (or, clay) cried out with a loud voice, saying, 'I swear unto thee by the name of Him that created the heavens, and the earth, and the things that are therein, that thou shalt not approach me to take me unto God.' And the angel Mouriel was not afraid at [the mention of] the Name of My Father when he heard it, and he paid no heed thereto, but he went to it, and he laid hold of it with firmness and determination, and he brought it to My Father [Who] rejoiced over it.

Mankind must be made of the dust of this earth, at least those who will be, or have had temporal bodies on this earth. This is so, because, in order to be governed by Anatural law@ our physical bodies must be made from the elements from the Asphere in which God has placed it@ (D&C 93:28) Other worlds may not have the same elements as ours therefore, the physical bodies there must be made from those other elements in order to have natural law (death, disease, pain, sickness, etc. etc.) govern them.

And He took the clay from the hand of the angel, and made Adam according to Our image and likeness, and He left him lying for forty days and forty nights without putting breath into him. And he heaved sighs over him daily, saying, 'If I put breath into this [man], he must suffer many pains.'

The plan of salvation is presented, and the Savior accepts the responsibility to become the redeemer of mankind.

And I said unto My Father, 'Put breath into him; I will be an advocate for him.' And My Father said unto Me, AIf I put breath into him, My beloved son, Thou wilt be obliged to go down into the world, and to suffer many pains for him before Thou shalt have redeemed him, and made him to come back to primal state.@ And I said unto My Father, 'Put breath into him; I will be his advocate, and I will go down into the world, and will fulfil Thy command.'

"And whilst He was wishing to put breath into him He took a book, and wrote therein [the names of] those who should come forth from him and who should enter into the kingdom which is in the heavens, according to what is written, AThese are they whose names are written in the Book of Life from the foundation of the World.@

The names of the righteous are written in the ALambs Book of Life@ before the foundation of this world.

And He put breath into him in this way; He breathed into his nostrils the breath of life three times, saying, ALive! Live! Live! According to the type of My Divinity.@   And the man lived straightway, and became a living soul, according to the image and likeness of God. And when Adam had risen up he cast himself down before [My] father, saying, 'My Lord and my God! Thou hast made me to come into being [from a state in which] I did not exist.'

The spirit of Adam (Michael) is placed into the created body now that the plan of salvation was accepted and the redeemer is made known. Adam is excited above stating that he can feel the difference that a body makes saying 'My Lord and My God! Thou hast made me to come into being [from a state in which] I did not exist.'

Thereupon My Father set him upon a great throne, and he placed on his head a crown of glory, and he put a royal scepter [in his hand],

---

Adam is given the priesthood, this is the 'wa'as' scepter in Egypt that represents the priesthood, and authority of god to be a prophet, priest, and king.

---

and My Father made every order [of angels] in the heavens to come and worship him, wether angel or archangel. And all the hosts of heaven worshiped God first of all, and then they worshiped Adam, saying, 'Hail, thou image and likeness of God!'

This perhaps, is the true doctrine behind the origin of the 'Adam God Theory' and is more complete once it is understood in the correct context. The Father has all worship Him first, as their God and Father of their spirits, He then has all of heaven (those coming to this earth) worship (bad translation, should be "give homage") to Adam the god and father of their physical bodies. Adam, or Michael, because of his righteousness and valency in the pre-earth life (see Alma 13:3-5) was chosen to become the first physical man on the newly created earth, and to hold all the keys, rights, and powers of the priesthood, under the direction of Christ, and our Father in Heaven. This places Adam as the 'Ancient of Days' the 'Grand Patriarch' the 'Prophet, Priest, and King' of all the spirits that will come to this earth. This choice of Michael, a younger but more righteous spirit doesn't set well with the 'Son of the Morning' an older spirit child. (Christ is the Firstborn. Could Satan be the firstling of the spirits that were to come to 'THIS EARTH', but Adam or Michael was more righteous and received the honor of being the first patriarch, and 'Ancient of Days' for this world? Could Abraham 3:27 be speaking of the one who would be the first patriarch? 'Michael' means is Hebrew 'like unto God.' This would account for the discrepancy between Moses 4, and Abraham 3.) This is a pattern seen throughout biblical history. Cain/Abel, Isaac/Ishmael, Jacob/Esau, Joseph/Reuben, Laman/Nephi, and Adam/Satan. The pattern is there for a reason.

And He intended that the order of the angels who were fashioned [before Adam] should worship him, and My Father said unto him (i.e. their chief), 'Come, thou thyself shalt worship my image and likeness.' And he, a being of great pride, drew himself up in a shameless manner, and said, 'It is meet that this [man Adam] should come and worship me, for I existed before he came into being.'

*The pride of Satan cannot allow a being younger than himself to rule over him. This same pride turns Cain against Abel, producing murder for gain, secret oaths and combinations, Master Mahan, and the first 'son of Satan, (perdition)'. D&C 29:36-37 states: 'And it came to pass that Adam, Being tempted of the devil--**for, behold, the devil was before Adam**, for he rebelled against me, saying Give me thine honor, which is my power; and also a third part of the hosts of heaven turned he away from me because of their agency; and they were thrust down, and thus came the devil and his angels.'*

"And when My Father saw his great pride, and that his wickedness and his evil-doing were complete, (had reached their highest pitch)

The Father gave Satan every chance. Agency would require Satan to know, and understand completely what the consequences would be for the exercise of his agency, or the consequence would not be righteous. Satan chose his path, his 'pride was complete' he would never turn back. He rebelled against God and was cast out.

He commanded all the armies of heaven, saying, 'Remove the writing [which is] in the hand of the proud one, strip ye off his armor, and cast ye him down upon the earth, for his time hath come. For he is the greatest of them all, (the rebellious angels) he is the head over them and is like a king, and he commandeth them as the general of an army [commandeth his] soldiers; he is the head over them, and their names are written in his hand.'

'The writing in his hand' is the priesthood authority that he had been give before his fall to perdition. This is the same writing in Pharaoh's hand, depicted in the statues in Egypt.

Thus is it with this cunning one, and the [names of the] angels were written in his hand. And all the angels gathered together to him, and they did not wish to remove the writing from his hand. And my Father commanded them to bring a sharp reaping-knife, and to stab him therewith on this side and that, right through his body to the vertebrae of his shoulders, and he was unable to hold himself up. And straightway My Father commanded a mighty Cherubim, and he smote him, and cast him down from heaven upon the earth, because of his pride, and he broke his wings and his ribs and made helpless, and those whom he had brought with him became devils with him.

The 'reaping-knife' is the ancient sign of Satan, as his middle finger is arched in the shape of the reaping-knife. This knife is used to preform the oath which he had taken in the pre-earth existence. He was stabbed from his shoulder, and cut to the vertebrae, across the body to his other shoulder. This completes the loss of his powers and priest hoods, as he had Aaltogether turned therefrom@ his oath and covenant of the priesthood which he had made with the Father. The braking of his wings symbolize that his power to move about was taken, he was on the earth to stay. This lone and dreary world became his kingdom, and he became, in name only, 'the god of this world.'

27

"And My Father made them take Adam into Paradise, and a multitude of angels sang hymns before him, and they left him there, and he continued to ascribe blessing unto God. And Adam lived alone in Paradise for one hundred years. And when he had completed the period of one hundred years--now Adam lived in the Paradise of Delight, and remained there alone, and the angels used to come to him every day--My Father said, 'It is not good to allow the man to live by himself, but let Us make for him a helper like unto himself.' And he brought a slumber upon Adam, who fell into a deep sleep, and he took out one of his ribs and filled up [the place thereof] with flesh, and He made a woman according to the form of Adam. And when Adam woke up out of his sleep he saw her, and he said, 'This now is bone of my bones, and flesh of [my flesh]; she shall be called "woman", because she was taken out of her male' Now it was Adam who gave names to all the cattle, and to the wild beasts and to the birds, and to every living creature which moveth upon the earth, and even to those which are in the waters; unto all of them did Adam give names, according to the command of My Good Father.

"And Adam lived in the Paradise of Delight, he and Eve his wife, for two hundred years; and they were virgins, and they were even as the angels of God. And when they had been living in the Paradise of Delight for two hundred years, Eve came forth and passed through the northern part of Paradise, close by the wall, in order to obtain fruit for the cattle and for all the [other] creatures, because My Father had told Adam and Eve to feed them according to His command, and they received their food from the hand of Adam and Eve. And the serpent himself came at the hour of evening to receive his food according to his wont, for the serpent was like unto all the [other] beasts, and he walked upon his feet just as did they. And the Devil lived nigh unto Paradise, and he lay in wait for Adam and Eve by day and by night, and when he saw Eve by herself he went into the serpent, and said within himself, 'Behold, I have found [my] opportunity; I will speak into her ear, and I will make her to eat of the tree, and I will cause them to be expelled from paradise, for I myself was expelled from Paradise for their sakes.'

"And the Devil spake unto Eve through the mouth of the serpent, saying, 'Why do ye not eat of the tree which is in the middle of Paradise, as ye do of all the [other] trees, for the fruit therreof is good?' And [Eve] said, 'God said unto us, Ye may certainly eat of every tree which is in Paradise with the exception of the tree of knowledge of the good and of the evil; in the day wherein ye eat thereof ye shall surely die.' And the serpent said unto her, 'Ye shall not surely die, but ye shall be like unto these gods, ye shall know the good and the evil, and ye shall [be able] to separate the sweet from the bitter. God spake unto you in this manner because when ye have eaten thereof ye shall become as gods.' And the Devil ceased not to speak into her [ear] until he had beguiled her and she ate of the tree. And straightway Eve became naked, and she knew that she was naked, and she took some leaves of the fig-tree, and covered her nakedness. And she went to Adam, and when Adam saw her, and saw that she was naked, he was exceedingly grieved, and he became very sorrowful in heart, [and shed] tears in great abundance. And he said unto her, 'Wherefore hast thou acted in this wise? Behold, from this day forward we shall die, and God will be wroth with us, and he will cast us forth from Paradise.' And Eve said unto him. 'Come thou and eat. If God shall blame thee, I will take everything upon myself before God,' And in this way Adam took, and ate, and he became naked, and he knew immediately that he was naked; and he covered his nakedness with fig-leaves.

"And straightway the voice of My Father came to him in Paradise, saying, 'Adam, where art thou' And he said, 'My Lord, I heard Thy voice, but I was afraid, and I hid myself because I was naked.' And My Father said unto him. 'Who told thee [so]? Hast thou eaten of the tree until thou hast become naked?' And Adam said, 'My Lord, the woman whom Thou didst give unto me as a helper made me eat, and I became naked.' And My Father said unto her, 'Wherefore hast thou done this thing?' She said unto Him, 'My Lord, the serpent led me astray; I ate, and I became like the gods.' And My Father said unto the serpent, 'Because thou hast done this thing, cursed art thou among all the beasts of the earth. Thou shalt walk upon thy belly all the days of thy life, and all thy seed [shall be accursed] throughout all generations on the earth. Thou shalt eat earth and ashes all thy time, and so shall all those that shall come forth from thee.' It was in this way that the serpent came to walk upon his belly, according to what My Father decreed for him. And He said unto the woman also, 'Because thou hast done this thing thou shalt bring forth children in sorrow and sighing, and thou shalt turn to thy husband.' And similarly He turned to Adam, and said unto him, ΛCursed be the earth because of thy deeds. Thou shalt eat thy bread by the sweat of thy face, and all those who shall come out of thee shall do likewise. Behold, thou shalt die from this day onwards, because thou art earth, and thou shalt return again to the earth. Thou shalt live in the world a life of nine hundred and thirty years, and when death cometh upon thee thou shalt turn to the earth again. Thy soul shall abide in Amente, *(Hades, or the spirit world)* and thou shalt sit in black darkness for four and a half thousand of years . . .

'And when five and a half thousand of years are fulfilled I will send My beloved son into the world, and he shall abide in a virgin womb, (her name shall be Mary). She shall give Him birth on the earth in lowliness and humility . . . he shall pass thirty-three and a half years in the world, and He shall receive every attribute of humanity, sin alone excepted. He shall perform innumerable mighty deeds and wonders, He shall raise the dead, He shall drive out the devils, he shall heal those who are sick of the palsy, he shall make the lame to walk, the deaf He shall make to hear, and the dumb He shall make to speak, He shall cleanse the lepers, and [restore] the arms that are withered, and He shall open the eyes of the blind by the word of His power, In short, there shall be no limit to the miracles which He shall perform, but in spite of all these men will not believe on Him. And at length, after all these things, they shall rise up against Him, and they shall deliver Him over unto death, and they shall give Him into the hand of the Governor, that is to say, Pilate, and he shall judge Him for thy sake. He shall be in the form of a servant for thy sake. They shall smite Him in the face for thy sake. They shall treat Him with contempt and vilify him for thy sake. The shall pass sentence of condemnation upon Him as if He were a sacrilegious person. They shall mount Him upon the wood of the Cross, between two thieves, for thy sake. They shall set a crown of thorns upon His head for thy sake. They shall make Him drink vinegar and gall for thy sake. They shall drive nails into His hands and feet for thy sake. He shall yield up His Spirit on the Cross. They shall pierce his side with a spear so that water and blood shall flow forth therefrom, and it is these which shall cleanse the sins of the world. They shall lay Him in a new tomb. He shall rise from the dead on the third day. He shall go down into Amente, He shall shatter the gate of brass, and break in pieces the bolts of iron, and shall bring thee up therefrom together with all those who shall be held there in captivity with thee. For thy sake, O Adam, the son of God shall suffer all these things until He hath redeemed thee, and restored thee to Paradise, unto the place whence thou didst come, for He made Himself to be thy advocate (or, protector), when thou wast clay, before He put spirit (or, breath) into thee.'

"It was I, the Son of God, Who suffered all these things until I delivered man from the hand of the Devil. And you have seen all these things with your eyes, O my holy Apostles. It was in this wise that My Father expelled Adam and Eve from Paradise. He shut the gate [thereof], and He placed a mighty being of fire to watch the gate of Paradise, so that no one might enter therein until all those things which He had proclaimed concerning Adam had been fulfilled.

"And the Devil went to meet Adam outside Paradise, and he said unto him, 'Behold, O Adam, I was cast forth from my glory through thee, and behold, I have made thee to be expelled from the Paradise of Delight because thou hast caused me to become a stranger to my dwelling-place in heaven. Know thou that I will never cease to contend against thee and against all those who shall came after thee from out of thee, until I have taken them all down into Amente with me."

Again Satan confronts Adam and Eve speaking of the pre-earth life where it was Adam/Michael that had caused Satan to be cast out of his former glory with his power, and priesthood. Satan ratifies to Adam, his goal to keep Adam and Eve and all their posterity from their glory, powers, priesthoods, and dominions, in exaltation and glory in the presence again of our eternal Father in Heaven. This is the quest for the celestial Eden, the Father's 'Garden of Delights.' (see the Apycolypse of Adam, re: the exaltation of Adam.)

"And when Adam heard these things he became very sad, and shed many tears both by day and by night. And My Father said unto Mouriel the angel, 'Behold, the man whom I created in My image hath transgressed the commandment which I gave him. He hath eaten of the tree and hath brought a great injury upon all mankind. For this reason I make the king over him, for it was thou who didst bring him to Me on this day, which is the thirteenth of the month Hathor.

'Thy name shall be a terror in the mouth of every one. They shall call thee Abbaton, the Angel of Death.

'Thy form and thine image shall be [associated with] complaining, and wrath, and threatening in all souls, until they have yielded up their spirits.

'Thine eye and thy face shall be like unto a wheel of fire which beareth waves and waves [of fire] before me.

'The sound of thy nostrils shall be like unto the sound of a lake of fire wherein burn fire and sulphur (or, naphtha).

'The sound of the noises made by thy lips shall be like unto the sounds of the seven thunders which shall speak with their tongues.

'Thy head shall be like unto these great pillars of fire which [reach] from heaven downwards.

'Thy teeth shall project from thy mouth the length of half a cubit.

'The fingers of thy hands and [the toes of] thy feet shall be like unto sharp reaping-knives.

'Seven heads shall be on the top of thy head, and they shall change their shapes and forms [continually].

'Their teeth shall project outside their mouths for the length of two palms, and they shall point towards the four quarters of the world. Thou shalt be suspended in the midst, and thou shalt sit upon a throne of fire.

'Thine eyes shall look down upon the earth, and upon whatsoever is in the depths of the waters; nothing shall be hidden from thee in heaven, nor from one end of the earth to the other, from the north to the south, and from the east to the west, among all the created things which I have made.

'Not one of them shall yield up his spirit until he hath see thee.

'Thou shalt shew compassion neither upon small nor great, and thou shalt carry all away mercilessly. The Powers shall be under thy control, and thou shalt send them after every soul. They shall strike terror into souls, and shall change their forms. When the period of their life hath come to an end thou shalt appear to them, and they shall look upon thee; and when they look upon thy face their souls shall not be able to abide in them, even for a moment, and they will be forced to yield them up. Thus thou shalt continue to be king over them until the period for which I have ordained the world [to last] shall be ended.@

"And when the angels saw him they were all greatly disturbed together, and they said, 'Woe! Woe be unto the sons of men who shall be born into the world! For behold, even we who are incorporeal shall perish through terror.' The Abbaton, the Angel of Death, cast himself down before My Father, saying, 'My Lord, behold Thou hast made me to be an object of terror unto all the angels. Now, therefore, O my Lord, I entreat Thee, and I beseech Thy goodness to grant that when the sons of men who shall be born into the world shall hear that thou hast made me to be an object of terror and fear they shall become afraid, and shall give charity, and alms, and gifts, in my name, and that the day whereon Thou didst stablish me may be written down in the Book, and that they may appear on [the day of] my commemoration, and may seek after mercy and rest for their souls. And now, O my Lord, let Thy Spirit stablish them. 'And grant unto me power over them, so that I may take them to the place of rest, and to the dwelling-place of all those who rejoice, and let them celebrate a festival in my honor upon the earth even as they celebrate festivals in honor of all my fellow angels. O my Lord, let Thy mercy help them!'

"And My Father spake, saying, 'I tell thee, O Abbaton thou Angel [of death], whosoever shall hold thee in terror and shall give alms and charities in thy name, or repent, write in the book [the day of] thy stablishing, that is to say, the thirteenth day of the month Hathor, the day whereon I established thee over Adam because of his disobedience, I will write their names in the Book of Life, and I will give them as a gift unto thee in My kingdom, and they shall never experience any kind of punishment (or, torture). But thou shalt not go unto them in this terrible form of thine, but thou shalt go unto them and treat them with gentle tenderness, until thou are able to bring them (i.e. their souls) out of the body. I will give thee power over them, and thou shalt take them to the place of rest, the dwelling-place of all those who rejoice, for I am God, the good and Compassionate towards My clay.' Then Abbaton, the Angel [of Death], cast himself down before My Father, and he spake unto Him, saying, 'I will purify them, O Lord, my God and my King, in the place of all those whom Thou hast made.'

"And now, O my holy Apostles, I have made you to know what My Father did in respect of Abbaton, the awful and terrifying [angel], [and how He set him] over the creation which He had made, because of the transgression of Adam and Eve; preach ye it to all mankind."

And John, answered and spake [unto him], saying, "My Lord and my God, Who hast sanctified me unto Thyself, Who hast made all my thoughts to cling unto Thee, when Thou shalt gather together all thy clay into the valley of Jehosaphat, in order that each one may receive according to what he hath done, whether it be good or whether it be evil, if Abbaton, the Angel of Death, shall come on that day, being in forms of his own person,-- if this be so, I say my Lord, there is not one soul that shall be able to stand before Thy awful throne. Behold, we shall perish through fright when we hear these things at Thy hand.

And the Saviour opened His mouth with a smile in the face of John, and he spake unto him, saying, "O John, My beloved, who didst cast thyself upon My breast because of the purity of thy heart, and the purity of thy body, dost thou not know that in the day of the Holy Resurrection that there shall be no death, because old things shall have passed away? And there shall remain only the second death for those who have to meet it. On the day of the holy Resurrection I shall come upon the clouds of heaven, and every eye shall see Me, and all peoples and tongues shall lament. And thousands of thousands, and tens of thousands of tens of thousands of angels shall be before Me. And My Cross shall advance before me, like a symbol of sovereignty before a king, according to what I have said unto you, 'The son of Man shall come in his glory, and with that which is of his Father, and all his angels with Him' I will command My chief Archangel, the holy Michael, and he shall blow a blast on his trumpet in the Valley of Jehosaphat, that those who are dead may arise incorruptible, and there shall not remain upon the earth one soul that shall not rise up, from Adam the first man even unto the last man that shall be borne into the world. And they all shall rise up in the valley of Jehosaphat, so that each one may receive in his body according to what he hath done, whether it be good or whether it be evil. And they shall stand [there] in fear and trembling awaiting the spirit of My Father.

"And as for thee, O My beloved John, thou shalt not die until the thrones have been prepared on the day of the Resurrection, because the thrones of glory shall come down from heaven, and ye shall sit upon them, and I will sit in your midst. All the saints shall see the honor which I will pay unto thee, O My beloved John. I will command Abbaton, the Angel of Death, to come unto thee on that day, and he shall not be in any form that will terrify thee, but he shall come unto thee in the form of a gentle man, with a face like unto that of Michael, and he shall take away thy soul and bring it unto Me. Thy body shall not be in the tomb for ever, neither shall the earth rest upon it for ever. All the saints shall marvel at thee because that shalt not be judged until thou judgest them. Thou shalt be dead for three and a half hours (days), lying upon thy throne, and all creation shall see thee. I will make thy soul to return to thy body, and thou shalt rise up and array thyself in apparel of glory, like unto that of one who hath stood up in the marriage chamber. Ye shall judge the world, according to what I have ordained for you, and ye shall sit upon thrones and shall judge the Twelve Tribes of Israel. And I said with [My] mouth unto Paul, 'We shall judge the angels before we come to the beings of the earth.' For on that day [when] everything shall stand in fear and trembling I shall say, 'Let them be separated from each other, even as a shepherd separates the sheep from the goats, the righteous on the right hand, and the sinners on the left,@ and not one shall make a sound (literally Agive his voice') until he who is chief in his day shall command him.

"I shall look upon all My clay, and when I see that he is going to destruction I shall cry out to My Father, saying, 'My Father, what profit is there in My Blood if he goeth to destruction?' And straightway the voice of My Father shall come unto Me from the seventh heaven, and none shall hear it except Myself, for I and My Father are one, saying 'Power belongeth unto Thee, O My Son, to do whatsoever Thou pleaseth with Thy clay.' And in that day I shall say, 'I rejoice because Thou didst cleave My covering, and didst gird me about with joy, and My right hand shall bless Thee because I am without sorrow.' I shall say unto you in that day, 'O My holy Apostles, and all My saints, whether ye be angels or archangels, or whether ye be prophets or righteous, and especially My Mother, and My chief Archangels Michael and Gabriel, I speak unto you, saying: No man who shall celebrate your commemoration upon earth, or shall give a loaf of bread in you name shall go to destruction.' And straightway all the saints shall rush forwards towards them, and each one shall seize upon those that belong to him. All those who have shewn love to you upon earth shall be brought back to the others who are on the right hand. Then shall the others cry out with loud wailings, and tears, and with suffering and sorrow of the heart, saying, 'O Lord the Merciful One, the son of the Merciful One, shew mercy upon us.' Thereupon straightway shall the Son of God shed tears over them, and he shall say unto them, 'My word remaineth with My Father.'

"And straightway My Father shall shut the door of heaven, and go His way. And I shall say them straightway, 'My Father doth not desire to shew mercy upon you.' And they shall cry out the more, saying, 'Have mercy upon us for the Devil would not permit us to repent. If we had known that these things were to be we should have repented even unto the shedding of blood.' And forthwith I shall utter curses upon Satan that day, and I will make them to seize him, and to fetter him in the bonds which cannot be broken, and I will curse that lying prophet who hath led astray all the nations, and Antichrist, the son of perdition, and they shall cast them into the Lake of Fire which burneth with fire and sulphur, together with all those who have been their followers in the world, and they shall never enjoy repose, day or night. Their worm shall not die, and their fire shall not be quenched.

"Now therefore, O My holy Apostles, behold I have shewn you everything which ye asked me to explain, and how Adam transgressed until death came into the world, and how Abbaton, the Angel [of Death], became king over all created things. And now ye shall proclaim the day of his commemoration, so that the sons of men may be afraid and repent. Speak ye unto all mankind, saying, 'Whosoever doeth that which is good shall rise in the resurrection. . . . . . life. Whosoever shall do that which is evil shall rise in the resurrection to judgment.' Then the Apostles worshiped the Saviour, saying, 'Our Lord and our God! Thou hast filled us with blessings, and Thou hast never disappointed us in any way, in [answering] the questions which we have asked of Thee.'" And the Saviour kissed them, and the angels bore Him up into heaven whilst they followed Him with their gaze. And the Apostles worshiped him and each one of them departed to preach what the Lord had commanded them.

(E. A. Wallis Budge, *Coptic Martyrdoms*, Vol IV, Pub. British Museum, London, 1977.)

4- The Cosmic Serpent

The Cosmic Serpent is a scientific book that discusses the asteroid impacts on the earth and other planets. It contains the most detailed and complete information in one volume. It appears that some of the events in the Book of Revelation are direct results of impacts of meteors or asteroids. The destruction in Third Nephi seems also to fall into this type of natural disaster.

p.76

It turns out that if the current population is typical, an Apollo asteroid of at least 1 km diameter will collide with the earth every 250,000 years or so. If such an asteroid has the density of water ice, its mass is 4 billion tons and for a mean impact velocity of 25 km/sec the impact energy is 3 million megatons. For a rocky constitution the energy will approach 10 million megatons. The unit of energy employed here is the "megaton equivalent of TNT", one megaton corresponding to the explosion of a million tons of TNT. The Hiroshima explosion had an energy of about a fiftieth of a megaton; a sizeable hydrogen bomb will release 1-10 megatons of energy; the Krakatoa eruption of August 1883 was about 50 megatons; and a major earthquake may involve the release of over 100 megatons.

p.96
The effect of a large land impact

The comet or asteroid will enter the atmosphere at hypersonic speed and a shock wave will hug its forward hemisphere and extend backwards as a long cylinder. Essentially it punches a hole in the atmosphere, the displaced air being thrust sideways from the cylinder at about the speed of the missile, creating a blast wave of about 10 million megatons. The great bulk of the kinetic energy of the asteroid therefore reaches the ground, and the crater develops in the manner already described. Much of the energy is expended in the fragmentation and shifting of the rock, a few per cent going into the creation of a high-temperature ball of vapour. A crater of about 200 km diameter is formed within a few minutes, ejecta being raised through several kilometers and deposited in part in a rim. The atmosphere around the crater will be violently disturbed by these rapid ground motions and by the expansion of the fireball. Further, the passage of ejecta ranging from kilometer-sized lumps to hot ash is expected and strong interaction will occur between these ejecta and the atmosphere. The proportion of energy ultimately deposited in the atmosphere is difficult to assess with precision. Certainly in an explosion, a considerable percentage of the original energy ends up as blast wave. A figure of 10 per cent is adopted below.

Complicated though the atmosperic disturbances must be in the region of the crater, the situation will have simplified within a few crater diameters, a few minutes after the explosion. Beyond 1,000 km, say, from the epicentre, a shock wave will have formed and be moving rapidly outwards. The situation may be characterized by a cylindrical shock front behind which the atmosphere has piled up into a dense, high-pressure hot shell. The shell snowploughs into the as yet undisturbed atmosphere ahead of it, gathering it up. If say 10 per cent of the impact energy is deposited as blast motion into the atmosphere within 500 km of the epicentre, then at 2,000 km distance a wind velocity of 2,400 km/hr of characteristic duration 0.4 hr is expected. If there is no back pressure behind the blast, that is if it is impelled forwards simply by its own momentum, then at 5,000 km

p.97
the wind velocity has dropped to 400 km/hr, enduring for 0.8 hr, and at 10,000 km from the epicentre, that is 90 degrees away, the wind speed is down to 100 km/hr and blows for 14 hours.

In addition to the dynamic pressure caused by the blast of air there is an instantaneous pressure and temperature rise due to the compression of gas immediately behind the shock front. The shock and blast inevitably deposit energy into the atmosphere, and this appears ultimately as heat. At 2,000 km the overpressure is 8.5 atmospheres and the air temperature is 480 degrees C. At 5,000 km the figures are 0.6 atm and 60 degrees C, dropping to 0.1 atm and 30 degrees C at 10,000 km. This intense heating expands the atmosphere behind the front, which rises to create a hot, low-density regime: the blast wave is thus followed by a partial vacuum, a rarefaction wave, of somewhat longer duration.

If all the nominal 100 million megatons of energy deposited in the atmosphere were manifested as wind motions, a mean wind velocity of 1,500 km/hr would be expected globally. If deposited as heat, then a global rise in air temperature of 43 degrees would be expected.

The heat-deposition problem is somewhat complicated by the fact that vaporized and melted rock, hot ash and so on will be flung out of

p.98

the crater, the vapor and small particles especially streaming along with the current. This represents an additional source of heat, but the consequences are difficult to assess.

p.99

About 100,000 cubic km of material is ejected by the impact, much of it in the form of fine dust, which is carried along by the violent motions of the atmosphere. Even in an undisturbed stratosphere, fine dust quickly spreads globally.

The falling speed of a particle ten-millionths of a centimetre across in the normal, undisturbed atmosphere is about 1 mm/sec at 50 km altitude, about 0.1 mm/sec at 30 km, and about 0.01 mm/sec at 15km. At the latter speed a falling time of five years is implied. Very roughly a particle a tenth as large has a tenth this falling speed and the converse. Sub-millimetre-sized particles would fall out within about a month.

p.100

A similar proportion of 100,000 cubic km would result in a blockage of sunlight with an Aoverkill@ factor of over 10,000 ! Thus, if this simple picture of dust suspension were valid, total blackness would be expected for two to three years after the impact, followed by a rather sudden clearing of the sky.

A drastic change in the chemistry of the atmosphere, probably of most consequence in the stratosphere, is also likely. Above about 2,000 degrees nitrogen and oxygen in the atmosphere combine to give nitric oxide. Each megaton injected into the atmosphere will produce between 1,000 and 5,000 tons of nitric oxide and this will be carried into the stratosphere. An injection of 100 million megatons therefore implies the creation of several hundred thousand million tons of NO. Between 15 and 40 km altitude, ozone (03) filters out biologically damaging ultraviolet solar radiation. The mass of ozone in the atmosphere is comparable with the injected mass of NO. The latter however, destroys ozone by a catalytic reaction in which 1 g of NO removes 100-200 g of ozone. The result of the impact would therefore be a complete removal of the ozone. While this hardly matters when sunlight is blocked by dust in any case, the question would become important if, by the time the dust clears, the ozone were still depleted. The timescale for the replenishment of ozone is twenty to thirty years.

Apart from these atmospheric effects, mention should also be made of a ground effect which may be of consequence well beyond the crater. The energy carried by the shock, penetrating the ground, shatters and heats the rock, expelling some of it to form a crater. But a small residue of this energy will spread beyond the rock-fragmenting region: once the tensile strength of the rock is greater than the shock pressure, the rock no longer fragments and the energy is transported by vibration. Probably 1 per cent or so of the total energy is thus carried away by seismic waves. For the impact being discussed, about 10 million megatons will go into these vibrations much of it as surface waves--earthquakes. The Rayleigh (corkscrew) and Love (to and fro) waves which comprise earthquake motions damp slowly with distance, the amplitude at 5,000 km still being a third of that near the epicentre; and at 90 degrees from the impact point the energy/km squared in the ground motions will still exceed 10 percent of that around the crater. A mean

277

global value of about 0.01 megaton/km sq. Is implied. This is at the extreme top end of earthquake intensity scales, and corresponds to great catastrophe with for example earth layers being overturned, clefts appearing in the ground and free-standing objects and creatures being thrown in the air.

p.101

To sum up, the immediate global effects are a violent scorching wind, the ejection of incandescent material, severe earthquake, possible a prolonged obscuration of sunlight, and exposure to ultraviolet radiation of germicidal intensity when the sky clears.

The effect of a large oceanic impact

Of course most impacting bodies will have crashed into seas or oceans. The consequences of ocean impact have been little studied and are not well understood, and in the description that follows one cannot even be sure that all the main features of the phenomenon have been included.

Experiments on crater formation in sand show that the sizes of craters in loosely bound material may be up to ten times those of the corresponding craters formed in rock. A very large, shallow crater, perhaps 500-1,000 km across, would be formed by the impact of a 10 km diameter asteroid, the crater "walls" being formed of water. The whole structure, because of the great dimensions, would take over an hour to form. Of course the ocean whose depth will be less than the diameter of the asteroid, is quite unable to absorb the impact momentum and a true crater will be formed in the sea bed, breaking the crust and exposing the underlying hot mantle material. The shattering of the ocean bed material will not be greatly affected by the overlying water but its excavation will be; in effect some of the ballistic energy of excavation will be transferred into water wave motion. Lifting and displacement of the underlying rock may be a prime input to the oceanic disturbance.

The filling in of the water crater will create a rebounding column of water mixed with solids, the whole reaching several kilometres in height. Because in the latter stages the inrushing water is flowing over lava some energy transfer is expected. It might be considered that a square centimetre column of water several kilometres deep will not be significantly affected by heating through contact with lava at one end; however the possibility exists that some of the heat energy is expended in overturning the lave, in which case a rapid convective mixing of the lava is possible. The heating then becomes a volume rather than a surface phenomenon and may be quite significant. The energy contasined in a 100-metre depth of lava a 2,000 degrees C, in a crater of radius 100 km, is about equal to the initial impact energy, and this must complicate the subsequent flow of the displaced water. We neglect the effect here.

The crater expert Gault and his colleagues carried out a calculation

p.102

in which a 1.4 km diameter asteroid struck the ocean at 25 km/sec. They found that 92 per cent of the impact energy went into splash, shock heating and wave formation. The ocean was evacuated to a depth of 6km over a radial dimension of 15 km. Neglecting turbulent dissipation of the wave energy, they found that the "ripples" spreading outwards had an amplitude of 1 km at 100 km distance from the epicentre, droping off in proportion to distance so that, for example, the wave amplitude was 50 metres at a distance of 1,000 km.

Approaching a shoreline, a wave slows down and increases in amplitude as it enters shallow water. There is a piling up of water as the forward part of the wave slows down. An increase in wave height by a factor of ten as the coastline is reached is expected so that the 50 metre wave would become 0.5 km in height.

The important question however, is the stability of these impact-generated waves. Development of the wave structure is a complicated technical problem and work carried out by Strelitz suggests that the waves may break up and dissipate in the ocean. The reason is that the waves are steep, not sinusoidal. Piling on to each other they evolve into a hydraulic bore--an almost vertical wall of water in an extreme case--which cannot maintain its shape and therefore breaks up in the open sea.

The steepness of the waves, in turn, comes from the small dimension over which the energy has been deposited; thus in the Gault calculation one has energy greater than that of any earthquake-induced tsunami dumped into a mere 200km sq. Of ocean. A normal tsunami may be induced by a sub-oceanic earthquake covering an area of 30,000 km sq. The waves generated are of great length and are very shallow: on a ship at sea one would scarcely notice the swell. These long wavelengths tend not to be destroyed by passage into shallow water and can therefore deposit their energy right on a coastline, with devastating effects.

The situation may be quite different with an asteroid of 10 km diameter, for in that case the collision energy is a thousand times as great and the submarine crater has an area comparable to that covered by a large earthquake. Thus the ground motions which will

p.103

couple into the overlying water will generate waves of length comparable to that generated by a normal earghquake. Of course the energy transported implies a much greater wave amplitude: 1,000 km from the epicentre, the wave would be on the order of 0.5 km in height. For a wavelength of say 100 km this still represents quite a shallow wave; pending detailed calculations or observations in the field, it seems likely that this wave energy can be transported over global distances at least until it reaches a continental shel or a coastline or a shallow sea, where it will rear up and transform into a breaker kilometres high. A run-up on to land would create a hydraulic bore of awesome dimensions, and a deep and catastropic inundation of the land.

(Victor Clube and Bill Napier, *The Cosmic Serpent*, Universe Books, New York, 1982)

5- The False Gods We Worship
President Spencer W. Kimball

1.   I have heard that the sense most closely associated with memory is the sense of smell. If this is true, then perhaps it explains the many; pleasing feelings that overtake me these mornings when I am able to step outdoors for a few moments and breathe in the warm and comfortable aromas that I have come to associate over the years with the soil and vegetation of this good earth.

2.   Now and then, when the moment is right, some particular scent - perhaps only the green grass, or the smell of sage brought from a distance by a breeze will take me back to the days of my youth in Arizona. It was an arid country, yet it was fruitful under the hands of determined laborers.

3.   We worked with the land and the cattle in all kinds of weather, and when we traveled it was on horseback or in open wagons or carriages, mostly. I used to run like the wind with my brothers and sisters through the orchards, down the dusty lanes, past rows of corn, red tomatoes, onions, squash. Because of this, I suppose it is natural to think that in those days we were closer to elemental life.

4.   Some time ago I chanced to walk outdoors when the dark and massive clouds of an early afternoon thunderstorm were gathering; and as the large raindrops began to drum the dusty soil with increasing rapidity, I recalled the occasional summer afternoons when I was a boy when the tremendous thunderheads would gather over the hills and bring welcome rain to the thirsty soil of the valley floor. We children would run for the shed, and while the lightning danced about we would sit and watch, transfixed, marveling at the ever increasing power of the pounding rainfall. Afterward, the air would be clean and cool and filled with the sweet smells of the soil, the trees, and the plants of the garden.

5.   There were evenings those many years ago, at about sunset, when I would walk in with the cows. Stopping by a tired old fence post I would sometimes just stand silently in the mellow light and the fragrance of sunflowers and ask myself, 'If you were going to create a world, what would it be like?' Now with a little thought the answer seems so natural: 'just like this one.'

6.   So on this day while I stood watching the thunderstorm, I felt - and I feel now - that this is a marvelous earth on which we find ourselves: and when I thought of our preparations for the United States Bicentennial celebration I felt a deep gratitude to the Lord for the choice land and the people and institutions of America. There is much that is good in this land, and much to love.

7.   Nevertheless, on this occasion of so many pleasant memories another impression assailed my thoughts. The dark and threatening clouds that hung so low over the valley seemed to force my mind back to a theme that the brethren have concerned themselves with for many years not - indeed a theme that has often occupied the attention of the Lord's chosen prophets since the world began. I am speaking of the general state of wickedness in which we seem to find the world in these perilous yet crucially momentous days: and thinking of this, I am reminded of the general principle that were much is given much is expected. (See Luke 12:48)

8.   The Lord gave us a choice world and expects righteousness and obedience to his commandments in return. But when I review the performance of this people in comparison with what is expected, I am appalled and frightened. Iniquity seems to abound. The Destroyer seems to be taking full advantage of the time remaining to him in this, the great day of his power. Evil seems about to engulf us like a great wave, and we feel that truly we are living in conditions similar to those in the days of Noah before the Flood.

9.   I have traveled much in various assignments over the years, and when I pass through the lovely countryside or fly over the vast and beautiful expanses of our globe, I compare those beauties with many of the dark and miserable practices of men, and I have the feeling that the good earth can hardly bear our presence upon it. I recall the occasion when Enoch heard the earth mourn saying, 'Wo, wo is me, the mother of men: I am pained, I am weary, because of the wickedness of my children. When shall I rest, and be cleansed from the filthiness which is gone forth out of me?' (Moses 7:48)

10.   The Brethren constantly cry out against that which is intolerable in the sight of the Lord; against pollution of mind, body, and our surroundings; against vulgarity, stealing, lying, pride and blasphemy; against fornication, adultery, the sacred power to create; against murder and all that is like unto it; against all manner of desecration.

11.   That such a cry should be necessary among a people so blessed is amazing to me. And that such things should be found even among the Saints to some degrees is scarcely believable, for these are a people who are in possession of many gifts of the Spirit, who have knowledge that puts the eternities into perspective, who have been shown the way to eternal life.

12.   Sadly, however, we find that to be shown the way is not necessarily to walk in it, and many have not been able to continue in faith. These have submitted themselves in one degree or another to the enticing's of Satan and his servants and joined with those of Athe world@ in lives of ever-deepening idolatry.

13.   I use the word *idolatry* intentionally. As I study ancient scripture, I am more and more convinced that there is significance in the fact that the commandment 'Thou shalt have no other gods before me' is the first of the Ten Commandments.

14.   Few men have ever knowingly and deliberately chosen to reject God and his blessings. Rather, we learn from the scriptures that because the exercise of faith has always appeared to be more difficult that relying on things more immediately at hand, carnal man has tended to transfer his trust in God to material things. Therefore, in all ages when men have fallen under the power of Satan and lost the faith, they have put in its place a hope in the 'arm of flesh' and in Agods of silver, and gold, of brass, iron, wood, and stone, which see not, nor hear, nor know@ (Dan.5:23) - That is, in idols. This I find to be a dominant theme in the Old Testament. Whatever thing a man sets his heart and his trust in most is his god; and if this god doesn't also happen to be the true and living God of Israel, that man is laboring in idolatry.

15.   It is my firm belief that when we read these scriptures and try to 'liken them unto ourselves,' as Nephi suggested (1 Nephi 19:23), we will see many parallels between the ancient worship of graven images and behavioral patterns in our very own experience.

16.   The Lord has blessed us as a people with prosperity unequaled in times past. The resources that have been placed in our power are good, and necessary to our work here on the earth. But I am afraid that many of us have been surfeited with flocks and herds and acres and barns and wealth and have begun to worship them as false gods, and they have power over us. Do we have more of these good things than our faith can stand?

17.   Many people spend most of their time working in the service of a self-image that includes sufficient money, stocks, bonds, investment portfolios, property, credit cards, furnishings, automobiles, and the like to guarantee carnal security throughout, it is hoped, a long and happy life. Forgotten is the fact that our assignment is to use these many resources in our families and quorums to build up the kingdom of God - to further the missionary effort and the genealogical and temple work; to raise our children up as fruitful servants unto the Lord; to bless others in every way, that they may also be fruitful. Instead, we expend these blessings on our own desires, and as Moroni said, 'Ye adorn yourselves with that which hath no life, and yet suffer the hungry, and the needy, and the naked, and the sick and the afflicted to pass by you, and notice them not.' (Mormon 8:39).

18.   As the Lord himself said in our day 'They seek not the Lord to establish his righteousness, but every man walketh in his own way, and after the image of his own God, whose image is in the likeness of the world, and whose substance is that of an idol, which waxeth old and shall perish in Babylon, even Babylon the great which shall fall.' (D&C 1:16).

19.   One man I know of was called to a position of service in the Church but he felt that he couldn't accept because his investments required more attention and more of his time that he could spare for the Lord's work. He left the service of the Lord in search of Mammon, and he is a millionaire today.

20.   But I recently learned and interesting fact: If a man owns a million dollars worth of gold at today's prices, he possesses approximately one 27-billionth of all the gold that is present in the earth's thin crust alone. This is an amount so small in proportion as to be inconceivable to the mind of man. But there is more to this: The Lord who created and has power over all the earth created many other earths as well, even Aworlds without number@ (Moses 1:33); and when this man received the oath and covenant of the priesthood (D&C 84:33-44), he received a promise from the Lord of 'all that my Father hath' (v.38). To set aside all these great promises in favor of a chest of gold and a sense of carnal security is a mistake in perspective of colossal proportions. To think that he has settled for so little is saddening and pitiful prospect indeed; the souls of men are far more precious than this.

21.   One young man, when called on a mission, replied that he didn't have much talent for that kind of thing. What he was good at was keeping his powerful new automobile in to condition. He enjoyed the sense of power and acceleration, and when he was driving, the continual motion gave him the illusion that he was really getting somewhere.

22.   All along his father had been content with saying, 'He likes to do things with his hands. That's good enough for him.'

23.   Good enough for a son of God? This young man didn't realize that the power of his automobile is infinitesimally small in comparison with the power of the sea or of the sun; and there are many suns, all controlled by law and by priesthood, ultimately - a priesthood power that he could have been developing in the service of the Lord. He settled for a pitiful god, a composite of steel and rubber and shiny chrome.

24.   An older couple retired from the world of work and also, in effect, from the Church. They purchased a pickup truck and camper, and separating themselves from all obligations, set out to see the world and simply enjoy what little they had accumulated the rest of their days. They had no time for the temple, were too busy for genealogical research and for missionary service. He lost contact with his high priests quorum and wan not home enough to work on his personal history. Their experience and leadership were sorely needed in their branch, but unable to Aendure to the end@ they were not available.

25.   I am reminded of an article I read some years ago about a group of men who had gone to the jungles of capture monkeys. They tried a number if different things to catch the monkeys, including nets. But finding that the nets could injure such small creatures, they finally came upon an ingenious solution. They built a large number of small boxes, and in the top of each they bored a hole just large enough for a monkey to get his hand into. They then set these boxes out under the trees and in each one they put a nut that the monkeys were particularly fond of.

26.   When the men left, the monkeys began to come down from the trees and examine the boxes. Finding that there were nuts to be had, they reached into the boxes to get them. But when a monkey would try to withdraw his hand with the nut, he could not get his hand out of the box because his little fist, with the nut inside, was now to large.

27.   At about this time, the men would come out of the underbrush and converge on the monkeys. And here is the curious thing: When the monkeys saw the men coming, they would shriek and scramble about them with the thought of escaping; but as easy as it would

have been, they would not let go of the nut so that they could withdraw their hands from the boxes and thus escape. The men captured them easily.

28. And so it often seems to be with people, having such a firm grasp on things of the world - that which is Telestial - that no amount of urging and no degree of emergency can persuade them to let go in favor of that which is celestial. Satan gets them in his grip easily. If we insist on spending all our time and resources building up for ourselves a worldly kingdom, that is exactly what we will inherit.

29. In spite of our delight in defining ourselves a modern, and our tendency to think we possess a sophistication that no people in the past ever had - in spite of these things, we are, on the whole, an idolatrous people - a condition most repugnant to the Lord.

30. We are a warlike people, easily distracted from our assignment of preparing for the coming of the Lord. When enemies rise up, we commit vast resources to the fabrication of Gods of stone and steel - ships, planes, missiles, fortifications - and depend on them for protection and deliverance. When threatened, we become anti-enemy instead of pro-kingdom of God; we train a man in the art of war and call him a patriot, thus in the manner of Satan's counterfeit of true patriotism, perverting the savior's teaching: 'Love your enemies, bless them that curse you, do good to them that hate you, and pray for them which despitefully use you and persecute you; that ye may be the children of your father which is in heaven.' (Matt. 5:44-45).

31. We forget that if we are righteous the Lord will either not suffer our enemies to come upon us - and this is the special promise to the inhabitants of the land of the Americas (see 2 Ne. 1:7) - or he will fight our battles for us (Ex. 14:14; D&C 98:37) This he is able to do, for as he said at the time of his betrayal, 'Thinkest thou that I cannot now pray to my Father and he shall presently give me more than twelve legions of angels?@ (Matthew 26:53) We can imagine what fearsome soldiers they would be. King Jehoshaphat and his people were delivered by such a troop (see 2 Chron. 20), and when Elisha's life was threatened, he comforted his servant by saying, AFear not; for they that be with us are more than they that be with them' (2 Kings 6:16). The Lord then opened the eyes of the servant, 'and he saw; and behold, the mountain was full of horses and chariots of fire round about Elisha.' (V. 17)

32. Enoch, too, was a man of great faith who would not be distracted from his duties by the enemy: 'And so great was the faith of Enoch, that he led the people of God, and their enemies came to battle against them; and he spake the word of the Lord, and the Earth trembled, and the mountains fled, even according to his command; and the rivers of water were turned out of their course; and the roar of the lions was heard out of the wilderness; and all nations feared greatly, so powerful was the word of Enoch.' (Moses 7:13)

33. What are we to fear when the Lord is with us? Can we not take the Lord at his word and exercise a particle of faith in him? Our assignment is affirmative: to forsake the things of the world as ends in themselves; to leave off idolatry and press forward in faith; to carry the gospel to our enemies that they might no longer be our enemies.

34. We must leave off the worship of modern-day idols and a reliance on the 'arm of flesh,' for the Lord has said to all the world in our day, 'I will not spare any that remain in Babylon.' (D&C 64:24)

35. When Peter preached such a message as this to the people on the day of Pentecost, many of them 'were pricked in their heart, and said unto Peter and to the rest of the apostles, men and brethren, what shall we do?' (Acts 2:37)

36. And Peter answered: 'repent, and be baptized everyone of you in the name of Jesus Christ for the remission of sins, and receive the Holy Ghost.' (V. 38)

37. As we near the year 2000, our message is the same as that which Peter gave. And further, that which the Lord himself gave 'unto the ends of the earth, that all that will hear may hear:

38.	'Prepare ye, prepare ye for that which is to come, for the Lord is nigh.' (D&C 1:11-12)

39.	We believe that the way for each person and each family to prepare as the Lord has directed is to begin to exercise greater faith, to repent, and to enter into the work of his kingdom on earth, which is The Church of Jesus Christ of Latter Day Saints.

40.	It may seem a little difficult at first, but when a person begins to catch a vision of the true work, when he begins to see something of eternity in its true perspective, the blessings begin to far outweigh the cost of leaving Athe world@ behind.

41.	Herein lies the only true happiness, and therefore we invite and welcome all men, everywhere, to join in this work. For those who are determined to serve the Lord at all costs, this is the way to eternal life. All else is but a means to that end.

President Spencer W. Kimball Ensign
June 1976

Made in United States
Troutdale, OR
11/02/2024